# BEYOND SURVIVAL

## STRATEGIES AND STORIES FROM THE TRANSFORMATIVE JUSTICE MOVEMENT

# BEYOND SURVIVAL

## STRATEGIES AND STORIES FROM THE TRANSFORMATIVE JUSTICE MOVEMENT

*Edited by*
Ejeris Dixon and Leah Lakshmi Piepzna-Samarasinha

AK
PRESS

"*Beyond Survival* is full of grounded, practical wisdom based in brave, thoughtful, collaborative efforts. It will be immensely useful to people trying to respond to the real crises our communities are facing with creative solutions that actually build healing and safety. *This* is the collection that so many of us have been waiting for, capturing the knowledge generated by grassroots experiments undertaken by bold, imaginative activists working to respond to and prevent violence. We will be using this as a reference book for building community responses to harm and violence for decades to come." —Dean Spade, author of *Normal Life: Administrative Violence, Critical Trans Politics, & the Limits of Law*

"I've been waiting for this book for so many years. Gritty, unsentimental, blunt, compassionate, and visionary, the wildly varied voices, insights, and experiences collected in this exceptional—and essential— anthology help chart new pathways through the harms of violence in its interrelated interpersonal, vigilante, and structural forms. Appearing at precisely the moment we need them most, these visions, questions, and practices will stir your imagination, fuel your own radical dreams, and open your heart to the possibility of transformed futures for us all." —Kay Whitlock, author of *Considering Hate: Violence, Goodness, and Justice in American Culture and Politics*

"*Beyond Survival* arrives just on time. Through the combined brilliance of Ejeris Dixon and Leah Lakshmi Piepzna-Samarasinha we are offered a beautiful invitation: away from any quick and easy solutions that don't ever do what they purport and toward a fundamental rethinking of what safety is, and a lifetime practice learning, relearning, and creating it through community with all the messiness it entails. This book is truly making the road by dreaming and I'm so grateful for it." —Tourmaline, filmmaker

"Somewhere between a call to action, a love letter, and a prayer, *Beyond Survival* is a gift to those of us working for justice. The voices in this collection are strong and compassionate, and their reflections are honest and open-hearted. Readers will feel challenged, inspired, and held by this critically important book. It will surely inspire change." —Beth E. Richie, author of *Arrested Justice: Black Women, Violence, and America's Prison Nation*

"*Beyond Survival* is a book for anyone yearning for transformation within themselves and across communities. If I had this book when I first began organizing, I would not have felt so alone and lost when seeking ways to confront conflict, harm, and violence without policing and punishment. As our movements evolve, so must what we consider as essential reading—*Beyond Survival* is clearly essential reading." —Charlene A. Carruthers, author of *Unapologetic: A Black, Queer, and Feminist Mandate for Radical Movements*

"If you're serious about toppling the pillars of white supremacy in the United States, start by reading *Beyond Survival*. In 1968, the Civil Rights Movement brought the earliest glimmers of democracy to the U.S. and the sharp thinking and activism of feminists of color have continued to forge pathways moving us forward, together. Deep societal inequalities ensure progress is met with push back, evidenced in the increased criminalization and targeting of the most vulnerable and marginalized among us. Those of us committed to a people-centered society grounded in accountability and transparency must create parallel systems that replace 20th century policing with 21st-century transformative justice. How do we get from here to here? Luckily for us, editors Ejiris Dixon and Leah Lakshmi Piepzna-Samarasinha have provided a blueprint, featuring some of the brightest minds making transformative justice a reality. While many articles and essays have highlighted the 'why' of transformative justice, the question of 'how' persists. Now, *Beyond Survival* boldly answers. Ejeris and Leah, along with the featured writers, have propelled transformative justice into today's stagnant policy discourse. The co-editors don't shy away from the messy parts, the hard work, or tenacity it takes to perform transformative justice, they embrace it. They know, like Audre Lorde before them, that survival 'sounds like a promise.' And to make the promise real, we need to know 'how' to survive. With interviews, stories of success, and unadulterated realness, *Beyond Survival* shows us how to keep going, how to keep pressing forward, how to survive until we are beyond the injustices of today." —Eric Ward, Executive Director of the Western States Center and Civil Rights Strategist

ISBN: 9781849353625
E-ISBN: 9781849353632
Library of Congress Control Number: 2019933781

AK Press
370 Ryan Avenue #100
Chico, CA 95973
www.akpress.org
akpress@akpress.org

AK Press
33 Tower St.
Edinburgh EH6 7BN
Scotland
www.akuk.com
ak@akedin.demon.co.uk

The above addresses would be delighted to provide you with the latest AK
Press distribution catalog, which features books, pamphlets, zines, and stylish
apparel published and/or distributed by AK Press. Alternatively, visit our websites for the complete catalog, latest news, and secure ordering.

Cover design and interior illustrations by Siana Sonoquie,
unless otherwise noted

Printed in the United States of America on acid-free, recycled paper

# CONTENTS

## Part Three:
## We Didn't Call It TJ, but Maybe It
## Worked Anyway? . . . . . . . . . . . . . . . 189

## Part Four:
## What Did We Dream Then,
## What Do We Know Now? . . . . . . . . 255

*To the ones who lived, the ones who didn't, and the future we are building for all of us*

# FOREWORD

## ALEXIS PAULINE GUMBS

"I love the word survival. It sounds to me like a promise."
—Audre Lorde[1]

"Freedom is not a secret. It's a practice."
—Alexis Pauline Gumbs

*Beyond Survival.* The title is poetic. Recursive. Survival already means to live beyond. Beyond what? Beyond disasters, systemic and interpersonal. Beyond the halted breathing of our ancestors. Beyond yesterday. And five minutes ago. Beyond that. The change-shapers and community-builders gathered together in this book are all visionaries. But that's not it. This book puts the "be" in "beyond."

This book, encyclopedic yet inevitably incomplete because it seeks to document generations of practice, is one we will continue to reference for a long time in order to be beyond the repetitive

---

1   This reflection was cut from an early draft of "Eye to Eye: Black Women, Hatred and Anger," by Audre Lorde (Audre Lorde Papers, Spelman College Archive).

violence of our current society, the violence we reproduce by our harm of each other and our denial of harm. So before you start using this book you must already know: You have survived. Numerous disastrous harms that could have destroyed you did not quite destroy you. You live. Beyond that, you must also acknowledge that the relationships, organizations, and spaces you have moved through have survived *you*, a person like other people, shaped by systems of harm. Breathe on that.

This is not a guidebook on how to be harmless.

This is not a glossary of words to prove you're down.

This is not a boilerplate for your organization's next grant.

This is beyond that.

This book does more than document a movement that is still moving. It seeks to accompany you and us on a journey beyond what we can imagine right now. It promises to be with you when you intentionally or unintentionally harm one or many people again. When your old hurts make it feel impossible to be in community. When conflicts we thought we resolved show up again. It acknowledges that there is no way to beyond but through.

This is a generous text, created by people who imagine that a more ethical and loving world can emerge in the middle of the worst muck of racialized, ableist heterocapital. The primary offering here is a space to be.

Be here.

Be all over the place.

Be messy.

Be wrong.

Be bold in your hopefulness.

Be confused in community.

Be reaching past isolation.

Be part of the problem.

Be hungry for after.

Be helpful in the midst.

Be so early in the process.

Be broken by belief.

Be bolstered by brave comrades.

Be unbelievably unready.

Be alive.

Let this book be with you, like air is with you on a screaming planet. Not clean, but necessary. Not comfortable, but supportive. Let this book be with you like our ancestors are with us, not perfect, but instructive. Not finished, but full. Let this book be with you like I am with you. Curious and unrealistic, like you are with yourself. Problematic and prophetic and possible. Eternally available for transformation based on your still having something to learn and to teach us.

I am grateful to Ejeris and Leah for holding this project like they have held our communities, with a femme fierceness and provocative honesty that turns their own lessons into shareable fire. Their faith in this work and their diligent practice have retaught my breathing into safer and safer scales. I am grateful to you for your vulnerable presence. For your healing and opening heart. Beyond.

# INTRODUCTION

## EJERIS DIXON AND LEAH LAKSHMI PIEPZNA-SAMARASINHA

## HOW AND WHY WE CAME TO THIS PROJECT

LEAH: It was 2014, 2015, 2016. *The Revolution Starts at Home: Confronting Intimate Violence in Activist Communities*—the zine I coedited with fellow activist writers Ching-In Chen and Jai Dulani that turned into a mega-zine and then turned into a book published by the longtime, much-lamented independent feminist of color South End Press—was back in print after South End went bust. I got messages—via email, Instagram, and OKCupid DMs, from strangers and acquaintances on the street or at a queer of color performance night—thanking us for creating such a resource.

I was glad it was working for them. But I was also increasingly…flummoxed? We had come up with the idea for *The Revolution Starts at Home* in 2004. The zine first came out in 2008; the book came out in 2011. Twelve, thirteen, fourteen years later, perhaps twenty years since feminists of color most recently started talking about ways to deal with abuse and violence outside of the state or traditional antiviolence nonprofit structures, it was still the only book out there for people who were like, "Something is happening and I don't want to call the cops, or can't—what do I do?"

5

And in those twenty years, the world has changed. We still live in a brutal white-supremacist settler colonial ableist cissexist state. But twenty years ago, when my nonbinary of color, already-been-to-jail lover put me in a chokehold and I couldn't call the cops without being deported and risking them killing me, nobody was talking about how to address violence without the state. It felt hard enough to get other young Black, Indigenous, people of color (BIPOC) I was in movement organizing with to believe that yes, abuse happens here, and it's real and not justified by oppression. Then, for the years that followed, getting other antiviolence workers at the crisis line where I worked to imagine nonstate approaches to partner abuse and sexual assault seemed like "crazy" talk.

Not only that, but getting any writing about non-state approaches to violence into the mainstream media felt like a wild dream. When we published *The Revolution Starts at Home*, our editor told us not to put "transformative justice"[1] in the title because no one would know what it meant. But twenty years later, all those hundreds of workshops, attempted accountability processes, late-night conversations, rallies, action camps, huge heated Facebook fights, minizines about consent handed out in the club, rallies held after murders, community databases and Safe Neighborhood maps, Safer Relationship classes, and safety team trainings have paid off. The world is still messed up, but it is also different.

In my experience, the years from 2010 to 2012 were a tough time for transformative justice (TJ). I was bitter and so were a lot of people I knew. They had tried TJ and it had been a huge disaster, or it hadn't worked perfectly, or it left them with more questions than answers. Some people got into vigilantism, or talked about it anyway, because, hey, beating the shit out of someone has

---

1  We had a long discussion about whether or not to capitalize transformative justice (TJ) throughout the book, and we decided on lower case for a few reasons. We want TJ to be an accessible practice that everyday people can use. We don't want to contribute to the "formalization" of TJ. We also want the work to be seen as real and valid, and we want the movement work to be respected. Whether to capitalize the term depends on your context, and we wanted to explain our intent here.

an impact you can see. Projects burnt out, and longtime organizers took long breaks from TJ work that often became permanent.

But at the same time we witnessed a rise in both reporting and activism around police and ICE violence and around stranger murders of BIPOC, especially Black and brown trans women, disabled people, and sex workers. With the rise of Black Lives Matter, the Movement for Black Lives, Idle No More, and organizing led by immigrant, Latinx, and other people of color to stop police and immigration violence, more and more people seemed to believe that prisons and police were socially destructive and unnecessary. I felt a turning point when I picked up a copy of *Rolling Stone* in 2014 and saw their article, "Policing Is a Dirty Job, but Nobody's Gotta Do It: 6 Ideas for a Cop-Free World."[2] Fifteen years after my partner put me in a chokehold and my comrades had no idea what to do, those "wing-nut ideas" were now highlighted in a mainstream, national magazine.

EJERIS: I'm not a writer. So when Leah approached me to coedit this book, I thought it was a joke and I turned her down. She asked again, in fact, I think she asked three times, and I eventually gave a fearful yes. Looking back, I'm grateful I said yes, grateful to coshape this project. And while writing is not my thing, I do know violence: living through my own experiences of survival; supporting hundreds of survivors; creating organizing strategies on police violence, sexual violence, intimate partner violence, and hate violence; and crafting antiviolence curricula and policy.

From 2005 to 2013 I worked on violence almost every single day for ten to twelve hours a day. And since 2013 I seem to work on violence every other day. I've worked on more murders than I can count, attended more funerals than birthdays, and have a drawer where I keep the endless stock of cards for grieving parents, partners, and chosen family. I would write, "I'm sorry you've lost your loved one. I'm a member of ____ organization. You're going to meet a lot of people in the next few weeks. I'm

---

2   José Martín, "Policing Is a Dirty Job, But Nobody's Gotta Do It: 6 Ideas for a Cop-Free World," *Rolling Stone*, December 16, 2014.

here to help and to promise that I'm someone that you can rely on." I didn't know if I had something to contribute to a book, but I knew that I had something to contribute to the story of the transformative justice movement.

Within my time connected to this movement, transformative justice and community accountability strategies have become dramatically more visible. I want to make sure that we captured stories that aren't always as visible. There have been conversations, arguments, and even declarations of what and who is or isn't transformative enough. I want to ensure that we highlighted the breadth of the work and varying types of transformative justice. I want to make certain that we let TJ be free, that we don't judge TJ, put TJ into boxes, or constrain TJ just because she became a popular kid. And I want people to know that for so many of us TJ is already in us, in our families and lived experiences, and is something that we just call life.

## WHY THIS BOOK

So many people experiencing violence or other emergencies don't want to call the police—or in some cases understand that they *should* not—but have no idea of what to do instead. In the years leading up to our decision to coedit this book, both of us witnessed many conversations where people would complain that there were "no resources" to explain how transformative justice or community accountability works. Both of us knew that there were resources, but you need to know where to look to find them. Accessing so many of the resources that we knew about required knowing who to ask, what workshops to take, where and when they were happening, and what terms to Google—and if you were outside a particular generation or movement context, knowing all that didn't come easy. Organizations don't always stay around and are often under-resourced, so if you don't know where to look, you may find only the remnants.

At the same time, there's been an upswing in the past five years of writing about transformative justice that sings its praises and talks about what a wonderful thing it is but is short on the specifics of how exactly you do it.

This project began because we wanted to offer a resource that could help explain not *why* but *how* to do transformative justice. In the recent upsurge of popular discussion of abolition and transformative justice, a number of essays and think pieces have eloquently addressed the whys of TJ: the violence of prisons and the fact that prisons and policing do not increase safety for survivors of violence who are Black, brown, queer, trans, broke, immigrant, disabled, or sex-working. They explain, mostly for people who don't have these experiences, that contact with the cops can end in our deaths. But they don't talk about the nitty-gritty work needed to create an alternative to policing. In working on this book, we wanted to open up the definition of TJ. Many people have told us that when they think of transformative justice, they think it is "a really long process where people talk about what happened, cry, get overwhelmed, and eventually stop answering their emails."

While processes are important—and we've included stories of some that, miraculously, worked!—we also wanted to fill in some of the million different ways "not 911" can look. So this book includes disabled-made toolkits for supporting people who are experiencing emotional crises without calling the cops; Trans Lifeline's story of running a national crisis line by and for trans people that, unlike every other suicide prevention hotline, never calls 911 without an explicit request; Oakland Power Projects' deep dive into how Black and brown people in Oakland deal with medical crises and overdoses; Audre Lorde Project's detailed toolkit for creating safer club and party spaces without police; and Audrey Huntley's descriptions of how she and other Indigenous women and Two-Spirit people led successful murder investigations into the deaths of Indigenous women when the cops failed to act, using ceremony and the skill of "just talking to people." Addressing violence while not engaging with police, prisons, and courts is a beautiful task that can also feel totally overwhelming. These pieces show some of the many ways people can dive in.

Theory without practice can be irresponsible, and it can drive people who need immediate solutions away from the support they need. We want to show the messy, beautiful, and unromanticized aspects of this movement. We want to highlight the stories and strategies of everyone who tried something just because they had to, because no one else was going to, because, like us, they didn't know if they would survive. We also want to provide space for reflecting on how far we have come and where we are as a movement. Whenever TJ organizers get together, we start telling the truly wild stories of all the shit we've seen, like the times a fight broke out during a process, the times we tried to figure out whether there is a TJ strategy for murder, or the times we raised funds and provided food, offered shelter, and paid medical bills for someone because we weren't sure what else to do.

This book includes interviews with some people who have been doing this work a really long time, and their reflections help us to see how far we have come. We lift up the memories of organizations and projects such as Sista II Sista, Challenging Male Supremacy Project, Young Women's Empowerment Project, Support NY, Philly Stands Up, the StoryTelling and Organizing Project (STOP), Chrysalis Collective, Community Against Rape and Abuse (CARA), and others, many of whom are now fading from collective consciousness and whose thousands of hours of often-unpaid labor are the reason we are here.

Recognizing that people sometimes talk about TJ as if it were an easy, wonderful, utopian thing, we've included frank stories of the real deal, the messy parts, the hard work, and how people are finding ways to do it anyway. We hope these stories inspire and encourage you. We hope this book gives you practical knowledge for deepening your own TJ practice, reminds you of strategies you may have already tried, and invites you to learn from those experiences as well as our own.

Finally, because the origin stories of books are often shrouded in mystery, we feel it's important to note that we cocreated this book waiting at gates for planes to take off, shouting messages to each other using voice-to-text on our phones, sitting through three-hour Zoom calls filled with the everyday hilarity of our lives, writing at three in the morning when we couldn't sleep, and surviving crises that nearly led to nervous breakdowns as we navigated the intensities of this world in our bodies and communities.

This book grew from the soil of a Black and brown queer feminist friendship and comradeship, grounded in mutual respect, honesty, and care. It was not cocreated from an ivory tower or a place of protected privilege. We want you to know that you can write your own book, too—at the kitchen table and in the waiting room, or sitting on the floor of Gate 38C with your phone plugged into the wall. You don't have to wait for permission or to be a "real writer" to do it. You can just move with intention and offer the world the brilliant tools you and your communities have crafted from hustle and brilliance. In our work of making the world that is coming, where prisons and police are a memory and we have many ways of preventing and addressing harm as human beings, we need nothing less.

## PART ONE

# MAKING THE ROAD BY DREAMING

## STORIES OF ACCOUNTABILITY

1

# BUILDING COMMUNITY SAFETY

## PRACTICAL STEPS TOWARD LIBERATORY TRANSFORMATION

*Ejeris Dixon*


"Mom, when you were growing up, did you ever call the police?"

"I can't remember any time that we did."

"What did you do if something violent happened?"

"It depended on the situation. Often, we could send for the uncles, brothers, fathers, or other family members of people involved to interrupt violence. However, there was this time when we had this family that lived on our block, where the husband was attacking his wife. And people were fed up, so some men in the community with standing—a minister, teacher, doctor, and others—decided to intervene. Those men stopped by the house to let the husband know that they wouldn't tolerate his behavior and it needed to stop."

\* \* \*

My mom grew up in New Orleans in the 1940s, 1950s, and 1960s. Her entire life was marked by experiences of state violence and Jim Crow segregation. The police, white citizens' councils, and the Klan intermingled to form the backbone of a racist political and economic system. Her experiences were not unique. Historically and currently most marginalized communities—including Black people, poor people, queer and trans people, and people with disabilities—have experienced violence and discrimination from police, emergency services, and the legal system.

Just as the use of state violence against Black communities is not new, neither are the ideas of transformative justice or community accountability. *Transformative justice* and *community accountability* are terms that describe ways to address violence without relying on police or prisons. These approaches often work to prevent violence, to intervene when harm is occurring, to hold people accountable, and to transform individuals and society to build safer communities. These strategies are some of the only options that marginalized communities have to address harm.

The work of transformative justice can happen in a variety of ways. Some groups support survivors by helping them identify their needs and boundaries while ensuring their attackers agree to these boundaries and atone for the harm they caused. Other groups create safe spaces and sanctuaries to support people escaping from violence. There are also community campaigns that educate community members on the specific dynamics of violence, how to prevent it, and what community-based programs are available.

As the powerfully inspiring movement to end anti-Black state violence continues to grow, we must ensure that our work toward community safety receives the same attention and diligence. As a person who has survived multiple forms of violence, I know that ending state violence alone will not keep me, my family, my friends, or my community safe. I'm excited by the campaigns that organizers are pursuing to divert money away from police departments and into community services. However, I want us to push this work one step further. I believe we can build community safety systems that will one day operate independently from the police and government.

The process of building community safety poses some critical questions to our movements:

- What is the world that we want?

- How will we define safety?

- How do we build the skills to address harm and violence?

- How do we create the trust needed for communities to rely on each other for mutual support?

I'd like to offer some answers to these questions in the form of principles for building community safety strategies. By acting on these principles, everyone can take steps to decrease our reliance on police and prisons.

## RELATIONSHIP BUILDING

From 2005 to 2010, I had the privilege of serving as the founding program coordinator of the Safe OUTside the System (SOS) Collective at the Audre Lorde Project. During that time, I worked alongside other queer and trans people of color living in Central Brooklyn to create a campaign to address state violence and anti-LGBTQ violence without relying on the criminal legal system. I learned that the process of building community-based strategies can fundamentally reshape our ways of engaging with each other.

Violence and oppression break community ties and breed fear and distrust. At its core, the work to create safety is to build meaningful, accountable relationships within our neighborhoods and communities. Within the SOS Collective, we made it a point to do outreach in the immediate area after incidents of violence. While it often felt terrifying to talk about the work of preventing and ending violence against LGBTQ people of color, we built strong allies and had life-changing conversations.

Time and time again, I've known people who were saved by the relationships they built. I've witnessed people selling drugs address and intervene in transphobic violence because of relationships. I know friends who've helped their neighbors escape from violent relationships based on the connections they have built together.

If and when violence occurs, the people who live closest are most likely to help us, and vice versa. Relationship building doesn't have to involve old-school door-knocking. It can be as simple as attending community events, saying hello and introducing yourself to your neighbors, or inviting your neighbors to events that you organize. It can be talking to your noisy neighbor about calling the cops. It's about the necessity of meeting the businesses and store owners in your immediate areas and on routes that you frequently use.

This strategy is not without complications.

For many people, particularly women, trans, and non-binary people, the act of engaging with strangers can open us up to harassment and even violence. At the same time, these challenges shouldn't prevent us from building relationships; they may merely shift the ways that we go about doing so.

Additionally, we must also be cognizant of the way that class, educational privilege, and gentrification can impact relationship building. Gentrification is its own form of violence within many low-income neighborhoods. Many gentrifiers/newcomers act fearfully and avoid shopping, attending events, or building relationships within their communities. Gentrifiers/newcomers who are also movement leaders tend to create movements and strategies not grounded in the lived experiences of the people most impacted by violence.

While I don't believe that we can separate ourselves from our privileges, we can leverage them toward justice. My educational privilege and relationships mean that I know a lot of lawyers and know about our rights during police encounters. I've made sure to share "know your rights" information with my neighbors, to observe the cops alongside my neighbors, and to give legal referrals.

Through these moments I've strengthened relationships with my neighbors and deepened trust.

## BOLD, SMALL EXPERIMENTS

Some of the most innovative transformative justice and community accountability projects have come from bold, small experiments. The Safe OUTside the System Collective started from the audacity of a small team of people who believed that we could prevent and intervene in violence without the police. For over a year, through weekly meetings, we discussed our experiences of violence and brainstormed responses. During these times, LGBTQ people of color were reporting physical attacks to us at least once a month, and two or three people were murdered each year in Central Brooklyn.

Meanwhile, the NYPD was operating like an occupying army. It was common to walk home from the subway and see officers stationed on every block or large groups of police officers walking down the street. We had no choice but to create a community safety campaign. Our campaign recruited local businesses and organizations and trained them to recognize, prevent, and intervene in violence without relying on law enforcement.

At first, we had no idea how to work on this, but we researched, experimented, and talked with the business owners themselves to understand how they already addressed violence and then worked with them to ensure that their strategies included LGBTQ people of color. At the time, we did not think we were doing something innovative. We just knew we needed to build new structures for our ultimate survival.

I believe that bold, small experiments rise and fall based on two fairly simple ideas: planning and perseverance. We have to be accountable enough to continue our experiments, to measure them, to hold ourselves to high standards, and to believe in them. Even within projects carried out completely by unpaid volunteers, we are using a very valuable resource: time. Often, those of us with the least money, time, or privilege put a disproportionate amount of our time into movement work. So as we continue our experiments, we need to talk about our goals, the resources we need, and how we are going to distribute those resources equitably.

The crucial questions are: What can you help build? What conversations can you start to increase the safety of your community? What new structures or collaborations will you create to decrease your reliance on the criminal legal system? Perhaps you want to think about one form of violence to work on and build your knowledge from there. You could start simply by having a dinner with your friends, family, and chosen family to discuss how you all can better support each other. Or you could raise the issue of police violence and harassment at your next tenants' association meeting and see if there's a way that your neighbors want to engage with each other rather than with the police. Next, you could research ways people can get emergency medical assistance outside of 911. The possibilities are endless.

No matter how small they are, our experiments should aspire to center the experiences of the most marginalized folks within our communities. One of the major challenges of the movements of the 1960s and 1970s was their inability to fully hold and implement an intersectional analysis. We need to make sure that our bold experiments center the experiences of Black people, Indigenous people, people of color, disabled people, trans people, poor people, low-income people, migrants, and all marginalized people. Starting small gives us the opportunity to collectively imagine community safety responses without telling anyone to wait their turn.

## TAKING TIME TO BUILD SKILLS

In order to ensure safety for our communities, we need to have the necessary skills, whether those are skills in deescalating violence, planning for safety, resolving conflicts, holding community accountability processes, or navigating consent. In each case, there is a core skill set that creates a foundation for addressing interpersonal and state violence within our communities. One of our largest failures in this arena seems to stem from arrogance.

There are times we believe we have the skills to address harm simply because we have a strong political analysis or a strong desire to address harm. There's a substantial distinction between having skills and learning skills, between being experts and practicing.

In activist and progressive communities, we're often accustomed to attending one training or reading one essay and then declaring ourselves leaders and educators on an issue. I believe the notion of instant expertise runs contrary to our liberatory values. Safety is not a product that we can package and market. Community safety is not a certification that we place on our résumés. We are invited to practice community safety skills with one of our most precious resources, our lives. In a world that is already trying to kill us with a multitude of oppressive strategies, we must be deliberate and vigilant in honoring where we each are in our journeys.

I've spent the last ten years practicing verbal de-escalation strategies to address violence on the street, at events, and at actions and protests. I am constantly learning and growing. Every incident is different; sometimes I can reduce or diffuse conflict, and other times I fail miserably. The strategies or tactics that work in one instance can go horribly wrong in others, even under similar conditions. Intervening in violence in the moment calls for using nonverbal communication to read, communicate, and negotiate safety. With each incident I am developing my instincts; by practicing I learn, despite the outcome.

We must practice community safety as we would practice an instrument or a sport. By practicing in slow, measurable, and deliberate ways, we build the knowledge we need to diffuse and address conflict within our communities.

We can also learn a great deal if we are open to engaging with people who have different politics than we do. I left the SOS Collective in 2010 because it was time for new leadership, and I was ready to continue learning in other settings. I took a job at a large LGBTQ antiviolence organization that wasn't involved with transformative justice or community accountability work. I did this intentionally and deliberately to see what I could learn from working outside my comfort zone.

When we make judgment into one of our primary organizing strategies, we reduce the trust needed to create safety. Some of the people with the most practice working on violence are deeply embedded within the criminal legal system or other punitive structures. I've had enlightening conversations about trends in homophobic and transphobic violence with prosecutors. I've also learned about de-escalating violence from bouncers and from school counselors. I deeply wanted to learn from people who had held down more incidents than I had.

This new experience expanded my knowledge and deepened my practice. I coordinated organizers in their efforts to implement advocacy and community-organizing strategies in response to more than forty murders of queer and trans people.

I had the opportunity to refine my process developing and presenting community-organizing options to recent survivors of violence and to surviving family members. Through this intense practice I created a process of rapid-response organizing in the aftermath of violence. I was able to use all the skills I had developed while doing community safety campaigns, and I gained a deeper, more nuanced understanding of organizing around trauma. The ability to work with survivors of intimate-partner violence, sexual violence, homophobic and transphobic violence, and police violence was invaluable, as was my experience working with survivors and organizers around the country.

I also want to acknowledge that in these times, taking time to practice can feel like a luxury. The urgency is real. We are dying. As a Black queer woman, I live and love in communities of survivors. But we will not create, implement, and achieve the measured and nuanced community safety systems we deserve through shoddy and rushed attempts. Instead, we must collectively weave our stories into strategies based on sharing what worked and what failed. Therefore, let me ask you: What has kept you alive so far? What are the lessons and themes and patterns that you can draw from? How can you practice safety? Where can you deepen your knowledge? And what unlikely allies can you recruit as learning partners?

# SPENDING LESS TIME JUDGING SURVIVORS

One day, while I was working at the Audre Lorde Project, I received an email that deeply upset me. We had recently attended a march organized by a mother whose gay son had been horrifically murdered. This mother had organized the march to raise awareness about her son's murder and was also passing out flyers that asked people to report information to the police. In response, I received this message from a critic: "I can't believe that you would support state-based responses. Can you tell us about how this is in line with your politics?"

I was incensed by the email. While I didn't believe that the state would bring justice in this case, I believe in supporting Black mothers. I particularly believe in supporting Black mothers who are brave, proud, and resilient enough to organize against homophobic violence in the face of devastating loss. I do not need to dictate the strategies surviving family members should use. Instead, I find ways to support them that are in line with my politics because I know that just as punishment does not transform behavior, neither does judgment.

When we make judgment into one of our primary organizing strategies, we reduce the trust needed to create safety.

When we say "Don't call the cops," we usually assume that we're talking to privileged, college-educated, upper-class, mostly white people who aren't aware of the impact that calling the police has on communities of color. We also need to push back against our societal conditioning that tells us policing and prisons make us safer. Yet when people of color and particularly Black people choose to call emergency services, it is an inherent negotiation. We come from generations of state violence. Many of us have family members in prison. Most of us have either directly experienced police violence or intimately know people who have. These are not flippant decisions. Yet when we create a culture of judgment so thick that we make it impossible for people to admit that they have called emergency services or needed to, there are critical impacts. I've had many queer people of color survivors or witnesses of violence come to me for support, distraught that they called 911. "I heard my neighbor screaming. I couldn't figure out how to safely intervene. Was I wrong to call 911?"

When people who've experienced life-threatening injuries or people witnessing violence decide to call an ambulance, we must acknowledge that we have yet to build an alternative to 911. However, if we create a culture in which people feel comfortable sharing stories about when they called emergency services but didn't want to, we actually learn about crucial needs for community safety projects.

I believe that we can practice transformative justice while simultaneously reducing the harm from the state. Remembering that one of the primary goals of our work is relationship building, we must ask ourselves who wins when we shame survivors for using the available options when all such options are violent.

Therefore, our work is to find ways to hold both compassion and critique while also building our awareness of when to use which tool. As a practical step I would suggest examining when and why we use judgment in our conversations with each other and whether we're seeking to educate or support. We can reframe both education and support in nonjudgmental ways. For instance, education can include sharing tools for de-escalating conflict that a person could try before calling 911. We can achieve compassion without judgment when we focus on making sure that people feel heard and understood and that they do not feel isolated. Compassionately discussing calling 911 with someone can sound like this: "I'm so sorry that happened. It seems like you didn't have very many options. If it's helpful, I'm happy to be someone you call on if you ever find yourself in that situation again."

I'd like to offer these ideas as sparks for our collective imagination. To do this right we must start small, build to scale, and allow ourselves to learn from both our successes and our failures.

In this piece I have discussed smaller steps toward community safety, but in order to be successful we must connect these strategies with larger liberatory movements. We must bring these ideas and conversations into our meetings, organizations, and movements. We need to take time to include them within our demands and campaigns strategies to build community safety and reduce harm. Even as we act urgently to resist the state violence that is killing our communities, we must also do slow work to develop community safety and resilience.

## 2

# BEYOND FIRING

## HOW DO WE CREATE COMMUNITY-WIDE ACCOUNTABILITY FOR SEXUAL HARASSMENT IN OUR MOVEMENTS?

*Amanda Aguilar Shank*

BEING A PRISON ABOLITIONIST IS A LIFE PATH, IT'S A FRAMEWORK that we develop together through doing and learning. This story is just one of thousands that I hope can help us learn together what happens when we apply our principles to the messy and complicated world(s) we live in.

Sometimes people have a misconception that abolition is entirely about firing the cops and burning the prisons. It is actually about knowing that the current systems we have put in place to address harm are actually causing additional harm. It is about realizing that we have a responsibility to align the ways we relate to each other with our values—from the most intimate relationship up to larger systems like the criminal and immigration systems.

Abolition is the visionary process of imagining and building the structures that we want to see replace the ones we are dismantling today. Yes, I want to see an end to the criminal and immigration systems as we know them today. I want to see the end to cops, prisons, imperialism, and militarization. I have seen how these systems harm me and my family and the families of millions in the name of safety for the few.

Yet interpersonal harm is a basic fact of human reality. We can't avoid being harmed and harming others. It's just that current systems we have in place perpetuate harm and increase suffering, while claiming to do the opposite. Abolition is a hopeful vision that means each moment where harm happens is an opportunity to transform relationships and communities, build trust and safety, and grow slowly toward the beautiful people we are meant to be, in the world that we deserve.

This past spring, as part of the counterattack against white supremacy and the Trump regime, Enlace, the organization where I work, was asked to cosponsor a rally. Usually, this would have been an easy decision. Dozens of organizations with whom we collaborate had cosponsored the rally, and the "United Against Hate" message was timely and unifying. But when I saw Voz Hispana on the list of anchor organizations, I was confronted, once again, by the experience of sexual harassment I had as a younger organizer. Once again, I was thrown back into the exhausting and frustrating process of pushing for accountability for somebody who had harmed me and others, when our movement does not yet have the tools to hold this accountability process in collective.

Francisco Lopez has recently emerged as one of the core leaders of Voz Hispana Cambio Comunitario. From about 2010 until 2013, I worked as an organizer on immigrant rights issues for another organization, in close collaboration with Francisco, who was then the executive director of a statewide immigrant rights coalition and was both more powerful and significantly older than me. In early 2013, Francisco began making unwanted sexual advances toward me; these advances occurred weekly over the course of several months. What started with Francisco coming on to me intensely one night, and me turning him down repeatedly, eventually became phone calls, emails, pulling me aside at events, telling me stories about his sexual history, and offering me a significant salary increase if I would work for him. When I asked him to stop over email, documenting the exchange, he attempted to diminish me publicly while continuing the advances.

On one week-long project out of town, he literally heckled me as I spoke in a public forum that I had helped organize ("you've talked enough already, get down!"), spoke over me in meetings, and refused to meet with me to share information I needed—then at night he would tell me almost jokingly that I should join him in his hotel room.

I felt many of the things that people in my position feel—isolation, shame, anger, confusion. I felt disillusioned with our movement spaces. As a young woman, harassment was not new to me, but I felt especially pained and naive to have expected something different in the movement. I considered going into a different line of work.

But I liked the work and believed in it. I just didn't want to work with Francisco. At this time, Ramon Ramirez was serving as board chair of the immigrants' rights coalition. I observed Ramon's leadership style over time. Entering a room, he would greet everybody, including young women with minor leadership roles, with respect. He would ask about family. He promoted women in his organization, spoke about their accomplishments, and stepped back to make space for women in public speaking and leadership roles. He talked frequently and publicly about the importance of advancing women and LGBTQ leadership, and about his own commitment as a cisgender man to unlearning sexism and homophobia.

I trusted Ramon and so, one day, mentioned Francisco's behavior to him. Ramon was livid. He told me that it wasn't the first time he had heard stories like the one I was sharing, but that nobody had wanted to come forward. I told Ramon that I was open to talking with other people who had similar experiences with Francisco. Sometime after that conversation, Ramon connected me with three other women who each had their own stories about Francisco's sexual harassment; one was a current staff member of the immigrant rights organization and two were former staffers.

In our group of four, we shared our stories and recognized patterns in Francisco's behavior going back many years. My feelings of shame and self-doubt fell away as I learned about Francisco pressuring other women in similar, sometimes identical ways to what I had experienced. Collectively, we created a list of behavior we had experienced from Francisco: kissing and attempting to kiss, harassing supervised employees and student interns, offering permanent employment and a larger salary during the period in which harassment was occurring, and pressuring to share a bed or hotel room while on professional travel. Over several weeks of talks, we broke our isolation, and it began to feel both possible and necessary to come forward together about our experiences.

Now, as part of a group of four women who had experienced similar behavior from Francisco, we brought written testimonies of our experiences to the board of directors of the immigrant rights coalition, and, soon after, Francisco quietly resigned his position as executive director. We did not go to the press or call him out publicly. One of the women in our group was still working at the organization and bearing extreme stress as a result of the situation. We also did not want to damage the reputation of the organization, harm the immigrant and Latinx community, or provide any more fodder to white supremacist organizations who are consistently on the offensive in our state.

In the end, Francisco left and rumors circulated. The immigrants' rights organization held discussions about gender justice—which continue today—and hired a new executive director. Each of us in our group of four moved on with our respective work. Francisco has never contacted us again.

In the end, this is a textbook "success." Justice was served, and the perpetrator was removed from his position of authority.

However, people do not simply disappear. Francisco has re-emerged now in Voz Hispana, which collaborates with several other immigrants' rights organizations. I continue to feel unsettled. I do not regret our actions that led toward accountability, but I continue to ask "what's next?" Yes, this abusive person has been cast out of an organization, but something more is required than the "throwaway" approach.

I believe our wider movement community is capable of holding a process of accountability where we (1) protect community members when the potential for harm from specific people exists and (2) hold open a door to a transformative healing process, including people on both sides of the harm.

## WE NEED TO SCALE UP ACCOUNTABILITY TO THE COMMUNITY LEVEL

Over the past several years, other impacted women, our allies, and I have used different strategies to leverage our networks and build accountability. I offer these up with hopes that they can be of use to others in similar situations and can build toward accountability processes that mirror our values.

### Stage 1

The first step that we took toward a community accountability process was in 2015. Francisco emerged in organizing spaces, and based on confidential conversations with several women, we were concerned that his behavior of sexual harassment may have continued. We drafted a letter, signed by the four women who came forward about our experiences, describing the behavior we had experienced. We felt vulnerable, since this was the first time our names were made public, and asked our allies to also draft a letter signed by a number of nonprofit directors and other community leaders. We circulated these "open letters" privately, but widely, through our networks. At the time, we felt that reaching out to the press could harm the movement as a whole, and we hoped that by one-on-one outreach we could create a critical mass of people who could act to promote women's safety.

After circulating the letters, we received a number of calls from people seeking more information about Francisco. One person ran a university internship placement program and had seen some red flags but was grateful to have additional information to back up her intuition. Others were working on projects with Francisco and were unsure about whether to continue.

Different people took different actions based on our letter. Some organizations stopped working with Francisco, others placed restrictions on his ability to access women one-on-one in their organization, others continued working with Francisco the same as they had before.

Our intention was to provide information that could help to alert and protect future women who may have been at risk of experiencing the same thing we experienced. This was a partial success.

For a time, it seemed that Francisco's work in our field lessened and that many people were taking precautions when working with him, though he did have a small core group that continued to align with him. Even though our names were now known to Francisco, none of the original four women was contacted by him or a proxy or ever received any acknowledgment or apology from Francisco. We had perhaps succeeded at limiting his reach and ability to continue the behavior, yet there was no sign that his behavior would change and no push to enter into an accountability process.

## *Stage 2*

Now in 2017, Francisco and Voz Hispana have again started to become more visible in organizing spaces and in the press. Voz Hispana has some shared turf with organizations where I work, along with one of the other women, making our jobs stressful and putting our dignity on the line as potential ally organizations side with either us or Voz Hispana.

I am contacted on a regular basis by organizations seeking information, asking to know more details and asking whether and how they should collaborate with Francisco and Voz Hispana. While I deeply appreciate when people reach out, every single one of these conversations is emotionally draining and takes time away from the important work that I love. Each time, I have to share our letters, hope that they get into the right hands, and direct well-meaning people about what appropriate action to take.

I am not the only one who is drained emotionally—the other women impacted, former board member allies like Ramon Ramirez, and others are also sinking energy and resources into this process. This extra load takes away from our work, work that is strategic, that is accountable to our communities, that is focused on changing the balance of power for marginalized communities and building frontline leadership. Our work is important, yet we find ourselves again and again engaging in a one-by-one process of educating and organizing around Francisco.

I long for some larger systems of accountability and guidelines about what is acceptable in our movement spaces and what the consequences are for those who choose not to live by our core values. I long for the ability to collectively hold those systems, for accountability to be a muscle that is practiced and strengthened over time by all of us.

### Stage 3

When I received the invitation to cosponsor the United Against Hate rally, I decided this time to honor my experience and the safety of other women in the movement, and to open the conversation a bit wider. Even after four years, it felt like a risk. As an AFAB cisgender woman of color I have been raised both in and out of movement spaces to put up with harassment and abuse, and to diminish myself in the face of male needs and ego. To begin to do otherwise is both liberating and frightening. I have pushed past these barriers because I believe the safety and leadership of women; trans people; and gender nonconforming people, women, and femmes is important. It is one of the key pieces that we need for our movements to be truly liberatory. Not only is it wrong for us to be harmed so constantly, but it limits our ability to grow toward our wildest visions of the future we need and deserve.

With this in mind, I sent the following email to the rally organizer:

> One lesson I have learned as an organizer is that there are no shortcuts, and sometimes we have to slow down in order to get things right, even when the realities we are facing are urgent and terrifying. To me this is called movement building. I hope to be engaged in a long future of movement building with you.
>
> That said, Enlace will not be able to endorse the Portland Stands United Against Hate rally

at this point. Voz Hispana is one of the primary "hosts" listed on the Facebook page. Voz Hispana is an organization led by Francisco Lopez.

Several years ago, Francisco left his job as Executive Director of [an immigrants' rights organization] after multiple women brought complaints demonstrating a pattern of years of physical and verbal harassment by Francisco towards women within the organization and supporters of the organization, including staff and interns that he supervised. I was one of those women.

To my knowledge Francisco has yet to be accountable to his behavior. I am not aware of any attempt by Francisco to acknowledge his actions, the impact of his actions, or make amends with the women impacted. This is concerning to myself and a number of movement leaders who have chosen not to work with him and organizations he represents. Since several years have passed, I believe this information must not be widely known, which is why I am sharing it now.

If we are going to build movements capable of winning, we have to win for all of us. This means fighting white supremacy, racism, transphobia, homophobia, sexism and economic oppression in all of their forms, even and especially when it means we have to look in the mirror. It means holding ourselves and each other accountable.

I hope that an accountability process will sometime be possible for Francisco, and that he may be willing to enter into that process. Until then, it is not possible for me to endorse collaboration with him and organizations he represents. If Voz Hispana were to leave the space, or if Francisco were to leave Voz Hispana, I would vote yes wholeheartedly to participating.

I hope that you all will hear this information with the seriousness that it deserves, and join me in a commitment to make our movement spaces safe and free from repeats of the oppression we face each day in our daily lives. It will not be done in a day, but every day we have the opportunity to do better.

The response from rally organizers was swift and appreciated. At a rally organizing meeting, my letter was read and another impacted woman offered a firsthand account of her experiences with Francisco. The rally coalition voted to suspend participation by Voz Hispana until an accountability process was undertaken. The rally organizers sent the following letter:

> It was brought to our attention that charges of sexual harassment have been leveled against the leader of your organization, Francisco. A few of the organizations endorsing this event and individuals involved in the planning are directly affected by this and asked that your group be removed as a co-sponsor due to repeated failed efforts to initiate an accountability process with Voz Hispana for Francisco. The issue of removing Voz Hispana as a co-sponsoring organization was proposed to a planning meeting which included over 40 representatives of the various endorsing organizations last night. The group voted unanimously to remove Voz Hispana as a co-sponsor due to the serious nature of the charges and to our group's commitment to the safety and rights of women in our social justice community.

Many in attendance recognized the important work that Voz Hispana does in this community and expressed the hope of working with Voz Hispana in the future if this issue was adequately addressed.

We had now gone from quietly circulating our letter, to constant one-on-one talks about Francisco Lopez, to engaging a coalition of over forty organizations in our sector, to moving dozens of organizations to stop working with Voz Hispana until an accountability process had taken place.

The rally organizers had an action plan and consulted with me and the other woman, but they did not place the burden of action on us. This is a clear example of what happens when allies step up *with* people impacted by harassment, and I hope other organizations will be able to take these bold steps in the future.

## OUR ORGANIZATIONS, COALITIONS, AND MOVEMENT SPACES NEED BOTH PROTOCOL AND THE WILL TO TAKE ACTION IN CASES OF SEXUAL HARASSMENT AND ACCOUNTABILITY

The response of the United Against Hate rally organizers in my experience was the exception, not the rule. More commonly, I am called on personally to guide and hold our movement accountable over and over. Partners call me asking whether they should work with Voz Hispana. Can they sponsor something that Voz Hispana is also sponsoring? Should they work with groups aligned with Voz Hispana?

It is exhausting to carry the weight of navigating the situation. This weight is lightened when people and organizations have a shared sense of what is acceptable and what constitutes accountability.

I am relieved at the ways people who harass are increasingly being publicly discussed and held accountable within the framework of the #MeToo movement, which often means being removed from positions of power. We need to start recognizing that each organization does not exist in isolation and that whether or not people who are harassing are on our payroll, they are our responsibility. We need community accountability.

If you are thinking, "yes, I want to be part of that solution" and are wondering how, here are some guidelines: If you are somebody who knows me and the situation with Francisco, please take these to heart. You can still call me, but I hope that the call will be to share the steps you are taking toward accountability rather than to ask me what to do.

- Start by believing survivors and allying with us. We are not the problem because we came forward with information about someone's abusive behavior. That behavior and subsequent lack of recognition or restitution are the real problems. Support those who have gone through harassment. Do the right thing, even when politics or positioning pressure you to do otherwise.

- Come up with a protocol in your organizations for how or if to work with people who have harassed and assaulted others in the movement. Decide not to help expand the visibility, leadership, and reach of people who are known to be harming other people and to be unaccountable.

- When you hear a rumor about harassment or assault, make it your job to approach the people who have committed harm or their organizations directly. Ask them what happened. Ask them what they are doing about it.

- Make it your job to approach people that you see working with people who have committed harm or their organizations when there is a history of harassment or assault. Describe your protocol to them and encourage them to develop one as well.

- Be public about the protocol and decisions you have made, even involving specific individuals.

- Be like Ramon Ramirez, particularly if you are a cis-male ally. Promote and lift up the leadership of women; trans people; and gender nonconforming people, women, and femmes. Talk about your commitment to dismantling sexism and homophobia when speaking publicly. Build a culture of respect for women, trans people, gender-non-conforming people, femmes, and all marginalized people.

- If you have access to funding, bring resources into the field of community-wide accountability and dismantling hetero-patriarchy. Do not fund organizations that have unresolved allegations of harassment. When situations are unclear or messy, default to siding with those who are marginalized.

## PATH BACK—
### WHAT IS THE TRANSFORMATIVE SOLUTION?

Accountability includes naming the behavior and impact of our actions, issuing an apology, and taking specific steps toward reconciliation or restitution.

I believe in the ability of people to grow and change. I have been harmed and have harmed people in the past, sometimes knowingly, sometimes unknowingly. None of us is perfect. Our first priority always has to be to protect people at risk of harm, but if we hope to build communities that are truly safe, we need to understand and transform the source of harm. Francisco's personal story is complex. Like my family, he lived through the brutal U.S.-backed civil war in El Salvador, experiencing imperialist political terror up close, watching his loved ones killed. Francisco has his own painful history, his own harmful patterns, his own demons to unpack, but also his own strengths. He is a powerful speaker and storyteller; he is funny, smart, and charismatic. When he has put his talents in service of his organizing and advocacy work, he is strikingly passionate and effective. On one level, he has harmed and betrayed people who trusted him. Yet on another he has demonstrated that he is willing to work to build a better world. He is a complex person, like all people, full of contradictions. I believe in a path back. I believe accountability can be a step toward greater wholeness, personally and as a movement. The project of building toward collective liberation is too important and too difficult to permanently cut people out when they make mistakes. We cannot afford it.

Simply firing and excluding people who harass is a practice that mirrors the ultimately ineffective approach of the criminal justice system. Today, such an approach may be the best blunt instrument that we have to increase safety in our communities. I believe it is almost always a step in the right direction. Still, I am troubled by the lack of options we have for exercising accountability.

I believe there is a path we can begin to walk toward building strong communities where sexual harassment and assault are simply not tolerated. I believe our movement is broad enough to offer a path back for those who violate our ethics and are ready to be held accountable. To develop this muscle, we need to start being more honest with ourselves and in public about the way that harm is being done and the ways that we are or aren't responding. We need to develop the capacity to struggle with each other, and we must be committed to learning this new skill movement-wide.

My work as a prison abolitionist has taught me that as much as we try to "throw away" people—through the prison industrial complex, through deportation, through violence—people do not simply "go away" when it is convenient or desired. Further, when somebody is "outside"—unaccountable, invisible, not a part of—there is very little possibility of reconciliation, transformation, or healing. Yet while I am hungry for a path back for those who do harm, it is not the burden of people harmed to continue to cover for, reach out, and hope for accountability from the people who have harmed them.

Covering for Francisco by remaining publicly silent about what he chose to do to me in 2013 has been a heavy burden that I am done carrying. Pushing for accountability, alone or in small numbers, with my own dignity at stake, has been another burden.

This article calls on each of you, readers, to help me to carry this weight. Will you accept my invitation?

## ENDNOTE

This piece was written and published in the fall of 2017, in the midst of the #MeToo movement. People who had experienced sexual assault and harassment were sharing their experiences and personal stories, and the public mood shifted from "This (sexual violence) is not acceptable!" to "Wow, this is literally every single woman and femme's experience" to "We must take action. Every man who has perpetrated sexual assault must be fired and blacklisted."

For me, the fervor of the mainstream #MeToo moment was exciting and necessary, but it failed to connect all the dots. In social justice communities, so many of us have histories of trauma that come from generations of people forced from our land, bent and twisted by patriarchy, slavery, and genocide. If we simply fire those unable to carry these histories, those who perpetuate harmful lessons they were forced to learn, we will lose.

Missing from the #MeToo conversation about blacklisting was the decades-old conversation in social justice communities about how to protect people who experience harm and abuse while creating a transformative path to wholeness—for the person harmed, the person who harmed, and the community as a whole. I decided to write about my experience mostly as a way to get it out of my body, get it out of the center of a local controversy, and turn it back to my community. My article says, "Help me, this is complicated, hold this with me."

I also wanted to find ways to insert abolitionary frameworks into a potentially transformative moment that felt like it was falling into the trap of protecting (mostly white cisgender women) victims by increasing the power and scope of the criminal (in) justice system. While there is something satisfying about knowing Hollywood mogul Harry Weinstein's ankle is finally chafing under an ankle monitor the same way the ankles of immigrants and POC parolees have been for years, we also know how this story ends. Any time the state steps in to deliver safety, it is always a white supremacist model of safety that sees our communities at the threats to be protected against. We never win when we expand the powers and resources of the state to control and punish.[1]

---

1   I'd like to thank all of my comrades in this work, but especially Walidah Imarisha, Nathaniel Shara, and Nyanga Uuka for their wise counsel, for directing me to resources, and for their writing and work in the field of transformative justice and abolition. Thank you also to Mariame Kaba, whose work deeply shapes my commitment to abolition and transformative solutions to harm. The work of transformation is collective work, and the knowledge we gather has wide and ancient origins. These talented people and many more have eased my personal journey and helped me clarify the ideas and beliefs presented in this article. It is a joy and honor to be part of this unfolding process with you all.

## 3

# ISOLATION CANNOT HEAL ISOLATION

## ONE SURVIVOR'S RESPONSE TO SEXUAL ASSAULT

*Blyth Barnow*

As a survivor I'm told that prisons are there to protect me. Keep me safe. My deepest desire is supposed to be incarceration for my abuser. I'm supposed to want him to suffer, to pay for what he did. But I've never wanted that. I wanted some healing. For me and for him. But you aren't supposed to say that. You aren't supposed to say that you love the person who harmed you. You get accused of loving him more than you love yourself. Like you can't do both. You are silently asked to choose. Your heart and your history, or your healing. You are told that healing means seeing him for what he really is, a rapist. But I knew him. I knew how much more he was. I loved him still. He was my friend, and being his friend meant I knew the ways he had already suffered. I wanted him to get the support he needed. I wanted to make sure this never happened again.

\* \* \*

It was five years after. I had just started talking about it. I was exploring my options. But everyone said I needed to file a police report. They said it wasn't about me. It wasn't about my politics. It was about keeping other girls safe. And what I heard, and what a few people had the gall to say, was that if he raped another girl then it would be my fault. So, I went.

I went to the town police station hoping nobody I knew had a parking ticket to pay that day. I took my mother with me. We were estranged, separated by our own legacy of violence, but I had nobody else to ask. We went to the window, a sheet of bulletproof glass between me and the female officer. I told her I wanted to report a rape. She was taken aback. She asked when it happened. I told her five years ago. She said she may not be able to help me. She'd have to look up the statute of limitations. A big book got thumbed through and closed. Six years, she said. Just in time.

We walked through the heavy gray door to meet the detective. A man. He sat casually on the corner of the desk. He asked me why I waited so long. Asked if I wanted to file a report. I said I wanted to know about the process. He said something like, file a report, the alleged perpetrator is notified, press charges, it goes before a judge. It is unlikely to go to trial, he said. You waited too long. And if it does, you are unlikely to win.

I asked if I could just put something on file. Something on record so that if another woman filed a report there would be precedent. She would be more likely to be believed. She could call on me. No, he said. Everyone has a right to know if they've been accused of a crime. He asked again if I wanted to file a report. Suggested that I should, seemingly unaware of what that would mean in this smallish Ohio town. I told him I was unsure. He gave me the form, and I stood to leave.

* * *

He was a year older than me. I could not imagine him in prison. Yet another privilege of his white skin and mine. He grew up working class at best, maybe poor. It was just him, his mother, his sister. He was never as tough as the other boys. Too tenderhearted, too sensitive. It was what I loved about him. A working-class sense of loyalty and responsibility had been bred into him. You never hit a woman, you never snitch on a friend, and you always lend a hand when someone is in trouble. He held true to all these codes—another thing I loved about him. But no matter how much heavy metal he listened to, his nerdy, thin-framed version of "boy" never stacked up to the masculinity he saw modeled. A masculinity rooted in the lie of white supremacy and patriarchy. A lie that says white men are more capable, more deserving. The lie that white men are naturally more powerful. In his mind it was his greatest fault. He was not strong enough. He couldn't fight, and he couldn't pull his mother and sister out of poverty. No matter how much he tried. So, he joined the air force, determined to be a better man.

A few months later he came home. He'd broken down during boot camp and got sent to the psych ward, a failure. And while he was there, he made a friend, a boy like him. A few weeks later he found that boy in a bathroom stall dead. It confirmed what he thought he already knew, that boys like him were too weak to live.

He told me that story the day before he raped me. His eyes glazed over, his muscles rigid. A friend and I gave him a beer and put him to bed. She and I slept in the next room over. I woke with a start in the middle of the night. He was standing in the doorway watching us. Numbly he said he just wanted to make sure we were still alive. I got up and walked him back to bed, crawled in with him, and held him as he cried. Because I loved him and that is what you do when a person has been shattered.

The next night I had a party. He drank too much and kept trying to kiss me. It was sad, to see a friend so undone. I kissed him a few times, rejected him more. All our friends watched.

When he raped me, I could see the way he was grasping for power, for some sense of control over his life. Part of me wanted to give it to him. The rest of me wanted to run. But I couldn't. I couldn't for all of the reasons that only a person raped by someone they love can understand. Shock, terror, fear, shock, shame, pity, shock, pain, embarrassment, shock, politeness, love, care, shock, disbelief, disbelief, disbelief.

\* \* \*

After leaving that police station I knew. I knew that the police, prison, a judge would never help me find what I was looking for. I would never be allowed to be a full person and neither would he. We would both be blamed and that blame could never move toward accountability. The process would be painful and neither of us would get what we deserved. So, I threw the police report out.

I always wondered if he knew what he'd done. I wanted to believe he didn't. There had been nothing mean and calculating about him before. So, I resolved to write him a letter, letting him know exactly what his actions were and what they had cost me. It was meant to be a gift to him. A truth for him to confront. Something to propel him toward help. For me it was meant to be a telling. A naming. A request for accountability. I struggled with the letter for months. Never knowing exactly what to say or how to say it. Wanting to hold his humanity and mine. It felt impossible.

One October night, I drove down to Kent to see an author speak. I had gotten the idea for my letter after reading one of her books. At the end of her lecture I went up to talk to her. I thanked her and told her about my planned letter. She scoffed. "Don't write him a fucking letter," she said. "He isn't worth it."

I was shocked and tried to explain my position.

She said, "How many hours have you spent thinking about this letter?"

I paused.

"How many hours do you think he's spent thinking about you?"

My breath caught.

She said, "Don't give him any more power over you. If you want to write a letter, write one to someone who deserves your time and energy. Someone who deserves the heart you will put into it. Write his mother or his sister." We talked for an hour or more. She was right about some things and wrong about others.

That night I drove home and my hands were entirely numb with fear. I had to drive with my forearms and elbows. I wrote the letters that night, and as I did, I reconciled a few things. One,

I would always believe he was worth it. Two, I deserved as much support as I wanted to give to him. And three, it was not my job to take the lead in his healing.

Letting go of that responsibility was the hardest step. Letting go of his process meant focusing on mine. It meant letting go of my own false sense of control. It meant letting go of the rationalizations that had protected me from the magnitude of harm done. It meant letting go of what protected me from the truth: he was one of my closest friends and he raped me. It was a choice, and no harm done to him in the past could excuse or explain it away.

That night I wrote him a letter. I also wrote to his mother and sister. I laid out what had happened, what he was responsible for, and I also told them that soon I would be writing a letter to all our mutual friends. I told them I was going to post these letters publicly. I waited for a backlash that never came. I expected him angry at my front door. I expected some sort of explosion, but there was nothing. There was silence. I never heard from him again.

\* \* \*

I began to feel like I'd made a mistake. I'd given him too much credit, been too naive. He didn't care. He could discard the letter entirely, take no action. I hadn't warned anyone. I hadn't helped to prevent another assault. So, a month later I did what I had promised, I wrote a letter to all of our mutual friends and told them what he'd done.

That's where I found the backlash, though never as much as expected. I lost some friends, got called some names. I stopped getting invited places. But I also got letters of support. I got thanked. I got notes from people telling me they loved me and cared about what happened to me. Though sadly too many of those notes also included disclosures of their own violence. An unexpected weight to carry.

\* \* \*

I don't regret it. It was a choice that honored my own dignity and his. But it was not perfect. It was hard and ugly and devastating. It was also powerful. I didn't get the accountability I had hoped for, but I learned. I grew.

I noticed patterns and coping skills. I saw the harm caused by my own isolation and sense of responsibility. I grew up working class, the girl child of a single mother struggling with addiction. I learned early about responsibility. My life, my mother's life, depended on it. By age three I had been put into foster care after the violence of her boyfriend's hand was no longer ignorable. I learned to be silent but strong. I made myself invisible and never questioned my ability to survive alone.

In the end, that was most damaging. Doing it alone. Believing it was all my responsibility. Not the assault. But the healing. The justice. The protection of nameless other girls. I leaned heavy into the skills I learned as a child, over responsibility, independence, sharp analysis, and self-sacrifice. Which meant I never asked for the support I was so desperate for.

Because what I needed, maybe more than his apology, was a community of people who could help me hold and honor all the stories that led to this one, who could help me uproot the layers of silence learned through too much violence. I needed to be asked what I wanted and what I was hoping for. I needed someone to help me craft those letters, someone to remind me that I could list expectations. I needed someone who was going to sit with me through the fallout. Someone who could read the responses people sent me and tell me to wait before reading them myself. I needed someone beside me to reflect the ways my own trauma, old and new, was informing the process. I needed someone who could show me love that was deeper and more nuanced than just hating him.

\* \* \*

The violence of poverty, white supremacy, militarism, assault— they are woven together. No court can ever pull them apart. A prison can never protect me. Isolation cannot heal isolation.

4

# EXCERPT FROM "BLACK QUEER FEMINISM AS PRAXIS: BUILDING AN ORGANIZATION AND A MOVEMENT"

*Janaé E. Bonsu of BYP100*

MANY OF US HAVE NEVER SEEN WHAT IT LOOKS LIKE TO BE TRULY free, but a common thread in our dreams of collective freedom is a world full of self-sustaining communities that do not rely on systems that perpetually harm us—police, jails, and prisons— to keep us safe or to hold each other accountable. Black people generally, and specifically Black women, have created microcosms of such a world before. Some examples of the collective actions and struggles of queer, Black women and other women of color to abolish oppressive and punitive systems while simultaneously developing models of community accountability include, but certainly are not limited to, organizations such as UBUNTU in Durham, North Carolina, whose members helped survivors of intimate partner violence by offering their homes as safe places to stay, providing childcare, researching legal options, and engaging in other supportive tactics; and the Safe OUTside the System (SOS) Collective of the Audre Lorde Project in Brooklyn, which created a network of "Safe Spaces" in Brooklyn for community members fleeing from violence, including local businesses in the community where employees were trained to counter homophobia and transphobia, as well as to interrupt violence without calling the police. These are but a couple of examples of community accountability processes that strive for Queer Black Feminist principles of collective action, prioritizing safety over the criminal justice system to address gender violence.[1]

Most of the community accountability processes also point to the concept of transformative justice—a process where the individual perpetrator, the abusive relationship, and the culture and power dynamics of the community are transformed rather than a process in which revenge, retribution, or punishment is enacted.[2] As conflict is an inevitable element of our internal relationships, BYP100 (Black Youth Project 100) has had to learn (and is still learning) to develop and implement approaches to making those conflicts generative and to holding our members accountable to the violence they may perpetrate. Conflict resolution and community accountability through a Black Queer Feminist lens is sensitive to avoid replicating punitive and carceral logics, which are inherently racist, classist, homophobic, transphobic, and misogynist. Community accountability emphasizes the belief in people's ability to transform and grow and does not deem people disposable. At the same time, we do not accept the notion that any member's growth should ever be at the expense of another member's physical, mental, or emotional well-being or sense of safety, especially in cases where there are significant power imbalances between the members in conflict. But sometimes values

---

1   INCITE! Women of Color Against Violence, "Community Accountability Working Document: Principles/Concerns/Strategies/Models," 2003, http://www.incite-national.org/page/community-accountability-working-document.

2   Kristian Williams, *Our Enemies in Blue: Police Power in America* (Oakland: AK Press, 2015).

alone are not enough to concretize justice and resolution outside of punitive systems; most mechanisms of our community accountability and conflict resolution processes were developed in response to harm committed.

The most significant precipitating events to the way that BYP100 handles harm in a way that is true to our Black Queer Feminist values came in November 2015 when a woman posted an open letter to BYP100 accusing one of our chapter leaders at the time of sexual assault. This statement was written and posted three days after the survivor brought her concerns directly to BYP100 leadership. The organization had no precedent for how to handle this, but our values require us to take reports of sexual violence very seriously, ensuring that we never place blame on victims/survivors and that we center the wishes of those who have been harmed. The survivor agreed to a community accountability process, and although no one who was involved had any prior experience, BYP100 members had a relationship with a practitioner outside of the organization with years of experience facilitating community accountability processes, and that person was willing to facilitate this one. After a yearlong process, the lead facilitator wrote an important takeaway about community accountability (CA) and healing:

> CA processes cannot erase harm. At best, they can reduce the impact(s) of harm and they can encourage people in their ongoing healing journeys. There is nothing "soft" or "easy" about this. CA processes test everyone and can be some of the most difficult physical and emotional work that we can undertake. Healing requires an acknowledgment that there are wounds. Healing requires parties who actually want to heal.[3]

---

3  For a full summary of the community and organization accountability process for this incident, see Transforming Harm, "Summary Statement Re: Community Accountability Process (March 2017)," Tumblr, http://transformharm.tumblr.com/post/158171267676/summary-statement -re-community-accountability.

This community accountability process also led to the formation of the BYP100 Healing and Safety Council (HSC). The HSC was created not only to build a clear process using a transformative justice framework to address harm involving a BYP100 member but also to provide support, training, and resources to BYP100 members and our contingent communities, and to bring healing into what it means to organize through a Black Queer Feminist lens.

In the *Stay Woke, Stay Whole: Black Activist Manual*,[4] the HSC grounds the importance of healing in our political work and offers a guide for harm prevention and intervention. In this sense, healing is not just reactive, but also proactive so that we are able to sustain ourselves for the long term. Organizing—especially in moments of rapid response and long nights of strategizing—can be extremely draining. The HSC explains that healing-centered organizing requires habitual self-care and collective-care. It also upholds the right of people to self-determining bodies, which, historically, Black people have not had—from access to restrooms and space to support for gender-nonconforming bodies if/when they get arrested in acts of civil disobedience.

Generally, group or chapter self-care in a BYP100 space and many other Black organizing spaces that I have been a part of draws from Indigenous and ancestral practices, including chanting, African drumming, burning sage, building altars, offering libations, grounding, and taking time to check in with one another before getting down to business. Most meetings are arranged as talking circles in which everyone can see each other (that is, no one is at the front of the room talking at people), and community agreements are made with consensus to be mindful of power dynamics and how we hold space with one another. These are but a few examples of how dealing with conflict, harm, accountability, and healing can reflect Black Queer Feminist values.

---

4   I drew information presented herein from BYP100's organizing manual, our healing manual, and conversations with my comrades. Shout out specifically to Charlene Carruthers, Asha Ransby-Sporn, Je Naé Taylor, Rose Afriyie, Kai Green, Mari Morales-Williams, and Damon Williams.

While this chapter details some elements of Black Queer Feminism in praxis for BYP100, it is by no means exhaustive or perfect. My goal here was to put forth that a Black Queer Feminist politic deepens our analysis of issues, requires centering the margins in our strategies and solutions, and provides this movement with strategic direction. I will not purport that BYP100 or any other anti-oppressive movement organization has it all figured out, nor will I say that our processes have not been messy. We have very real organizational limitations. Sometimes accountability processes are not resolved through restorative justice. Sometimes our people are dealing with mental health needs that cannot always be met within the organization. Sometimes our struggles are practically, structurally, strategically, and politically too real for us to know how to deal with in real time. However, it is in the missteps, in the callouts and call-ins, and through trial and error that our ideologies and actions become more aligned. That is why constant reflexivity of praxis is so important. We are building the plane as we fly it, and hindsight is and will always be 20/20.

5

# FROM BREAKING SILENCE TO COMMUNITY CONTROL

## COMMUNITY-CONTROLLED DATABASES, MURDER INVESTIGATIONS, AND CEREMONY TO FIND MISSING AND MURDERED INDIGENOUS WOMEN, GIRLS, AND TWO-SPIRIT PEOPLE

*Audrey Huntley*

MY WORK SUPPORTING THE FAMILIES OF MISSING AND MURDERED Indigenous women and girls, trans and Two-Spirit people (MMIWG2S) to organize around the violent disappearances of their loved ones began in 1999. I had moved back to Turtle Island from Germany and found myself living in Vancouver's Downtown Eastside when I first learned about the Memorial March to honor Indigenous women who had died violent, premature deaths in the neighborhood. All of the recognition of MMIWG2S by the mainstream media and government that has happened in the last few years goes back to the grannies and aunties of this Vancouver community who began holding ceremony on February 14, 1991. They have been demanding justice every year since, and the marches and ceremonies have spread across the country, today taking place in over twenty cities across Canada, all focused on showing love for those who are gone and care for those left behind. In Toronto we gather at police headquarters to underline the complicity of the state and the impunity accorded to those who disappear MMIWG2S. We don't ask for permission to be there, but assert our sovereignty as Indigenous peoples living in the Dish with One Spoon Covenant and adhering to traditional laws of governance to gather wherever we want to on our lands. Attendance at this beautiful gathering, where we share strawberries and water in the dead of winter with temperatures often hovering around minus thirty degrees, has grown over the years: when we started, we were 100 to 150 people, but in recent years we have grown close to a thousand.

Public mourning is a powerful act that flies in the face of the societal indifference that has surrounded MMIWG2S for too long. The power of these marches and ceremonies lies in the reclamation and practice of public ceremony and grief, breaking through the shroud of silence surrounding these murders. In Toronto, Wanda Whitebird, a long-standing elder and community organizer in prison justice and Indigenous community, has conducted the prayers since the strawberry ceremony was shared with us by Darlene Ritchie, an Oneida woman, fourteen years ago. The love for community expressed in the drums, songs, and sharing of medicine resonates with all who enter the space and reverberates far beyond it. As Wanda says every year, we have a commitment to our sisters on the other side to show up every February 14, whether there are fifteen or fifteen hundred of us. We will never stop, and they will always be there waiting to join us.

This year, 2019, marks our fourteenth ceremony and the sixteenth year that No More Silence has been engaging with the Toronto community, documenting the violent deaths and disappearances of MMIWG2S and working to build the strength of Indigenous women and trans and Two-Spirit community members to resist violence. Since 2013, we have researched the disappearances of two hundred women and Two-Spirit community members in Ontario and created a community-led database documenting the lives and deaths of MMIW in Ontario. We released our final report on the research we've conducted for this database at our latest February 14th feast, the research was initiated in collaboration with Families of Sisters in Spirit and the Native Youth Sexual Health Network. We can keep track of our missing and murdered women, girls, and Two-Spirit people better than the state, which has an interest in keeping the numbers low. More importantly, we want to honor their memory. We want the information to be controlled by the community and accessible to the community and for the community—not locked away in a government database.

When we began doing this work, we didn't have a good grasp on how many deaths and disappearances had happened. There hadn't been any comprehensive research done on how many missing and murdered Indigenous women there actually were in Canada, until Amnesty International's *Stolen Sisters* report in 2006 raised awareness about this issue in the mainstream media. Beverley Jacobs (Mohawk), president of Native Women's Association of Canada (NWAC) at the time and a fierce advocate for Indigenous women, coauthored the report and contributed enormously in supporting family members through the Sisters in Spirit program. NWAC was able to do research for a number of years and documented 580 cases of MMIWG2S. However, the Conservative federal government cut NWAC's funding in 2010, and the data was handed over to the Royal Canadian Mounted Police (RCMP), the federal police force of Canada, along with ten million dollars to create a centralized missing person project—which didn't even focus on women, never mind Indigenous women.

We didn't need to demonstrate more cases in order to take this issue seriously, but we did know that mainstream society needed to be confronted with hard facts in order to get journalists to cover these stories, pressure governments to act, and raise awareness overall. And we wanted to know; we think that it is part of a community's responsibility to keep track of their own.

What distinguished us for a long time and still distinguishes us from other people who do this work was the understanding of settler colonialism as the inherent root of the violence. Our definition of who to include in our research has broadened over the years. For example, we've often been asked to include people's loved ones who committed suicide, such as a young girl, Jewel, Jamie Jamieson's daughter, who hung herself after being bullied for several weeks. In her mother's view, she was killed by the bullying. We started thinking about it as death by colonialism. We understand that there can be no solution outside of completely dismantling the settler colonial state.

For a very long time, we were very isolated within Toronto's Native community because of these stances. A lot of the Native community agencies are government-funded and did not want to be associated with those types of politics for fear of losing their funding. We also included in our work voices that have sometimes been marginalized within Native communities, such as members of the Native Youth Sexual Health Network, a group of young women and Two-Spirit people doing national organizing around Indigenous sexual and reproductive justice, and members of NaMeRes (Native Men's Residence), the local Indigenous men's shelter. We centered those who are most vulnerable and experience the highest levels of violence: trans and Two-Spirit people and sex workers. Maggie's, a sex work advocacy group, has been part of our organizing committee for several years, and we're proud to have a Two-Spirit women's big drum at our feast. This has caused some in the community to stay away, and we're OK with that. We understand that settler colonialism operates in a cis-sexist and heteropatriarchal framework, and we need to tear that down, too.

I have also had the opportunity to take the issue of MMIWG2S to the mainstream when I was employed by CBC television. I was fortunate to get approval for a cross-Canada research trip called the Traces of Missing Women Project in 2004. I set out from Toronto in the summer traveling west with the aim to gather the memories of loved ones who had been disappeared. I was more than a little anxious about wearing the hat of a CBC reporter and how that might make it more difficult to get folks to go on camera and talk to me. At that point, mainstream media either ignored violence against Indigenous people, or their depiction of the violence was riddled with racist stereotypes, with headlines like "Missing Prostitute's Body Found in Parking Lot." However, there was a lot of attention paid to the horrific serial killings that had occurred over the span of many years at a pig farm close to Vancouver. The 2002 arrest of one man, R. Picton, for the murders dominated headlines and framed the killings of dozens of women, of whom 60 percent were Indigenous, as the work of a madman, an aberration. His victims—who had been taken from the Downtown Eastside, were poor, involved in street economies such as sex work, and struggled with addictions—were not accorded any humanizing details of their lives. I wanted to provide a different point of view.

I set out on my road trip with my camera gear and wolf dog in a little Ford Fiesta, with pink posters that I hung up in the communities where I stopped and an 800 number where people could call me. I had promised myself that I would let families come to me and not breach anyone's privacy or ability to grieve by making cold calls. To my surprise, I was inundated with requests to share about community members' missing and murdered loved ones on my way. Not a single community was unaffected.

I believe the trust and desire to share with me came about because I used medicines and ceremony and followed the spiritual guidance of my elder, Wanda Whitebird, and her teachings. Before I left, we had a sweat and we blessed the tobacco ties for that journey, and then she instructed me, "Every time you cross into a new territory, put your tobacco down, and the sisters on the other side will decide who comes to you and whether they want their stories told."

I had been practicing ceremony for about four years at that point, and I'd had life-changing experiences in the lodge. But when that was my instruction, I was a little nervous, quite frankly. Like, really? That's all you got for me? I was by myself, and my dog, going off on this journey, and I had really no idea if anybody was going to talk to me. Having lived in the Native community for some time in Vancouver and the Downtown Eastside, I knew about people's animosity toward media and researchers, and I knew that it was justified because of the horribly exploitive experiences the community has had with them. But there were more people wanting me to come to them than I had geographical ability and time to speak with. I would be in northern British Columbia, and people on Vancouver Island would want me to come.

I ended up interviewing over forty-five family members of MMIW2S in a period of seven weeks covering fifteen thousand kilometers. I discovered there was a huge need for people to share their stories. They were already traumatized by the loss, and it was compounded by societal indifference to their stories and people's lack of interest and care. But I ended up getting only three minutes of airtime to share the footage from that trip. This was heartbreaking, so I used the footage to make an independent film called *The Heart Has Its Own Memory*. I decided to shoot only people's hands holding the tobacco ties I gave them. This was partly because people in the Downtown Eastside were sharing truths about the Hells Angels' involvement in the pig farm murders and needed to protect their identity, but also because I wanted the viewer to visualize the women who were gone as their loved ones shared.

Out of that experience, my boss recognized that MMIW was a story that needed telling and gave me the resources to work on a feature-length investigative documentary. I chose to focus on Norma George, whose naked dead body was found in a parking lot outside Vancouver in 1993. I was close with her sister who lived in the Downtown Eastside and believed it would be a healing experience for the family, and I really wanted to find out what had happened to her. This was the second time I experienced the incredible presence of spirit in doing this work. Both Norma and her brother Tom—who had been killed by the same people a few months before her—were with me every step of the way. They showed up in many ways and as crows, over and over again. I didn't even realize it until I was back in Toronto in the edit suite and saw that there were always crows in the footage.

Once we got started, I discovered that investigating a murder isn't that hard. It just involves a lot of talking to as many people as you can. In the course of about a year, I got tons of information about Norma's life. I was able to find and get her Bible and give it to her mother after fourteen years. She had this Bible that she made a lot of notes in throughout her young life that was really important to her. From talking to people, I found out that she used to stay in a rooming house in the Downtown Eastside with a man, and he was still living there. He was reluctant to talk; I never did get him to open the door to his room, but I stood outside and we talked through the closed door, and after three visits he slid the Bible out. (It also involved a six-pack of beer, but I never told my executive producer about that.) I was able to give Norma's Bible back to her mother, and that was a beautiful thing. All kinds of things like that happened. If you just start talking to people, it's amazing how much stuff will come out and how suddenly you will unearth things.

I put down a lot of tobacco during that year. I had also learned on the Traces of Missing Women trip to feast the women on the other side, so I continued that practice. I made sure to give them water to drink. I hadn't done this on the research trip, and it was startling when at the sweat to close off the journey Wanda received a message that the women were thirsty and that I had neglected that piece—they weren't angry, but it did get pointed out and we poured a lot of water at that sweat. And now I remember to always include a drink!

Everything we learned about Norma's life was really important to her family. They hadn't been able to complete their grieving ceremonies because they had received the body in a sealed coffin and were instructed by RCMP not to open it. People were in shock and followed those instructions, despite the fact that it was their tradition to do open-casket wakes. Not having done this meant they couldn't move forward with their process to place a headstone on her grave as well as on her brother's. They kept those headstones in a closet in their home for over fifteen years. As a result of the documentary airing on national television and some advocacy work I did with the RCMP, a team was sent to Northern BC to meet with the family and a community elder. They showed them autopsy photos so that they could identify Norma and complete their process and place the headstones. That was a big deal for the entire community, which had been stuck in this grief, and it was very important for Norma's mom to complete that ritual. She got to do the headstone ceremony only a year before she herself passed into the spirit world. People need to complete their ceremonies. I never knew about the power of ceremony until I put everything on the line at work.

Norma's case had been cold for thirteen years, and I didn't set out thinking we would find out what happened to her. But we were able to solve her murder and her brother Tom's. It was an off-camera interview with the coroner who worked on Norma that confirmed the suspicions we had been putting together. He had taken us to the place her body was dumped and mentioned the proximity of a certain clubhouse—it was one of our first shoot days, and I remember barely noticing that a dead crow lay where she had died. The coroner revealed information about the police investigation that confirmed who was responsible for her death. We had already pieced things together from the many conversations we'd had with her family and friends, and it all pointed in one direction.

The family was both devastated and relieved to have some answers. The guilty parties were untouchable, however, and since going public would have endangered her surviving family and friends, we changed the nature of our documentary. Instead of presenting the results of the investigative work, we told the story of her sisters, who were estranged and whose lives had taken different turns, and how they were reunited after thirteen years with a visit to Norma's grave in Takla Landing.

Making this film about Norma, *Go Home, Baby Girl*, was an amazing experience and confirmed two things for me. First, all work around MMIWG2S must be founded in ceremony and work with spirit—taking direction from the sisters on the other side. Second, investigations are best conducted by those closest to the disappeared—loved ones or community—not the policing institutions of the settler colonial state. I have seen families achieve the impossible under horrific circumstances because they don't quit in their quest for justice. Take the members of Cheyenne Fox's family, who are suing the Toronto police. When twenty-year-old Cheyenne fell from the twenty-fourth floor of a downtown condo, the police concluded her death was a suicide just a few hours after she died. There was nothing to indicate that she had killed herself, and she had been in the presence of a man who was never held for questioning. Cheyenne was a loving mom of a beautiful toddler whom her family insists she would never have willingly left behind.

The community was outraged at the police finding, and advocacy calls to investigators uncovered that there were two people in the apartment below who say they saw a woman dangling for five seconds or so. That didn't sound like someone jumping to their death at all. The family worked hard with the assistance of Aboriginal Legal Services to reverse the coroner's finding of suicide, which was a small victory. They continue to speak out against the police handling of their daughter's case and will be in court in 2019.

While those close to victims though not necessarily family—are best positioned to uncover the circumstances of their death and to solve their murders because they know them best, there is the dilemma of being overcome with shock and traumatic grief. It can be overwhelming for the individuals involved, who become so paralyzed that it is difficult to take action. This was something even I have felt myself. I was in Toronto when the death of Bella Laboucan-McClean, the youngest sister of a friend I had been close to when I lived in Vancouver, occurred. Bella had just graduated from design school and was excited to be going to London, England, to intern. She was vibrant and creative and defied all the stereotypes of the at-risk victim. She too fell thirty-one floors to her death from a downtown condo. I couldn't believe it at first. I found it harder to respond and take the steps that needed taking. Wanda Whitebird and I visited our friend who was Bella's roommate, at her apartment, and the shock and grief were so palpable and huge. It breaks my heart looking back to admit that it effectively shut us down and immobilized us. There was so much more I wish No More Silence had done to hold the police accountable for doing their jobs, but it was all we could do to organize a spirit-release ceremony at the site of her death to coincide with her body being returned to her community.

People are in such shock by violent tragic loss that even monitoring whether the cops are doing their jobs feels almost impossible, never mind people doing the job themselves. So that can't be the solution. The family members can't be expected to take this on—they are too busy dealing with the concrete horror. Cheyenne Fox's family should not have to be speaking out against the police when the father is already dealing with the horrific task of picking up his daughter's body to bring her home from Toronto to the reserve, and when his sons have to be the ones to pick up her dead body off a gurney and drive her north in the back of their own pickup truck. That's absolutely horrible. Families need more people who are close to them, they need a community structure that can develop some skills and knows what steps to take.

I spent 2016 working on a video resource to fill a bit of that gap. *Not Just Another Case: When Your Loved One Has Gone Missing or Been Murdered* was made with community members for community members and is proving to be a useful tool in assisting those who need to navigate the nightmare of violent loss. I was able to interview families and advocates across the county, from Newfoundland (including Innu women from Labrador) to BC. Community members shared painful experiences navigating the disappearance of their loved ones with the aim of helping others going through this horror. The video is designed to assist with the search for someone who is missing and to help families navigate the worst-case scenario if those who are missing are found murdered. Folks share important information on how to find someone while respecting Two-Spirit people's pronouns and chosen names, best practices for dealing with police, and surviving a trial.

One family's experience in investigating the murder of their loved one stands out. I met Kaykaitkw Harron (Syilx and Nlaka'pamux) in Vancouver, and she shared about how they mobilized community in the interior of BC to find her cousin, Roxanne Louie, when the police were failing. This young woman explained that they were pounding on the RCMP's door every day, occupying the space to ensure they were doing their job. They also contacted everyone they knew in Roxanne's circles and encouraged them to share with police. The family encountered a typical racist response by police who thought that Roxanne "was out partying," and this was also reported in the media. Kaykaitkw stresses how important it is to stop reinforcing those stereotypes and talks about how even community members who had internalized this view took a step back from looking for her because of this. She notes, as do many others in the video, that when a loved one who is usually in contact with folks everyday stops being in touch, something is wrong and action is required right away.

The importance of public vigils to create media presence cannot be understated. Roxanne's family held a Walk of Faith and ceremony in the hopes that she would come back to them safely. They actually marched through the neighborhood of Roxanne's in-laws, who they suspected were involved in her disappearance. This applied pressure to those who had committed the crime to come forward. This incredible community effort led by her family led to a confession so that Roxanne's body was recovered and her killers were tried and convicted of murder, a rare outcome. This would never have happened were it not for the strength and conviction of her family and the community support they rallied around them.

The last segment of the video presents community responses that support healing. I had the privilege of attending the Mihkowapikwaniy Memorial Storytelling and Youth Leadership Camp in Little Buffalo, which Bella Laboucan-McLean's family started in her honor. Community members spend four days on the land practicing traditional activities, leading up to a traditional round dance and ceremony for the family. Kids participate in media workshops, moose-hide tanning, fish scaling, beading, drum making, and stick games. Grief recovery practitioners and healers are available for the families, and an honor dance closes off the ceremony.

Bella's sister, Melina Laboucan, states that reconnecting with land and culture is part of the healing and restoration that families and communities need to go through. I wholeheartedly agree.

I chose the wise words of Alex Wilson, Two-Spirit advocate, to end the video on this powerful note: "There's an energy or spirit that exists in Indigenous people that is intimately connected to the land that we're on—there is hope in dismantling the system. I think it is absolutely possible, and I think that a community-based response is the way that is going to do that."

All My Relations.

# 6

# WHAT TO DO WHEN YOU'VE BEEN ABUSIVE

## ANNOTATED EDITION

*Kai Cheng Thom*

As I sit in my bed and begin to type (beds are my favorite typing places), there is a part of me that says, "Don't write this article."

There is a part of me that still resonates deeply with the fear and shame that surround the topics of abuse and intimate partner violence—the taboo that most communities have around talking not just about the fact that people experience rape and abuse, but that people we know and care about might be rapists and abusers.

Perhaps most secret and shameful of all is the fear that we, ourselves, are or have been abusive—the fear that we could be those villains, those monsters in the night.

Nobody wants to be "an abuser." No one wants to admit that they have hurt someone, especially when so many of us have been hurt ourselves.

But the truth is that abusers and survivors of abuse do not exist, and have never existed, in a dichotomy: sometimes, hurt people hurt people. In this rape culture we live in, sometimes it can be hard to tell the difference between the hurt you are experiencing and the hurt you are causing someone else.

In the years since this essay was originally published, we have seen, as a result of the #MeToo movement, an enormous shift in the intensity and frequency with which intimate partner violence and abuse is discussed in public. While this movement has brought about positive change and exposed many abusive people in power, it has also highlighted the complexity and epidemic nature of abuse. It has shown us, irrefutably, that survivors can also abuse.

It has shown us that we cannot think of abusers as incomprehensible monsters who must be exterminated—because abusers are also our heroes, lovers, friends, family. It has shown us that, more urgently than ever, we must find new ways of responding to and healing from violence.

\* \* \*

Seven years ago, when I first started training as a support worker for survivors of intimate partner violence, I was sitting in a training workshop when someone asked what our organization's policy was on taking requests for support from people who were abusing their partners and wanted help stopping.

The answer was brusque and immediate: "We don't work with abusers. Period."

Fair enough, I thought. After all, an organization created to support survivors of rape and abuse should center survivors, not the people who hurt them. The only problem was, I wondered, what happens when people are both survivors and abusers? And if we don't work with abusers, who does?

Note: I am not, in this article, talking about whether or not a relationship can be "mutually abusive." This is a conversation for another time. Rather, I am suggesting that people who are survivors in one relationship are capable of being abusive in previous or later relationships.

The question of whether a relationship can be mutually abusive is probably an important one to address, for the practical reason that many violent relationships break down into a debate over which person is the abuser and which is the survivor. Sometimes, the distinction is very easy to make because one person clearly has more power than the other. Often, however, things are more complex—for example, when both people in a relationship experience high levels of social oppression or marginalization.

While I do not have a clear answer to this question, I do wonder if it is more important to focus on identifying and ending violent patterns of behavior than on assigning blame. If a loved one hurts me, for example, I may be justified in defending myself. I can still take responsibility, however, if my defensive actions result in disproportionate amounts of harm—which doesn't prevent my loved one from taking responsibility in their own turn.

Seven years later, as a therapist who has worked with many individuals who are "recovering" or "former" abusers, I am still looking for the answers to those questions. There are extremely few resources and organizations out there with the mandate, will, or knowledge to help people stop being abusive.

But doesn't the feminist saying go, "We shouldn't be teaching people how not to get raped; we should be teaching people not to rape"?

And, if so, doesn't it follow that we shouldn't only support people who have survived abuse but should also support people in learning how not to abuse?

When we are able to admit that the capacity to harm lies within ourselves—within us all—we become capable of radically transforming the conversation around abuse and rape culture. We can go from simply reacting to abuse and punishing "abusers" to preventing abuse and healing our communities. Because the revolution starts at home, as they say. The revolution starts in your house, in your own relationships, in your bedroom. The revolution starts in your heart.

The following is a nine-step guide to confronting the abuser in you, in me, in us all.

# 1. LISTEN TO THE SURVIVOR

"Listen to the survivor" may seem to imply that there can only be one survivor in a given situation, or that the first person who calls out the other has to be the survivor of an abuse dynamic. This is not necessarily true. Today, I might give this section the title "Learn to Listen When Someone Says You Have Hurt Them."

When one has been abusive, the very first—and one of the most difficult—skills of holding oneself accountable is learning to simply listen to the person or people whom one has harmed:

- Listening without becoming defensive.

- Listening without trying to equivocate or make excuses.

- Listening without minimizing or denying the extent of the harm.

- Listening without trying to make oneself the center of the story being told.

When someone, particularly a partner or loved one, tells you that you have hurt or abused them, it can be easy to understand this as an accusation or attack. Very often, this is our first assumption—that we are being attacked.

This is why so many perpetrators of abuse respond to survivors who confront them by saying something along the lines of, "I'm not abusing you. You are abusing me, right now, with this accusation!"

But this is the cycle of violence talking. This is the script that rape culture has built for us: a script in which there must be a hero and a villain, a right and a wrong, an accuser and an accused.

What if we understood being confronted about perpetuating abuse as an act of courage—even a gift—on the part of the survivor?

What if, instead of reacting immediately in our own defense, we instead took the time to listen, to really try to understand the harm we might have done to another person?

When we think of accountability in terms of listening and love instead of accusation and punishment, everything changes. Listening without becoming defensive does not necessarily mean relinquishing one's own truth. We must be able to make room for varying perspectives and multiple emotional truths in our hearts.

## 2. TAKE RESPONSIBILITY FOR THE ABUSE

After listening, the next step in holding oneself accountable is taking responsibility for the abuse. This means, simply enough, agreeing that you and only you are the source of physical, emotional, or psychological violence you have directed toward another person.

Remember, however, that you are not responsible for the violence that someone else has done to that person, or for harm that they have done to themselves. Taking responsibility means learning boundaries, which means accepting the weight of your own actions, no more and no less. It is not helpful to overstate the amount of harm you have done to another person, nor to collapse into a puddle of martyrdom. Taking responsibility means engaging critically with your actions, not delegating all of the thinking to somebody else.

A simple analogy for taking responsibility for abuse is taking responsibility for stepping on someone else's foot: There are many reasons why you might do such a thing—you were in a hurry, you weren't looking where you were going, or maybe no one ever taught you that it was wrong to step on other people's feet.

But you still did it. No one else—only you are responsible, and it is up to you to acknowledge and apologize for it. The same holds true for abuse: no one, and I really mean no one—not your partner, not patriarchy, not mental illness, not society, not the Devil—is responsible for the violence that you do to another person. A lot of factors can contribute to or influence one's reasons for committing abuse (see the point below), but in the end, only I am responsible for my actions, as you are for yours.

## 3. ACCEPT THAT YOUR REASONS ARE NOT EXCUSES

There is an awful, pervasive myth out there that people who abuse others do so simply because they are bad people—because they are sadistic, or because they enjoy other people's pain.

This is, I think, part of the reason why so many people who have been abusive in the past or present resist the use of the terms "abuse" or "abuser" to describe their behavior. In fact, very, very, very few people who abuse are motivated to do so by sadism. In my experience as a therapist and community support worker, when people are abusive, it's usually because they have a reason based in desperation or suffering.

Some reasons for abusive behavior I have heard include:

"I am isolated and alone, and the only person who keeps me alive is my partner. This is why I can't let my partner leave me."

"My partner hurts me all the time. I was just hurting them back."

"I am sick, and if I don't force people to take care of me, then I will be left to die."

"I am suffering, and the only way to relieve the pain is to hurt myself or others."

"I didn't know that what I was doing was abuse. People always did the same to me. I was just following the script."

"No one will love me unless I make them."

All of these are powerful, real reasons for abuse—but they are never excuses. There is no reason good enough to excuse abusive behavior. Reasons help us understand abuse, but they do not excuse it. Accepting this is essential to transforming culpability into accountability and turning justice into healing.

## 4. DON'T PLAY THE "SURVIVOR OLYMPICS"

As I mentioned above, communities tend to operate on a survivor/abuser or victim/perpetrator dichotomy model of abuse. This is the belief that people who have survived abuse in one relationship can never be abusive in other relationships.

I find that social justice or leftist communities also tend to misapply social analysis to individual situations of abuse, suggesting that individuals who belong to oppressed or marginalized groups can never abuse individuals who belong to privileged groups (that is, that women can never abuse men, racialized people can never abuse white people, and so on).

But neither of the above ideas is true. Survivors of abuse in one relationship can, in fact, be abusive in other relationships.

And it's easier for privileged individuals to abuse others because of the extra power social privilege gives them, but *anyone* is capable of abusing *anyone* given the right (or rather, wrong) circumstances. It can be easy, when confronted with the abuse we have perpetrated, to play "survivor Olympics."

"I can't be abusive," we may want to argue. "I'm a survivor!" Or "The abuse I have survived is so much worse than what you're accusing me of!" Or "Nothing I do is abusive to you because you have more privilege than me."

But survivors can be abusers, too. Anyone can be abusive, and comparing or trivializing doesn't absolve us of responsibility for it.

## 5. TAKE THE SURVIVOR'S LEAD

When having a dialogue with someone who has been abused, it's essential to give the survivor the space to take the lead in expressing their needs and setting boundaries. You should also take time to think about your own needs and boundaries without making the person you have harmed take care of you. This is why having support in the community is crucial. If basic needs are going unmet, no one can heal from abuse, nor can anyone truly be accountable.

If you have abused someone, it's not up to you to decide how the process of healing or accountability should work. This doesn't mean that you don't get to have rights or boundaries, or that you can't contribute actively to the process. It means that you don't get to say that the person you have hurt is "crazy" or that what they are expressing doesn't matter.

Instead, it might be a good idea to try asking the person who has confronted you questions like these: What do you need right now? Is there anything I can do to make this feel better? How much contact would you like to have with me going forward? If we share a community, how should I navigate situations where we might end up in the same place? How does this conversation feel for you, right now?

At the same time, it's important to understand that the needs of survivors of abuse can change over time, and that survivors may not always know right away—or ever—what their needs are.

Being accountable and responsible for abuse means being patient, flexible, and reflective about the process of having dialogue with the survivor.

Having been witness to many community accountability processes that have seemed to create more harm for those involved, I must emphasize that survivor-led does not mean that those who identify as survivors are necessarily experts in transformative justice, nor that the identified survivor in a dynamic of abuse should get to dictate what happens to the identified abuser.

Survivors, understandably, may wish to get revenge on abusers and so may ask for violence to be done in the name of justice (also, abusers may wish to get revenge on survivors who name them and may try to manipulate the situation by making counterclaims of abuse). I have seen calls for abusers to be beaten up or put in life-threatening situations. This is a replication of the criminal justice system, which prioritizes retribution over recovery from violence. Criminal justice is interested in assigning blame and executing punishment, while transformative justice challenges the notion that punishment is inherent to justice.

I feel strongly that as long as punishment remains at the center of our thinking around accountability and justice, survivor-led processes are doomed to fall into the trap of individuals desperately trying to avoid accountability out of fear. Survivor-led, to me, means that survivors get to lead their own process of recovery, that survivors are given space to tell their stories and speak their needs (which criminal justice usually does not allow).

It does not mean that people who may have been deeply wounded are suddenly handed full responsibility for a community dialogue and rehabilitation process. Survivor-led does not mean that the community gets to abdicate its responsibility for providing support, safety, expertise, and leadership in making healing happen.

## 6. FACE THE FEAR OF ACCOUNTABILITY

Being accountable for abuse takes a *lot* of courage. We live in a culture that demonizes and oversimplifies abuse, probably because we don't want to accept the reality that abuse is actually commonplace and can be perpetrated by anybody. A lot of people paint themselves into corners denying abuse because, to be quite honest, it's terrifying to face the consequences, real and imagined, of taking responsibility. And there are real risks: people have lost friends, communities, jobs, and resources over abuse. The risks are especially high for marginalized individuals—I am thinking particularly of Black and brown folks here—who are likely to face harsh, discriminatory sentencing in legal processes.

If we are ever to see the dream of transformative justice become a widespread reality, we must collectively resist the culture of disposability that says that people who have done harm are no longer people, that they are "trash," that they must be "canceled."

While consequences for harmful behavior are a necessary outcome of accountability, those consequences should not include actions that are themselves abusive. If you have placed your trust in the community by allowing it to make a decision about how you should take accountability, that trust is a sacred responsibility. The leaders of a process of justice are responsible for not abusing their power, just as you are responsible for not abusing yours.

I can only suggest that when it comes to ending abuse, it's easier to face our fear than live in it all of our lives. It's more healing to tell the truth than to hide inside a lie. When we hold ourselves accountable, we prove that the myth of the "monster" abuser is a lie.

## 7. SEPARATE SHAME FROM GUILT

Shame and social stigma are powerful emotional forces that can prevent us from holding ourselves accountable for being abusive. We don't want to admit to "being that person," so we don't admit to having been abusive at all.

Some people might suggest that people who have been abusive ought to feel shame—after all, perpetrating abuse is wrong. I would argue, though, that this is where the difference between guilt and shame is key. Guilt is feeling bad about something you've done; shame is feeling bad about who you are. People who have been abusive should feel guilty for the specific acts of abuse they are responsible for. They should not feel shame about who they are because this means that abuse has become a part of their identity. It means that they believe that they are fundamentally a bad person—in other words, "an abuser."

But if you believe that you are an "abuser," a bad person who hurts others, then you have already lost the struggle for change—because we cannot change who we are. If you believe that you are a fundamentally good person who has done hurtful or abusive things, then you open the possibility for change.

## 8. DON'T EXPECT ANYONE TO FORGIVE YOU

Being accountable is not about earning forgiveness. That is to say, it doesn't matter how accountable you are—nobody has to forgive you for being abusive, least of all the person you have abused. In fact, using the process of "doing" accountability to manipulate or coerce someone into giving their forgiveness to you is an extension of the abuse dynamic. It centers the abuser, not the survivor. One shouldn't aim for forgiveness when holding oneself accountable.

Rather, self-accountability is about learning how we have harmed others, why we have harmed others, and how we can stop.

But...

## 9. FORGIVE YOURSELF

You do have to forgive yourself. Because you can't stop hurting other people until you stop hurting yourself. When one is abusive, when one is hurting so much on the inside that it feels like the only way to make it stop is to hurt other people, it can be terrifying to face the hard truth of words like *abuse* and *accountability*. One might rather blame others, blame society, blame the people we love, instead of ourselves.

This is true, I think, of community as well as individuals. It is so much easier, so much simpler, to create hard lines between good and bad people, to create walls to shut the shadowy archetype of "the abuser" out instead of mirrors to look at the abuser within.

Perhaps this is why self-accountability tools like this list are so rare. It takes courage to be accountable. To decide to heal. But when we do decide, we discover incredible new possibilities. There is good and bad in everyone. Anyone can heal, given the right circumstances, and everyone can heal, given the same. *You are capable of loving and being loved. Always. Always. Always.*[1]

---

1   Author's Note: This article was originally published under the title "9 Ways to Be Accountable When You've Been Abusive" on the website *Everyday Feminism* on February 1, 2016. In the years since, a number of personal experiences and community events have caused me to rethink some aspects of the piece. While I stand behind its primary assertions, it feels important to me to address certain issues of nuance and practical application. On receiving the invitation to re-publish it in this collection, I was also offered the chance to make significant edits. My intention is both to remain accountable to the original version of the text, and to show clearly where my thinking has shifted over time   just as all of our beliefs and practices in the area of transformative justice are, and must be, evolving conversations.

# 7

# TRANSFORMING FAMILY

## A STORY OF ACCOUNTABILITY

*Amita Swadhin*

I REMEMBER THE BLACK-AND-WHITE CHECKERED LINOLEUM TILE staring up at me. The heft of the phone receiver in my hand. The dial tone droning in my ear. My mother's hand frozen around the handle of the knife drawer. My father's hand about to strike my face.

I remember my clarity in that moment: I didn't want to kill him. I didn't even want to hurt him. Wanting that would make me just as bad as him. I just wanted him far away from me, my mom, and my sister, forever. I was sure I was going to die in that moment, but at least I would die certain that I was nothing like him. I was fourteen years old. My father and my rapist were the same person. I felt so much self-loathing, worried that somehow my blood was tainted, that I was inherently monstrous because my father was. "Devil's spawn" was a phrase that flashed through my head constantly, even though I knew I had never consented to my father's violence. School, television, and my insular Indian American community had taught me we are only as good as the families we come from. What did it mean that one of my makers was a monster who tortured me (and my mother and my sister and even the cat) brutally yet banally?

I didn't die that day and my father was eventually removed from our home. When my father hit me in the kitchen in front of my mother, we had already been engaged with the state for a year. I had disclosed sexual abuse to my mother when I was thirteen, afraid for my nine-year-old sister because my father had stopped raping me when I was twelve. My mother called a therapist for me, and the therapist called the New Jersey Division of Youth and Family Services. Mandated reporting. It was a total nightmare.

I had not yet found the words to tell my mother the full extent of violence I had survived. I was deeply riddled with shame, assuming that I was damaged because my father had raped me, sexually assaulted me, made me engage with his body sexually, and forced me to watch pornography hundreds of times from when I was four until I was twelve. I needed so much tenderness, love, and support. I needed a team of adults who could keep me safe while honoring my agency and autonomy.

Instead, I got the state: two white social workers in my living room, just a few days after I had barely disclosed to my mother that Dad had abused me for many years; a white female police officer who was icy cold; two white prosecutors, one who threatened to prosecute my mother for being complicit in my abuse. I didn't feel safe enough to tell these white people anything. My father said he had "molested" me, one time. He got five years' probation and no jail time.

Deep down, I suspected my mother knew about my father abusing me. I would go on to spend years of my adulthood unraveling her excuses and integrating the truth of her knowing. But even so, I had more flashes of clarity as a teenager: I didn't want to harm my mother. I'd grown up seeing my mother brutalized by my father. I remembered our family vacation to the Florida Keys when I was twelve. We all shared a hotel room with two beds. I remember waking up to my mother's soft pleas in the night: "Please, no, Vashisht, not here, the girls are here." I remember shutting my eyes tight and inching closer to my peacefully sleeping sister. I was prepared when he raped my mother. I knew I wasn't his only victim.

The day after my father hit me in the kitchen, I flew to Michigan to spend the summer in a high school debate camp. My sister got sent to suburban Cleveland, where we usually spent our summers with our Naani. While we were away, my father held my mother against the wall by her neck and threatened to kill her unless she could get him off probation. By then, my mother had been working in a doctor's office for ten years. Although my father was an anchor in the local South Asian community, he didn't have any social ties to her mostly white coworkers. So, my mother packed a bag, put the cat in a carrier, gave the parakeets extra food, and stayed with her coworker Sylvia for a week. Sylvia helped her file an order of protection, and the police escorted my father out of our house in handcuffs. My mother filed for divorce, but declined to press charges.

The divorce was finalized in 1995, just before I left for college. Months later, we got word from my father's nephew's wife (a white woman who was considering leaving my abusive cousin): my father had married an Indo-Guyanese woman he'd met through the Hindu temple he had joined when he moved forty minutes south of our home. I remember wondering whether we had a moral obligation to warn this woman. I quickly decided—no. She was a grown woman in her mid-thirties. My father stopped stalking my mother as soon as he started pursuing his new wife. He was someone else's problem now.

Within a few years, we got word through my cousin's wife that my father had a son. Again, I felt a twinge—should I warn my stepmother? But my father had moved all the assets from his carpet store into her name, and was fighting my mother in court over crumbs. My stepmother signed the meager child support checks. Every semester, I cried when my mother fretted that I might have to drop out of school because, even with my student loans and my work-study job, she was having a hard time paying my tuition. My hatred for my stepmother, an accomplice to my father's financial abuse, outweighed any concern I had. I rationalized any worry away by reminding myself my father had never (to my knowledge) sexually abused a boy.

But in my senior year of college, we got another call from my cousin's wife: my stepmother was pregnant again. It was a girl.

Fast forward to 2006. I was on the dance floor at Cattyshack, a lesbian club in Brooklyn. The DJ was another Punjabi woman, a little older than me. Years prior, we had pieced together that our fathers were friends when I was a kid, and when I disclosed my survivorship to her, she'd sheepishly told me her father had stayed friends with mine all these years. During her first break of the night, she made her way right over to me.

"I saw your dad," she said by way of greeting. "At Christmas. He came over to my parents' house. With his kids…Your sister's name? Sulakshmi. She's six."

When, at age sixteen, I cut my father off, his older brother made it clear to me that I was no longer a part of that family. Blood supremacy is the notion that blood ties are paramount, even at the expense of one's own well-being. It is the violence that allows patriarchy, ageism, and every other form of violence to persist generationally through incestuous rape, in my family and in so many others. I had done so much work to free myself from blood supremacy. So why did I care so much about this girl with whom I shared nothing but blood ties? The thought remained lodged in my subconscious.

Meanwhile, my inner compartmentalization persisted. While I was "out" as a survivor to my closest friends and colleagues, I wasn't "out" to the general public. In grad school, my complex PTSD flared up worse than it had since college. To cope, I decided to finally tell my story publicly, while helping other survivors tell theirs too. I collaborated with an off-off-Broadway theater group, Ping Chong + Company, to create *Secret Survivors*, an ensemble piece featuring me and four other survivors of child sexual abuse.

Through creating and performing *Secret Survivors*, I learned to hold my entire narrative at once. I confronted the members of my mother's family one by one, challenging their complicity in what had happened to me. And slowly, I reached the conclusion that

I needed to move far away from my mother to truly be free from her emotional abuse and gaslighting. I prepared to move to Los Angeles because my then-partner lived there.

One thing kept nagging at me, though: my never-contacted half sister. I knew by now she would be about twelve years old. I remembered how lonely and scared I'd felt at twelve. I remembered how it felt to choke on my silence, to endure, to gaslight myself. I knew we actually shared more than blood ties. We shared the same perpetrator.

I found Sulakshmi on Facebook, but I knew some parents, maybe including my father, monitored their children's social media accounts. I was scared of potential retaliation by my father, so I made a fake profile, pretending to be one of my own childhood best friends. And I sent Sulakshmi a message, with a link to a clip of *Secret Survivors*:

> Hi Sulakshmi. You don't know me, but my name is Amy, and I am one of your sister Amita's best friends from childhood. I'm not sure if you know about Amita, but she's your oldest sister, and she knows you exist. She survived a lot of abuse from your father when she was a kid, and she hopes you're not being abused by him, too. But if you are, and if you want to talk to her, I'd be happy to introduce you. Here's a clip of a theater project she made, telling her story. Take care, Amy.

It took Sulakshmi two months to write "Amy" back: "Wow. I had no idea. I'm not even sure where to start. I feel like my whole life is a lie. Yes, it happened to me too. Please put me in touch with Amita."

I immediately switched Facebook profiles and sent Sulakshmi a message from my actual account, assuring her I would support her.

As soon as I sent the message, I knew it was time to alert my family. I was now less worried about retaliation from my father, but I was also about to move to Los Angeles in two weeks. They'd be left behind in New Jersey, forty minutes north of where my father lived. They had a right to know.

I told my mother first. She was upset the cycle had repeated itself, but glad that Sulakshmi wouldn't have to face the healing process alone. Unfortunately, my mother reneged her support as soon as I told my stepdad. He felt I'd endangered my "real family" by risking my father's retaliation to intervene in "a stranger's life." I accused him of being a hypocrite, donating money to help orphans in India but not being brave enough to help a twelve-year-old girl heal from the violence of the same man who had so deeply harmed his own wife and stepdaughters.

That next week was one of the hardest. I spent my time packing boxes, grieving, and dissociating, sometimes all at once. My close friends, who were more like a network of platonic life partners, took public transportation from Brooklyn to suburban New Jersey to help me pack my things and ship them to Los Angeles. They kept me company on the phone into the late hours of the night. They reassured me I was loved, and commended me for reaching out to Sulakshmi. They helped me believe that even though everything about my relationship with my family was changing—again—somehow it would all be OK in the end.

Sulakshmi wrote back to me a month after I moved to Los Angeles, and we began an infrequent correspondence through Facebook Messenger. Within six months of our first communication, she asked me to help her mother understand the severity of the violence she'd endured. As soon as Sulakshmi had received "Amy's" message, she'd disclosed to her mother that our father had abused her. Her mother confronted our father immediately, and forced him to move out of the house. But Sulakshmi was worried that she would still have to see him, as her mother chose to stay married to him.

We spoke on the phone about what she wanted. She was clear, even at the tender age of twelve, that she didn't want police involvement. Her older brother had already been criminalized for marijuana possession and for supposedly making a teacher feel unsafe. The police had been terrible during that situation, and she was inclined not to trust them. She was also clear that she didn't want our father locked in a cage; she just didn't want to see or talk to him again.

Despite my clear commitment to prison abolition and transformative justice, I would be lying if I said I didn't feel a tinge of regret at a missed opportunity for revenge. But the bigger part of me wanted to spare her from state violence, from the harrowing experience of being put on trial as a young survivor. I told Sulakshmi about my experience with mandated reporting, and told her that I would help her the way she wanted to be helped.

We set up another call for me to finally talk to my stepmother. Sulakshmi stayed on the phone while she and I spoke. It was surreal. I remember telling my stepmother, "My father raped me. He beat and raped my mother for years. I heard from my cousin's wife that he also beat you when you were pregnant." She denied this, and was incredulous about my recounting of my father's history. But I was relentless. "Sulakshmi says he didn't rape her, but he did sexually assault her for years. I don't believe in calling the police, but what my father did is very, very illegal. Either you will guarantee that Sulakshmi will never have to see or talk to him again, or I will call the police." She promised. And eight years later, that promise still holds.

It took two more years of regular phone and Skype conversations until I was ready to meet Sulakshmi in person. By then, she was fifteen. We spent hours talking on a bench in Central Park and at the Metropolitan Museum of Art. We have so many things in common, things that I don't share with my sister with whom I grew up, and that Sulakshmi doesn't share with her brother. We are both poets, both activists, both really into school, both very extroverted people. We look like sisters too. We have the same eyes. Our father's eyes.

Since that first meeting, Sulakshmi and I have spent at least a week together once a year. When she was thirteen, she told me she wanted to be a survivor activist like me, but she knew she'd have to wait until she turned eighteen because of mandated reporting. When she finished high school, I flew her to California as a graduation present. Together, we shared our story at the first Mirror Memoirs conference for LGBTQI people of color who survived child sexual abuse, at the California Coalition Against Sexual Assault's statewide conference, and in the Living Bridges archive curated by fellow survivor activist Mia Mingus. We wanted people to understand transformative justice can be practiced even when intervening in the case of a minor who has been sexually assaulted or raped by a parent with whom they still live.

When I think about my journey toward transformative justice, I think about all the steps I took away from my past without knowing where they would lead. Shortly after I moved to Los Angeles, my father was scheduled to be a keynote speaker at a New Age event on healing and mysticism (if you've seen *Kumaré* or *Wild Wild Country*, you have some idea of the guru my father aspires to be). The event happened to be in front of the Queens Museum in New York City, where one of my best friends was the public events director. She told the event organizers she would pull their sound permit if they didn't pull my father from the lineup. Several of my friends attended the event to distribute flyers with my father's name on them, along with statistical information about the prevalence of child sexual abuse. I watched these events unfold from Los Angeles in awe—I'd never had any loved ones hold my father accountable. One of my friends, Bushra Rehman, even wrote a piece documenting the series of events for the *Feminist Wire*.

Six years later, I was preparing to give a keynote in New Mexico to a statewide coalition of direct service providers working with survivors of intimate partner violence and sexual violence. The day before my talk, I received a Facebook message from a stranger—a young Sikh American man who said my father had been visiting his gurudwara, marketing himself as a spiritual healer. This young man's "Spidey sense" had gone off when my father made plans to conduct a "healing ritual" for his younger sister. With a little Googling, he found Bushra's article, printed it out, and used it to confront my father in front of his father and sister. "Do you know this woman? Is she your daughter? Did you do the things she says you did?" He told me that my father admitted to being my father, but denied his violence. "I believe her, though," this young man replied. He convinced his parents to cancel the ritual. Then he printed out copies of the article and distributed them throughout the temple. "Your father will never be welcome in our gurudwara again. Thank you for your work. Keep doing what you are doing," he wrote.

Seeds bloom in the most unexpected ways. That's what transformative justice has taught me. If I'd cooperated with those prosecutors all those years ago, my father would have been incarcerated—and Sulakshmi would never have been born. Being able to heal with her, to laugh with her, to resist with her has been such an unexpected gift—one I would not have known to dream of when I was thirteen. Every time we are together, the veils of time part. For her, I can be the adult I needed when I was younger. By reaching for her, I've simultaneously interrupted my father's cycle of harm and created an everlasting bond of healing—something no judge or jail could ever provide.

PART TWO

# WE GOT THIS

## TOOLKITS AND ROAD MAPS

# 8

# PHILLY STANDS UP!

## A PORTRAIT OF PRAXIS, AN ANATOMY OF ACCOUNTABILITY

*Esteban Lance Kelly and Jenna Peters-Golden with
Qui Alexander, Bench Ansfield, Beth Blum, and
Dexter Rose of Philly Stands Up! Collective*

THE ALCHEMY OF OUR ACCOUNTABILITY WORK IS A SERENDIPITOUS mixture: part art, part science. To be sure, the skill and complexity involved in working on accountability processes is difficult to finesse. Nevertheless, we affirm that average people, regular folks in communities all across North America, can develop and exercise their own processes for making justice in sexual assault situations possible for their communities. In doing so, our communities can meet more success, by any measure, than the state ever has in addressing the chaos of issues stirred up by incidents of sexualized violence.

What we now know, we learned through trial and quite a bit of error. Some of the mistakes and missteps we've made throughout the years enabled, and in some cases exacerbated, pain toward survivors and communities. We take responsibility for these mistakes. Very few of us in the history of Philly Stands Up (PSU) came to the group with any prior formal experience working on sexual assault issues, let alone working with people who have caused harm. We are average people, figuring out how to do thorny work, and our achievements stem from being committed to our values and purpose. We believe that people who have caused harm can change and that we all can play a crucial role in catalyzing that shift.

In recognition of our peers and mentors in the past and present who have figured out and passed along lessons such as these—specifically Indigenous, Black, and brown communities with women at the front—it is with a great sense of humility that we share some of the logistical guts of what we've devised for our process of working on sexual assault situations. We are grateful to all the other organizers, thinkers, neighbors, and comrades whose wisdom and experience has been in collaboration with ours.

We see the input of energy and emotional attention to these processes as the core ingredients for supporting meaningful change. Our dedication to working with people who have perpetrated assault is rooted in our solidarity with survivors of harm, and our commitment to recognizing the humanity within us all. It demands naming that most of the people with whom we work have also survived sexual or physical violence in their lifetimes.

When we say that we work to hold people who have perpetrated sexual assault accountable[1] for the harm they have done, this means that we strive for them to do the following:

1. Recognize the harm they have done, even if it wasn't intentional.

2. Acknowledge that harm's impact on individuals and the community.

---

1   Our working definition is based on generationFIVE's articulation of accountability in their document, *Toward Transformative Justice: A Liberatory Approach to Child Sexual Abuse and Other Forms of Intimate and Community Violence* (San Francisco: generationFIVE, 2007).

3. Make appropriate restitution to the individual and community.

4. Develop solid skills for transforming attitudes and behavior to prevent further harm and make contributions toward liberation.

We conceptualize roughly five phases to an accountability process: the Beginning, Designing the Structure, Life Process, Tools We Use, and Closing a Process.

## PHASE 1. THE BEGINNING

People find us in many ways: we are known through our educational workshops, our contributions to zines, and also through word of mouth, the Internet, and personal connections with individual members in PSU.

Sometimes a person who has caused harm gets in touch with us and says something like, "I really messed up, and the person I hurt told me I need to work with you guys." Sometimes they say: "A few years ago I was abusive. I sexually assaulted someone and I wasn't really ready to deal with it until now." In our workshops, people are often surprised to hear about these situations in which people contact us of their own volition, sometimes years after committing harm. The reality is that, with time, we grow. With growth, with opportunity, many of us summon the courage to reflect on past behavior and see problems that we need to engage with.

Another possibility is that someone might say, "I was sexually assaulted by *so-and-so*, and I want to hold them accountable." They would then task us with tracking down *so-and-so* and attempting to initiate an accountability process. Beyond these cases, there are instances when someone who is neither the survivor nor the person who caused harm gets in touch with us on behalf of either party.

In any event, once we have touched base with the person who has caused harm, we sketch out the situation and discuss it as a group. We first find out if two collective members are able to take on this situation (we learned early on to always work in pairs). If so, we discuss what we know about the situation, and we honestly assess if we are equipped to handle it. There is always the possibility that we can't handle pieces of the situation. Sometimes we are not qualified for one reason or another and by trying to work on it we might cause more harm than good. Sometimes PSU members decline to engage a situation because some of its aspects feel emotionally triggering.

After we have assessed the situation, we schedule a meet-up with the person who has caused harm. We typically meet in places that are public but run a low risk of encounters with people we know; examples include parks, train stations, hotel lobbies, food courts, or outdoor cafés.

## PHASE 2. DESIGNING THE PROCESS

Next, we design a process based on what the situation warrants. Often, we have a document listing "demands." Demands are actions the survivor needs from the community or the person who caused harm in order to be safe and to heal. Below is a sample list of common demands:

- "Pay for my STI testing/abortion/doctor's appointment."

- "Deal with your drug/alcohol problem."

- "If you see me out somewhere, it's your responsibility to leave the premises."

- "Don't talk to me or contact me."

- "For now, don't go to the meetings of such-and-such organization in which both the survivor and person who has caused harm are members."

- "Disclose to all the people you are sleeping with or dating that you sexually assaulted someone and are in an account-ability process."

- "Write me a sincere letter of apology."

Demands are the central document in our accountability process. In situations where we have a list of demands, they fundamentally drive the design for our process. Our goals as facilitators of the process are to meet the demands laid out by the survivor—and in some cases the community at large—both in letter and in spirit. In designing a particular process, we bear several principles in mind.

First, we try to involve the person we are working with in the design of the process. If they can help brainstorm our objectives, timeline, and tactics, then they feel more invested in everything to come. As collaborators in a process rather than participants in an externally imposed program, they might be more reluctant to bail on commitments.

Second, in order to engage the person who caused harm, we figure out methods that specifically work for them. If they are a visually oriented person, we make drawings or word maps to describe what we are talking about in a meeting. If they hate to read, we might record a reading for them. If they have trouble sitting still or focusing for a long time, we might plan to talk while walking around the block. In our engagement efforts, we have even arranged meetings consisting of street skating and board games. Be accommodating and creative! The goal is to enlist this person in meaningful and sustained accountability and change—think like an educator, an organizer, and an artist.

We also use the meetings as an opportunity to model the behavior we are trying to encourage in the person with whom we are working. We demonstrate preferred behavior by, for example, articulating and maintaining explicit social and physical boundaries, striving for clear communication, practicing empathy, showing respect (which is perceptibly appreciated among people who have been ostracized in the aftermath of sexual assault), and exemplifying utter honesty. If the person we are working with misses a meeting or arrives late, we will discuss the need for better communication and help them understand how their actions were inconsiderate. Together, we lay down ground rules for how we want to communicate with one another, which gives us concrete agreements for holding folks accountable. We can then use their progress in adhering to agreements in creating positive momentum and endorsing their capacity to grow and change.

## PHASE 3. LIFE STRUCTURE

When needed, we emphasize fostering balance and creating structure in the person's life. If they are unstable, then it becomes difficult for them to be present in the work we are doing together. In such situations, it is crucial for us to take account of the broader challenges in their lives. The more grounded they are, the better their chances of following through on their accountability process.

Toward that end, we create space for them to have a personal "check-in" at the beginning of each meeting. This is a moment for them to share anything they wish about their daily lives, emotional state, or logistical hurdles. The check-in allows us to hear, for example, about their progress in finding a therapist or stable housing, or about job interviews or family visits. At times, we have actively passed along job prospects, accompanied people in looking for viable housing, and given people rides to therapy appointments. This humbling and more fundamentally "human" work has helped us to see what it truly means to acknowledge that we are all in community together, that a politics of trust depends on everyday support and interdependence, and that nobody rests outside of these principles in a just society.

## PHASE 4. TOOLS WE USE

Each process is unique. Most meetings consist primarily of talking. We talk about stories, the instances of assault that took place, relationship patterns, and countless connected issues. We employ several general tools as guides in the meeting space:

- *Storytelling*: We ask to hear stories, encourage discussion about dynamics or emerging themes, and use these didactically, sometimes revisiting their stories. Storytelling offers opportunities for us to pause and imagine the same story from the survivor's point of view. By deconstructing the story in this way, we can often push for new levels of understanding, building empathy and rewriting narratives that prevent people from taking full responsibility for their actions.

- *Writing*: Giving "homework" is a good way to maintain continuity between meetings. Sometimes people write down recollections of an instance of abuse, record what certain words mean to them, keep a log of times they felt frustration or anger (those are common emotions we work with), or maintain a journal about how the accountability process is going for them.

- *Role-Playing*: Taking a cue from Augusto Boal's Theatre of the Oppressed, we sometimes act out scenarios that have occurred or that could occur. Role playing is great for building skills of perception and empathy, and is a safe way for people to try out new behaviors and understand past ones.

- *Reading/Listening/Watching*: Most situations that we come across call for further education. There are countless helpful texts, films, lectures, podcasts, and so on that shed light on patriarchy, consent, substance abuse, internalized oppression, and the dynamics of power, privilege, and oppression. Here, our role is to tailor any resources to the person we are working with.

## PHASE 5. CLOSING A PROCESS

Improving ourselves is lifelong work for everyone, and certainly for folks who have a history of perpetrating violence. Most of our accountability processes last between nine months and two years, and they could potentially continue ad infinitum. In retrospect, the processes that last longer than a year have often felt too long. This begs the question, "When is it time to wrap up a situation?" Much like therapy, there is no objective answer to this, but here are some indicators for when it might be appropriate to wind things down.

One obvious signal that it's time to close out a process is when both the letter and the spirit of the demands have been met. If a demand is "write me a letter of apology," it won't do for the person who has caused harm to draft an apology within the first few months of their process when there is anger, resentment, and disbelief permeating the letter. Although hastily dashing off an apology may technically satisfy a demand, communicating sincere contrition is the true spirit of the demand. This can only be achieved once hard work and requisite time have gone into understanding one's role in the assault, and once the person has gained a sense of empathy for how the assault affected the survivor(s) and the community.

If a demand calls for sobriety or a reduction in the use of illicit substances, then fulfilling the true spirit of the demand would require both cutting back substance use and moving toward a true understanding of how the survivor (or community) came to this demand. We would look for the person who caused harm to recognize whether drinking or using creates conditions for impaired judgment and abusive behavior. Making that connection and changing their relationship to that substance would therefore be true fulfillment of the demand.

Another indicator that it's time to transition out of a formal process is that the person who has caused harm has demonstrated their capacity to navigate through "gray zones." Here, it is important to feel confident that they have practiced this shift in their everyday life and that this change is profound and lasting.

Often we would hesitate to wind down an accountability process unless we are sure that whomever we are working with has developed responsible and sustainable systems of support in their life. We look for clues that they have not just one or two, but plenty of decent friends with whom they can speak honestly. This can include housemates or family members they trust for support when challenges come up, particularly with issues related to this work. We also work to ensure that they are familiar with the resources available to them around the city.

Usually, "ending" a process looks more like phasing it out. Over time we go from meeting each week, to twice a month, to once a month, until finally we are only meeting to check in periodically. After an accountability process, the people with whom we have worked know that we are here for them whenever they need us.

9

# GOAL-SETTING TOOL

## DEALING WITH STRONG NEGATIVE FEELINGS AND FANTASY DURING GOAL SETTING

*Creative Interventions*

IT IS COMMON FOR PEOPLE TO HAVE STRONG NEGATIVE FEELINGS, fantasies, or unrealistic expectations linked to goals about situations of harm. At some point during the goal-setting phase, it is good to let a full range of feelings be expressed no matter how far-fetched they may seem to you. Considering the entire range of goals generated in response to a situation of harm may help people express strong negative feelings and fantasies—as well as other goals that may be more realistic. For example, the survivor may express goals such as the following:

- I wish the person doing harm were dead or experience the same harm they did to me.

- I wish the person doing harm could be publicly humiliated or hurt so that they would know they could never do this again.

- I wish this had never happened to me.

- I wish that I would feel the same as I felt before this ever happened.

Allies may express ideas such as the following:

- I wish the survivor would have walked away.

- I wish the survivor would cut off all contact with the person doing harm.

- I wish the survivor would just move on.

- I wish someone else would deal with this.

The person who did harm may want things like these:

- I wish everyone would just forgive me and forget about this.

- I wish everyone would understand that I was under a lot of pressure and cut me some slack.

- I wish everyone would know that the survivor deserved it—anybody would have done the same thing if they were in my shoes.

- I wish this had never happened.

While extreme responses and fantasies may be normal, we ask you to think about the following in assessing whether or not you want to pursue a goal:

- Values. Does this goal fit your values?

- Risk assessment. Will pursuing this goal lead to more harm for yourself or others, or will it lead to retaliation?

- Realistic or achievable. Is it actually possible to achieve this goal?

## GOAL-SETTING GUIDED
## QUESTIONS AND CHART

The following section includes some basic questions you can think through in moving toward goals. They can be asked individually or as a group.

If this process is survivor-driven—that is, if the process will prioritize the goals of the survivor—then this may be focused around the survivor's or victim's needs and desires. Others can think about these questions for themselves as individuals and also focus on the needs of the survivor and the community.

### Guided Questions

- What do I want for myself?

- What do I want for the survivor or victim (if I am not the survivor or victim)?

- What do I want for other important people (children, other family members, friends, organizations, and so on)?

- What do I want for the person doing harm (if I am not the person doing harm)?

- What do I want for the larger community? It may be useful to name who we mean by the community.

- What do I *not* want? You can ask this question using the same categories above.

- What is important to me? This can include values, ways things will happen, or people.

- What are the most important wants (or goals)? Is there anything that is an absolute "must have" or "must do"? Is there anything that is an absolute "must not"?

- Have I considered things such as safety, financial needs, connection to people or relationship, and other things that are important to me?

- Do these goals fit with my values? Is there anything I would add or leave out after thinking about this?

- Are some goals more achievable than others? Which are most achievable? Is there anything I would add or leave out after thinking about this?

- Will pursuing any of these goals lead to more harm to myself, the survivor or victim, the person doing harm, or others, or will it lead to retaliation? Is there anything I would add or leave out after thinking about this?

- What goals might be fantasies? Is there anything I would add or leave out after thinking about this?

- What would I consider a success? What goals would I consider "good enough"?

- Can I divide these goals into long-term and short-term goals? (If doing so makes sense, you can do that.)

After answering the guided questions, see if you can write your goals in the following chart. The chart will be easier to refer to and share with others.

## ⊞⊕ GOAL SETTING CHART

After answering the guided questions, see if you can write your goals in the following chart. The chart will be easier to refer to and share with others.

| Goals/Wants (or Don't Want) Add a * if necessary/important | For Whom? | Is This Goal Realistic? (Yes, No, Maybe) | Short-Term or Long-Term? | Anything Else? |
|---|---|---|---|---|
| I Want: | | | | |
| I Don't Want: | | | | |
| Limits or Bottom Lines: | | | | |

**REMEMBER:** Limits or Bottom lines may be a limit that you draw for yourself in order to stay involved in the intervention. They might be personal limits such as the amount of time you can spend. They might be limits to how the intervention takes place. (See What Is Goal Setting? for more about Bottom lines).

## 10

# EXCERPTS FROM *ENDING CHILD SEXUAL ABUSE: A TRANSFORMATIVE JUSTICE HANDBOOK*

*Staci K. Haines, Raquel Lavina, Chris Lymbertos, RJ Maccani, and Nathan Shara*

WE ARE WRITING THIS IN THE AUTUMN OF 2018, AFTER A SUMMER of seeing families separated at the border, another policy in a long history of traumatizing children, adults, and communities. The U.S. Supreme Court nomination hearings of Brett Kavanaugh showed us, yet again, the deep patriarchy and white supremacy that lives at the core of this nation—and reminded us of Anita Hill's bravery. #MeToo went viral a year ago, and since then, hundreds of thousands of people have told their stories of sexual violence. Sexual assault is also being grappled with within progressive social movements. Many of us have been engaged with processes to support healing for survivors, hold offenders accountable, and deepen feminisms within movement organizations ... all while attempting to stay aligned with our social justice values.

Many times, in the throes of this era, we have wished that transformative justice, as a politic and a practice, existed at a larger and more accessible scale. There are many survivors in need of trauma healing; many allies in need of a clear, politically grounded, and visionary strategy; and many movement organizations in need of tested and usable transformative justice (TJ) approaches that address personal, collective, and systemic change.

## WHEN WE LOOK AT TRANSFORMATIVE JUSTICE, WE SEE THAT THREE THINGS ARE NEEDED:

1.  Social analysis and organizing: We need to understand the intersectional, systemic causes and scale of sexual violence. To change it, we need organizing, movement building, and systems change guided by a liberatory vision.

2.  Trauma healing and transformation: We need knowledge and practice in the predictable impacts of trauma, and the ways to heal both individually and collectively. We need to know how to use this understanding in our organizing, resilience building, and leadership development. We need many spaces where folks can heal. Lastly, we need folks who are skilled in working with people who offend and moving them toward accountability and transformation.

3.  People: We need ongoing TJ processes and formations that are made up of folks who have these skills. These formations need to be surrounded by others, who have their backs and can add to the resources and skills. This is no small practice, and we need thousands of us.

This may sound overwhelming, but it is such an amazing call. Do we have the skills and scale we need? Not yet. Is there the collective will and commitment? Yes, we see it every day. Transformative justice is an ongoing opportunity to align our politics and practice, our healing and organizing, and is a means to stay true to the long road toward love and justice.

Following are segments from generationFIVE's *Ending Child Sexual Abuse: A Transformative Justice Handbook*. These are highlights from the sections on "Safety, Healing, and Agency" and "Accountability and Transformation of Those Who Abuse."

May this add to the collective transformative justice practice.

## SAFETY, HEALING, AND AGENCY

The people most directly impacted are at the heart of transformative justice. In child sexual abuse, this means the children currently experiencing sexual abuse, children and young people who were sexually abused in the past, and adults who experienced sexual abuse during childhood or adolescence. Though the resources, questions, and skills needed to ensure safety, healing, and agency for any one survivor vary depending on the context and conditions surrounding their experiences, a commitment to survivors' safety, healing, and agency is central to both the vision and the practice of transformative justice.

## INTERVENING IN CHILD SEXUAL ABUSE

Children cannot and should never be expected to prevent abuse they experience. The responsibility for abuse lies with the person or people doing the harm, and with the adults in a child's life who can stop it.

Children know that something wrong is happening but may not know what words to use, and also may be frightened that no one will believe them or that they will be punished if they tell.[1]

Adults in a child's life can get overwhelmed by feelings of horror and rage when learning that a child we care about may be experiencing sexual abuse. It's crucial to seek support *and* take action to protect the child or children in the situation. An adult's

---

1  Katy Anonymous, "Why Child Sexual Abuse Can Never Be Your Fault," *Pandora's Project*, 2009, www.pandys.org/articles/sexualabuseisnotyourfault.html.

initial response can make a huge difference in a child feeling safer immediately.

If you believe a child is being sexually abused or a child has just disclosed to you that they are being sexually abused:

- *Prioritize the child's safety and well-being.* While you will have intense feelings of your own, the child's well-being has to be the center of any interaction. Staying calm and present will support their safety and healing in both the short and long term. Let them know that they did the right thing in sharing with you.

- *Communicate to the child that the abuse was not their fault.* It is very common for survivors to assume that the abuse happened because of something they did or failed to do, such as "I wasn't supposed to talk to strangers and I did," or "I liked them, and they were nice to me." It is very important that the child consistently hears that the abuse was not their fault.

- *Assure the child that you will do whatever you can to prevent the abuse from happening again.* It is vital for adults to demonstrate to the child that they deserve protection, including by limiting contact with the person who has been abusive.[2] "Be careful though, not to make absolute promises that the abuse will stop," caution advocates from Stop It Now, an organization working to prevent child sexual abuse (CSA), "Broken promises are harmful to any child—especially one who is already feeling betrayed." But we can strive to eliminate all opportunities for the abuse to occur again, such as preventing the person doing the harm from

---

2   "How Should I Respond to the Child," *Stop It Now!*, www.stopitnow.org/ohc-content/how-should-i-respond-to-the-child.

being alone with the child or with other children in the family or community.

- *Seek additional support, resources, and help.* Intervening in child sexual abuse is not a single event, but requires an ongoing commitment to keep showing up over time to support healing, accountability, and transformation. Start identifying potential allies, resources, and supports early.

- *Assess the risks and present danger in the situation,* as well as your ability to respond to that danger, along with the ability of other allies in the situation.[3] Again, engage support where you don't have it. Sometimes those closest to the abuse are not the most resourced to help.

- *Positively affirm the child's sharing and be responsive to the child's pace.* A child may share a lot at once, and then not want to talk about the abuse the next time you speak with them. Allowing the child's pace to dictate the process is another way of affirming and restoring the child's sense of choice and self-determination.

- *Support the child's resilience.* We all have inherent resilience. This is not numbing or dissociating or "getting through." Resilience can be found in experiences that have us feel more alive, more hopeful, and more connected, and that have us feel we are more than the violence we experienced.

---

3   The Creative Interventions tool "Staying Safe. How Do We Stay Safe?" is a useful resource for making these assessments. See *Creative Interventions Toolkit: A Practical Guide to Stop Interpersonal Violence*, June 2012, http://www.creative-interventions.org/wp-content/uploads/2012/06/4.B.CI-Toolkit-Tools-Staying-Safe-Pre-Release-Version-06.2012.pdf.

Create opportunities for the child to do things that they like and that build their resilience like playing, making music and art, and engaging in spiritual practice.

Because child sexual abuse occurs in secrecy and isolates people from each other, we see honest and respectful connection as a core element of healing. This means, among other things, that people who have been sexually abused need access to spaces where they are supported and allowed to share what has been kept secret, and where they can experience belonging, compassion, and dignity.

Over and over, people who have been sexually abused report that what they need is to:

- Tell their own stories about their own experiences, within a context of trust and safety.

- Experience validation that the harm they experienced was and is real.

- Observe that the person who sexually abused them feels remorse and is accountable for their actions.

- Receive support that counteracts isolation and self-blame.

- Have choice and input into the resolution of the harm they experienced.

- Be accepted and encouraged, not shamed and blamed, for coming forward by their families, peers, and communities.

\* \* \*

"Recovery from trauma requires creating and telling another story about the experience of violence and the nature of the participants, a story powerful enough to restore a sense of our own humanity to the abused."
—Aurora Levins Morales, *Medicine Stories*[4]

Over the last decade, advocates, activists, and organizers have risen to the challenge of using a transformative justice model rather than models dictated by the criminal justice system. We have learned that to center the needs of survivors and change the conditions that support abuse, there are skills, practices, tools, resources, and messages we can provide, including the following:[5]

* Access to a safe, compassionate listener with whom it feels possible to acknowledge that the abuse happened—or to begin exploring the possibility that maybe it did.

* Education about child sexual abuse. Meaningful political education on the realities of child sexual abuse, its prevalence, and the relationship between CSA and broader systems of oppression (white supremacy, patriarchy, class oppression, religious oppression, ableism, adultism, homophobia, xenophobia, and so forth) are all critically important in supporting survivors to heal shame and locate accountability where it belongs.

---

4  Aurora Levins Morales, *Medicine Stories: History, Culture, and the Politics of Integrity* (Cambridge, MA: South End Press, 1998), 15.

5  This list is based on the Generative Somatics trauma-healing process developed by Staci K. Haines and Generative Somatics. See generativesomatics.org for more information, particularly the document "Arc of Somatic Transformation." http://www.generativesomatics.org/sites/default /files/GS0311_SomaticArc.pdf

- Opportunities to regenerate a sense of safety, in part through making choices and exercising self-determination. This includes relearning boundaries, or learning them for the first time.

- Opportunities to find or rebuild more authentic connection and relationships, which are based on what the person healing cares about and wants in relationship.

- Opportunities to practice mutual intimacy and sexuality, with resources and supports to navigate triggers or memories that may arise within the context of a sexual relationship or intimacy.

- Support in identifying and cultivating resilience.

- Support and guidance to heal shame and cultivate self-forgiveness. For many survivors, one of the most difficult aspects of healing is the process of coming to believe that it was not and is not our fault that someone sexually abused us.

- Support and guidance to learn centered accountability. Nothing about the experience of being sexually abused was your fault. And, out of our survival strategies and trauma reactions, we may have caused harm to other people in our lives.

- Actions that shift conditions within a family, community, and society. Getting involved in social and climate justice can be healing and can change the social and economic conditions that perpetuate violence in many forms. For many of us, taking action to end child sexual abuse or other forms of violence and injustice is a powerful expression of our collective survival, our resilience, and our right to be whole and to thrive.

## ACCOUNTABILITY AND TRANSFORMATION OF THOSE WHO ABUSE

Our stories matter. The stories we tell, and the stories we don't tell. What we keep hidden inside of ourselves can shape our experience of the world, and managing these aspects of our history can limit our energy, as well as our imagination about what is possible for our future. Choosing to put attention on the things that scare us—things we may feel ashamed of or which we don't understand—can be an act of both courage and resilience.

Accountability is central to any practice of justice. Transformative justice interventions seek concrete accountability from individuals who act abusively and also engage community members in creating conditions that invite and demand real accountability and change.

The vast majority of people who sexually abuse children deny their behavior. Given current punitive interventions, there is very little incentive for any of us to acknowledge sexually abusive behavior to others. It is vital that we create spaces and encouragement for people who have sexually abused children, or who feel they might sexually abuse children in the future, to be able to share and come forward. TJ asks us to transform the dominant paradigm of accountability that we have inherited.

Most of us have been deeply shaped by the false notion that in order for people to behave better they need to feel worse and be punished. In practice, we see that humans are, in fact, far more likely to change in desirable ways when they are more resourced, not less.

For example, at this time, there is no existing support within the United States for treating people with pedophilic urges.

Individuals who self-identify as having these desires have had to self-organize their own anonymous online support groups for nonoffending pedophiles. In contrast, Prevention Project Dunkelfeld developed a program in 2005 in Berlin, Germany, that offered treatment and support to anyone who stepped forward to seek help with pedophilic urges.

By March 2018, 9,515 people sought help from all over Germany, 2,894 people traveled to one of the sites for diagnosis and advice, 1,554 were offered a place in a therapeutic program, 925 participants have started the therapy, and 360 have successfully completed it. More than half reported having previously attempted to find therapy without success. Since 2011, the project has grown into a nationwide network called "Don't Offend" with twelve centers that provide free weekly group therapy. The project's slogan is "You are not guilty because of your sexual desire, but you are responsible for your sexual behavior."[6]

Another inspiring model for supporting accountability and transformation is Circles of Support and Accountability (CoSA), which was started in Canada by Mennonite pastor Harry Nigh, whose friend had been convicted for repeated sexual offenses. Alongside other parishioners, Nigh developed a support group model within which four to six trained volunteers from the community form what they call "an inner circle" around the person who caused harm. This circle meets regularly to facilitate getting the practical needs of the core member (the person who caused harm) met (such as finding housing and other services), to provide emotional support, and to challenge behaviors that may be associated with a risk of reoffending. CoSAs currently exist in several countries, as well as six U.S. states.[7]

---

6   Don't Offend, "Do You Like Children in Ways You Shouldn't?" 2019, https://www.dont-offend.org/.

7   Mennonite Central Committee (Canada), "Circles of Support and Accountability," 2019, https://mcccanada.ca/learn/more/circles-support-accountability-cosa.

# A TJ APPROACH ATTEMPTS TO MAKE PROACTIVE ACCOUNTABILITY SAFE AND COMPELLING

Our vision challenges us to create a collective culture of growth and dynamic support. One that acknowledges and supports each individual's inherent dignity and worthiness of connection, while simultaneously demanding rigorous self-accountability and mutual accountability. We aim for forms of accountability that enable transformation—transformation of survivor experience, of sexually abusive behavior, of bystander engagement, and of the broader conditions that allow child sexual abuse to continue.

We see that abuse happens when one person believes, consciously or unconsciously, that their needs, wants, and preferences take precedence over others. People engaging in abusive behaviors are often numb to, or seemingly unable to feel, the impacts of their behaviors on others.

A process of accountability and transformation requires that the person who has been harmful:

- Stops doing the harm.

- Feels empathy and remorse for the pain and impact of their actions.

- Takes measures, like restitution or reparations, to address the harm caused.

- Takes measures to prevent future harm.

- Works to understand the root causes of their harmful behavior.

- Engages in the ongoing work of accountability, healing, and integration.

- Takes action and organizes to support others to heal or to be part of changing community and social conditions that allow for CSA and other forms of violence.

While the impulse to villainize or banish may be understandable, we must engage, name the harm, and call upon this person's dignity in order to hold standards that support safety, connection, and dignity for everyone involved, and above all for those most directly impacted by the harm.

For many people, the idea of giving attention to the healing needs of a person who has been sexually abusive is difficult to tolerate, particularly when there are limited resources available for survivors. It is important to center the needs of those most directly impacted by the harm in a situation. We also hold that recognizing and attending to the humanity of those who harm is a central aspect of transforming our families, communities, and society. Seeing and dignifying the healing needs of people who abuse also runs counter to the idea that some people "out there" are "monsters" who are expendable or need to be "weeded out." By standing for everyone's need for healing, we challenge the dehumanizing logic that is central to systems of oppression, domination, and abuse. By standing for everyone's need for healing, we maintain our commitment to a vision of true liberation.

# 11

# PODS AND POD-MAPPING WORKSHEET

*Mia Mingus for the Bay Area Transformative Justice Collective*

DURING THE SPRING OF 2014, THE BAY AREA TRANSFORMATIVE Justice Collective (BATJC) began using the term "pod" to refer to a specific type of relationship within transformative justice (TJ) work. We needed a term to describe the relationship between people who would turn to each other for support around violent, harmful, and abusive experiences, whether as survivors, bystanders, or people who have harmed. These would be the people in our lives that we would call on to support us with our immediate and ongoing safety, accountability and transformation of behaviors, or individual and collective healing and resiliency.

Prior to this, we had been using the term "community" when we talked about transformative justice, but we found that, not surprisingly, many people do not feel connected to a "community" and, even more so, most people did not know what "community" meant or had wildly different definitions and understandings of "community." For some, "community" was an overarching term that encompassed huge numbers of people based on identity (for example, "the feminist community"). For others, "community" referred to a specific set of arbitrary values, practices, or

119

relationships (for instance, "I don't know them well, but we're in community with each other"). Some defined "community" simply by geographic location, regardless of relationship or identity (such as "the Bay Area community"). We found that people romanticized community, or, though they felt connected to a community at large, they had significant and trustworthy relationships with very few actual people who may or may not be part of that community. For example, someone might feel connected to "the queer community," but, when asked, could name only two or three people from that "queer community" they felt they could trust to show up for them in times of crisis, vulnerability, or violence.

Although "community" is a word that we use all the time, many people don't know what it is or feel they have never experienced it. This became increasingly confusing when we used terms such as "community accountability" or "community responses to violence" and encouraged people to "turn to their communities." And this became even more complicated in dealing with intimate and sexual violence because so many people are abused by someone they know and thus the violence, harm, and abuse was often coming from their "community."

We needed a different term to describe what we meant, and so "pods" was suggested and it stuck. This is not to say that we don't use the term "community" still—we do, but we needed to create new language for our work.

We knew that people who experience violence, harm, and abuse turn to their intimate networks before they turn to external state or social services. Most people don't call the police or seek counseling or even call anonymous hotlines. If they tell anyone at all, they turn to a trusted friend, family member, neighbor, or coworker. We wanted a way to name those currently in your life that you would rely on (or are relying on) to respond to violence, harm, and abuse.

# POD

Your pod is made up of the people that you would call on if violence, harm, or abuse happened to you; if you wanted support in taking accountability for violence, harm, or abuse that you've done; if you witnessed violence; or if someone you care about was being violent or being abused.

People can have multiple pods. The people you call to support you when you are being harmed may not be the same people you call on to support you when you have done harm, and vice versa. In general, pod people are often those you have relationship and trust with, though everyone has different criteria for their pods.

Once we started using the term "pods," we realized a bunch of things:

- Most people have few solid, dependable relationships in their lives. Much of this is the result of the breaking of relationships, isolation, fear, and criminalization that capitalism requires. We found that for many people, mapping their pod was a sobering process, as many thought their pod would be larger than it actually was. Most people have just one or two people in their pod. We reassure people that this is not a popularity contest, but rather a chance to reflect on why we have so few relationships with the deep trust, reliability, and groundedness we need to respond well to violence.

- Many people have fewer people they could call on to take accountability for harm they've done than to support them when they have been harmed. Though competent support for surviving violence is rare, accountable support for those taking accountability for harm they have done is even harder to find. More often than not, people end up colluding with abusers or reinforcing the shaming and blaming of survivors in their attempt to support someone in taking accountability for harm—if they stay in relationship with people who have harmed or been violent at all.

- Asking people to organize their pod was much more concrete than asking people to organize their "community." The shared language and concept of "pod" made transformative justice more accessible. Gone were the fantasies of a giant, magical "community response," filled with people we had only surface relationships with. Instead, we challenged ourselves and others to build solid pods of people through relationship and trust. Doing so pushes us to be specific about what those relationships look like and how they are built. It places relationship-building at the very center of transformative justice and community accountability work.

- "Pod people" don't fall neatly along traditional lines, especially in situations of intimate and sexual violence. People don't necessarily turn to their closest relationships (such as partner, family, or best friends). This is true both because these relationships are often where the violence is coming from, and because the criteria we would use for our pod people are not necessarily the same as those we use (or get taught to use) for our general intimate relationships. We have different and specific kinds of relationships with our pod people; in addition to relationship and trust, they often involve a combination of characteristics such as a track record of generative conflict, boundaries, the ability to give and receive feedback, and reliability. These are characteristics and skills that we are not readily taught to value in U.S. society and don't usually have the skill set to support in even our closest relationships.

- Building analysis was much easier than building the relationship and trust required for one's pod. Once people started to identify their pod, it became clear that most of the people they would call on were not necessarily political organizers or activists and usually didn't have political analysis. This was true even for political organizers and activists who were mapping their own pods. Using the language of "pods" was a way to meet people where they were and reveal what was already working in their intimate networks. People already had individuals (even if it was just one person) in their lives they would turn to when violence happened. So, this is where we needed to focus our work, instead of trying to build new relationships with strangers who might share a political analysis but had no relationship to each other, let alone trust. We set out to build through our relationships and trust. We then worked to support our folks in cultivating a shared analysis and framework for understanding intimate and sexual violence through, most notably, our transformative justice studies.

- The BATJC focuses on transformative justice responses to child sexual abuse. Growing and deepening our pods helps us build where children already are. Using the concept of pods is a way to reach children where they are because a five-year-old is not going to reach out to us for support, nor should they be expected to spearhead a community accountability process. The more we can grow our own pods and have conversations about protecting and supporting the children and youth in our lives, the better prepared we will be to respond to child sexual abuse in our intimate networks.

- Relationship and trust, not always political analysis, continue to be two of the most important factors in successful TJ interventions, whether in supporting survivor self-determination and healing or in accountability processes. Though shared language, values, and political understandings can be very useful in responding to violence, these are easier to build where relationship and trust already exist. By building where there are already authentic relationships and trust, rather than trying to piece together shallow versions, we help to set the conditions for successful TJ responses and also for the likelihood that people will respond to violence at all.

Many people do not have any pod people. This a reality for many oppressed and isolated communities and individuals because of how capitalism, oppression, and violence shape our lives. For example, many disabled people are extremely isolated because they lack access and resources; many immigrant women of color are isolated because of language or documentation; and adults, youth, and children who are surviving current abuse such as domestic violence may be isolated by their abusers.

We hope that by beginning to build and grow pods where they already exist (or could exist), we can build the conditions to support people who do not have pods. By growing the number of people in the Bay Area who can recognize, talk about, prevent, and respond to violence, we hope to make it more likely that people in need of support will find it in their daily lives. We also believe that orienting from a place of growing pods can help us gradually move away from the structures that keep people isolated. In this way, building our pods is useful for ourselves and the people in our immediate circles, but it is also part of building a network of pods that could support anyone experiencing violence.

Here is our Pod Mapping Worksheet. We use this as a template to help people start to identify who could be in their pods. We invite people to fill out multiple worksheets for their different pods. This is only a basic template; people are welcome to create their own pod maps.

- Write your name in the middle gray circle.

- The surrounding bold-outlined circles are your pod. Write the names of the people who are in your pod. We encourage people to write the names of actual individuals rather than categories, such as "my church group" or "my neighbors."

- The dotted lines surrounding your pod are people who are "movable." They are people that could be moved into your pod but need a little more work. For example, you might need to build more relationship or trust with them. Or maybe you've never had a conversation with them about prisons or sexual violence.

The larger circles at the edge of the page are for networks, communities, or groups that could be resources for you, such as your local domestic violence direct service organization, your cohort in nursing school, your youth group, or a transformative justice group.

Your pods may shift over time as your needs or relationships shift or as people's geographic locations shift. We encourage people to have conversations with their pod people about pods and transformative justice, to actively grow the number of people in their pod, and to support each other in building their pod. Growing a pod is not easy and may take time. In pod work, we measure our successes by the quality of our relationships with one another, and we invest the time it takes to build things like trust, respect, vulnerability, accountability, care, and love. We see building our pods as a concrete way to prepare and build resources for transformative justice in our communities.

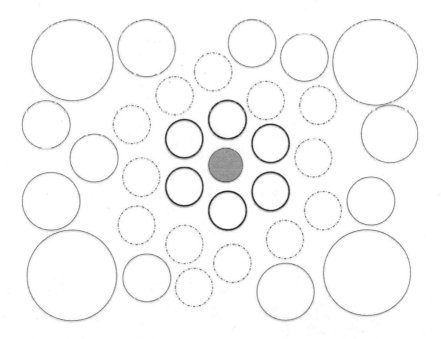

# 12

# WHEN IT ALL COMES CRASHING DOWN

## NAVIGATING CRISIS

*The Fireweed Collective (formerly known as The Icarus Project)*

WHEN YOU OR SOMEONE CLOSE TO YOU GOES INTO CRISIS, IT CAN be the scariest thing to ever happen. You don't know what to do, but it seems like someone's life might be at stake or they might get locked up, and everyone around is getting more stressed and panicked. Everyone knows a friend who has been there, or has been there themselves. Someone's personality starts to make strange changes, they're not sleeping or sleeping all day, they lose touch with the people around them, they disappear into their room for days, they have wild energy and outlandish plans, they start to dwell on suicide and hopelessness, they stop eating or taking care of themselves, they start taking risks and being reckless. They become a different person. They're in crisis.

# THE WORD "CRISIS" COMES FROM A GREEK ROOT MEANING "JUDGMENT."

A crisis is a moment of great tension and a moment of meeting the unknown. It's a turning point when things can't go on the way they have, and the situation isn't going to hold. Could crisis be an opportunity for breakthrough, not just breakdown? Can we learn about each other and ourselves as a community through crisis? Can we see crisis as an opportunity to judge a situation and ourselves carefully, not just react with panic and confusion or turn things over to the authorities?

## CRISIS RESPONSE SUGGESTIONS

*Working in teams.* If you're trying to help someone in crisis, coordinate with other friends and family to share responsibility and stress. If you're the one going through crisis, reach out to multiple people and swallow your pride. The more good help you can get, the easier the process will be and the less you will exhaust your friends.

*Try not to panic.* People in crisis can be made a lot worse if people start reacting with fear, control, and anger. Study after study has shown that if you react to someone in crisis with caring, openness, patience, and a relaxed and unhurried attitude, it can really help settle things down. Keep breathing, take time to do things that help you stay in your body, such as yoga and taking walks, be sure to eat, drink water, and try to get sleep.

*Be real about what's going on.* When people act weird or lose their minds, it is easy to overreact. It's also easy to under-react. If someone is actually seriously attempting suicide or doing something extremely dangerous like lying down on a busy freeway, getting the police involved might save their life. But if someone picks up a knife and is walking around the kitchen talking about UFOs, don't assume the worst and call the cops. Likewise, if someone is cutting themselves, it's usually a way of coping and doesn't always mean they're suicidal (unless they are cutting severely). Sometimes people who are talking about the ideas of death and suicide are in a very dangerous place, but sometimes they may just need to talk about painful feelings that are buried. Use your judgment and ask others for advice. Sometimes you just need to wait out crisis. Sometimes you need to intervene strongly and swiftly if the situation is truly dangerous and someone's life is really falling apart.

*Listen to the person without judgment.* What do they need? What are their feelings? What's going on? What can help? Sometimes we are so scared of someone else's suffering that we forget to ask them how to help. Beware of arguing with someone in crisis; their point of view might be off, but their feelings are real and need to be listened to. (Once they're out of crisis they'll be able to hear you better.) If you are in crisis, tell people what you're feeling and what you need. It is so hard to help people who aren't communicating.

*Lack of sleep is a major cause of crisis.* Many people come right out of crisis if they get some sleep, and any hospital will first get you to sleep if you are sleep deprived. If the person hasn't tried Benadryl, herbal or homeopathic remedies from a health food store, hot baths, rich food, exercise, or acupuncture, these can be extremely helpful. If someone is really manic and hasn't been sleeping for months, though, none of these may work, and you may have to seek out psychiatric drugs to break the cycle.

*Drugs are also a big cause of crisis.* Does someone who regularly takes psych meds suddenly stop? Withdrawal can cause a crisis. Get the person back on their meds (if they want to transition off meds they should do so carefully and slowly, not suddenly), and make sure they are in a safe space. Meds can start working very quickly for some, but for others it can take weeks.

*Create a sanctuary and meet basic needs.* Try to de-dramatize and de-stress the situation as much as possible. Crashing in a different home for a few days can give a person some breathing space and perspective. Perhaps caring friends could come by in shifts to spend time with the person, make good food, play nice music, drag them outside for exercise, spend time listening. Often people feel alone and uncared for in crisis, and making an effort to offer them a sanctuary can mean a lot. Make sure basic needs are met:

food, water, sleep, shelter, exercise, and, if appropriate, professional (alternative or psychiatric) attention.

*Calling the police or hospital shouldn't be the automatic response.* Police and hospitals are not saviors. They can make things worse. When you're out of other options, though, you shouldn't rule them out. Faced with a decision like this, get input from people who have a good head on their shoulders and know about the person. Have other options been tried? Did the hospital help in the past? Are people overreacting? Don't assume that it's always the right thing to do just because it puts everything in the hands of the "authorities." Be realistic, however, when your community has exhausted its capacity to help and there is a risk of real danger. The alternative support networks we need do not exist everywhere that people are in crisis. The most important thing is to keep people alive.

## ADVANCE DIRECTIVES

If you know your crises get bad enough to get you into a hospital, you should use a psychiatric advance directive or power of attorney. Basically, it's like a living will for crisis: it gives you power and self-control over what happens to you when you go into a crisis. If you start to lose your mind and have a hard time speaking for yourself, people will look at your advance directive to figure out what to do.[1]

There is an elaborate advance directive form at the Bazelon Center for Mental Health Law and a simpler one at the Copeland Center for Wellness and Recovery website, or you can just write a letter and sign it. Write down who you want contacted if you are in crisis and who you don't want contacted, what hospital you prefer to go to, what medications you do and don't want to be given, what health practitioner you want to work with, and any

---

1   Bazelton Center for Mental Health Law has templates available at http://www.bazelon.org/our-work/mental-health-systems/advance-directives/. For the forms: http://www.bazelon.org/issues/advancedirectives/templates.htm, and http://www.mentalhealthrecovery.com/pdfs/crisisplan.pdf.

special instructions for supporters, such as "take me out into the woods," "help me sleep with these herbs or those pills," "feed me kale," "when you ask me questions, give me a long time to answer, be patient and don't walk away," or "make sure I can see my pets as soon as possible."

Write your directive, get it signed by someone and write "witness" by their name, and date it. Distribute copies so that relevant people are able to access it, such as with a therapist or health practitioner, with family, with people close to you, or with people in any support or activist group you're in. Then, when you go into crisis, people can use your directive as a guide for responding to the situation, and it can be used to help convince hospitals, doctors, and so forth to respect your choices about how to be treated. (Directives have some legal weight, but not as much as a living will. Ongoing reforms in mental health law may strengthen the role of directives in the future.)

## ON SUICIDE

While it's easy to romanticize certain sides of bipolar disorder, it is a dangerously incomplete picture. if you believe the statistics, one in five untreated manic-depressives commits suicide. In the medical establishment's opinion, bipolar disorder is a highly lethal disease. Whether or not you choose to see things this way, the stark fact remains that the extremes of bipolar mood swings have driven thousands and thousands of people to kill themselves, and these swings can happen with astounding speed.

There is no accepted theory about why one person who is suicidal ends up doing it and another doesn't. There is no perfect answer to what you should do when someone is suicidal, and no reliable way to prevent someone from killing themselves if they really want to. Suicide is, and will probably always be, a mystery. There are, however, a lot of things that people have learned, things that come from a real sense of caring and love for people who have died or who might die, and truths people have realized when they were at the brink and made their way back. Here are a few we've collected:

- Feeling suicidal is not giving up on life. Feeling suicidal is being desperate for things to be different. People are holding out for a better person they know they can be and a better life they know they deserve, but they feel totally blocked. Discover the vision for a better life, and see how it is only possible to realize that vision if you stick around to find out what can happen. Turn some of that suicidal energy toward risking change in life. Find out what behavior pattern or life condition you want to kill instead of taking your whole life. Is there a way to change those patterns that you haven't yet tried? Who can you turn to for help changing those patterns?

- People who are suicidal are often really isolated. They need someone to talk with confidentially on a deep level, someone who is not going to judge them or reject them. Did something happen? What do you need? Be patient with long silences; let the person speak. Let people ask for anything, an errand, food, a place to stay, and the like. Often, suicidal people don't want to be honest because they're so ashamed of what they are feeling, and that is an incredibly hard thing to admit. Be patient and calm.

- People need to hear things that might seem obvious: You are a good person. Your friendship has helped me. You are a cool person and you have done cool things, even if you can't remember them now. You have loved life and you can love it again. There are ways to make your feelings change and to make your head start working better. If you kill yourself, nothing in your life will ever change. You will hurt people you love. You will never know what could have happened. Your problems are very real, but there are other ways to deal with them.

- Suicidal people are often under the sway of a critical voice or belief that lies about who and what they are. It might be the voice of a parent, an abuser, someone who betrayed them, or simply the negative version of themselves that depression and madness have put in their brain. Usually this voice is not perceiving reality accurately. Get a reality check from someone close and stop believing these voices. You aren't a "failure," and change isn't impossible. *And you are not alone.* Other people have felt pain this deep and terrible, and they have found ways to change their lives and survive. You are not the only one.

- There are ways to get past this and change your life.

## 13

# WHY NO NONCONSENSUAL ACTIVE RESCUE?

*Trans Lifeline*

THE TRANS LIFELINE IS A GRASSROOTS HOTLINE AND MICRO-grants organization offering direct emotional and financial support to trans people in crisis—for the trans community, by the trans community. Founded in 2014 as a peer-support crisis hotline, the hotline was, and still is, the only service in the country in which all operators are transgender.

*"Are you going to call someone on me if I tell you how I'm feeling?"*

That is one of the most common questions we get from callers. And one of the most common questions we get from people who work in crisis intervention and the general public is why our answer is generally no. We will only call authorities in three circumstances: if a caller asks us to, if there is a credible threat to a third party, or to comply with laws regarding suspected child abuse and neglect.

Since we launched, Trans Lifeline has abided by three unwavering principles:

1. All our operators must be trans.

2. We believe in the power of peer support from shared experience.

3. We do not call emergency services to assist a caller in danger without their request.

In these principles we stand out starkly from many other hotlines, and we are often asked why it is so important to us to abide by the third principle. "How can you save lives if you can't intervene?" Active rescue, or the practice of a crisis hotline choosing to dispatch law enforcement or emergency services to a caller's location, is a very common occurrence on suicide hotlines in the United States. Operators are often trained on the theory that any caller who mentions suicidal ideation is at risk and requires immediate intervention. While at first glance this might be an understandable blanket policy, nonconsensual active rescue entails a number of risks that are made significantly more severe when a caller is trans.

In October 2015, Trans Lifeline surveyed about eight hundred trans people across the United States regarding their experiences with suicide hotline use. Approximately 70 percent of the respondents stated that they had never called a suicide hotline. Over half of those respondents specified that they had been in crisis, but they did not feel safe calling a hotline. Approximately a quarter of respondents stated that they had interacted with law enforcement or emergency personnel as a result of a crisis call, while one in five had been placed on an involuntary psychiatric hold.

Respondents were also asked to rate, on a scale of one to five, how comfortable they felt interacting with doctors, nurses, paramedics, firefighters, and police officers. The average response for each profession was under three, with police officers being the lowest, between one and two. Over and over again, we hear from our community—including our own volunteers—that one of the main deciding factors in whether they reach out for help is whether they will have to deal with active rescue. Trans Lifeline does not engage in nonconsensual active rescue because, in our community, active rescue can place our community at increased risk for suicidality.

According to the National Transgender Discrimination Survey, at least a quarter of respondents reported being denied equal treatment or being harassed, disrespected, or assaulted in a hospital, and at least one-fifth of respondents reported mistreatment in a mental health setting. Nearly half of respondents reporting having been harassed, asked to leave a public space, or assaulted after having to present incongruent identity documents. Well over half of respondents stated that they would not be willing to go to police for help because of how they would be treated for being trans. Over half of respondents who had interacted with police who knew or suspected that they were trans reported being misgendered, verbally harassed, or physically or sexually assaulted by officers.

In the United States, police training does not tend to prioritize mandatory crisis intervention. These trainings are often optional, limited, and overshadowed by training that encourages disproportionate responses, including frequent use of force, for individuals in mental health crises. In simpler terms, forcing any person in crisis to interact with armed police officers poses a risk of that person being harmed or killed. Law enforcement and emergency personnel training on how to respectfully and competently interact with trans people in crisis is functionally nonexistent. The risk of harm or use of deadly force predictably increases when the person in crisis is a person of color or disabled.[1] For trans people in rural or conservative areas, where cultural competency tends to be lower both in the general population and among law enforcement officers, the risks of abuse are further exacerbated for very poor and homeless trans people, and, not surprisingly, they are highly represented among Trans Lifeline callers.

---

1    The Autistic Self-Advocacy Network's "ASAN Joint Statement on the Death of Kayden Clarke" speaks to the death of a suicidal trans man, at the hands of police. Autistic Self Advocacy Network (ASAN), "ASAN Joint Statement on the Death of Kayden Clarke," February 8, 2016, https://autisticadvocacy .org/2016/02/asan-joint-statement-death-of-kayden-clarke.

Beyond the risk of harm from law enforcement, nonconsensual active rescue poses several other risks for our community. Young callers frequently share that they have experienced nonconsensual active rescue after sharing suicidal ideation with another support line. Many of these young people are not out to their families, and the active rescue effectively makes the decision for them, which can result in abuse, rejection, or, on some occasions, sudden and unexpected homelessness.

Hospitalization following active rescue can add an additional layer of risk. Around one-third of trans people live below the poverty line, a rate twice that of the general population. For many callers, being charged for an ambulance or hospital bill can make the difference between survival and being out on the street. Depending on where a caller lives, a history of involuntary commitment can also preclude them from receiving gender-affirming medical treatment (such as surgery) in the future, or greatly decrease their chances. In looking at suicidality and risk factors specific to our community, we find that some of the most prominent factors that contribute to ongoing suicidality are alienation, transphobic treatment (especially by people in positions of power, helping professions, or family), perceived burdensomeness, lack of access to material resources, and exclusion from medically transitioning or living authentically in one's affirmed gender. These factors overlap with the risks posed by nonconsensual active rescue. In other words, were we to engage in nonconsensual active rescue, we could increase the suicidality risk factors for a caller.

Finally, we must consider the impact of nonconsensual active rescue policies on callers who are not in immediate crisis. In our experience, peer support is impossible to provide without rapport, trust, and respect for the caller's agency. Countless callers have told us that they would not be comfortable speaking to us about anything from walking their dog to getting top surgery to coming out to family unless we assure them that we will not call authorities without their consent. Once we give that reassurance, callers are able to trust us—often enough to share more difficult thoughts too.

Reflexively responding to suicidal ideation by calling in non-consensual active rescue amounts to handing off a caller to someone else, which is generally not what callers seek or even what would benefit them. In our experience, suicidal people are some of the most resilient people: suicidal ideation usually doesn't occur to a person arbitrarily. For many in our community, chronic suicidal ideation is a response to trauma and can be managed. When we validate each other's feelings, share lived experiences, and speak candidly about crisis and suicidality, we have a higher rate of success than we would if a caller felt their trust violated by nonconsensual active rescue. At Trans Lifeline, we view people in crisis as human beings with agency and the ability to have a conversation without a need for nonconsensual intervention, and we see positive results from that approach.

Many of these results, which are too often ignored in suicide prevention culture, apply to all people   not just trans people. Any person in crisis is likely to experience it as a result of real, material circumstances, and we see it as our duty to speak to those circumstances from a place of trust and support. Law enforcement can place people at risk, especially callers who are poor, people of color, or living with physical or mental illness. Laying the groundwork for support without the risk of nonconsensual intervention can save lives—and, ultimately, saving lives is the mission we serve.

# 14

# MAYBE YOU DON'T HAVE TO CALL 911?

## KNOW YOUR OPTIONS

*Oakland Power Projects*

OAKLAND POWER PROJECTS BUILDS CAPACITY TO INVEST IN PRACtices, relationships, and resources that build community power and well-being. We can make our families and neighborhoods safe and healthy without relying on the cops.

Critical Resistance's Oakland chapter spent more than two years fighting a successful campaign against gang injunctions in Oakland, California, as part of the Stop the Injunctions Coalition. In the spring of 2013, as the city abandoned its two temporary injunctions (in North Oakland and the Fruitvale) and moved on to other policing schemes that continued to fail the people of Oakland, Critical Resistance (CR) began to consider taking up new work. Through a steady and intentional process, Critical Resistance members talked to close allies from the Stop the Injunctions Coalition to get a sense of the perceptions and experience of the current policing landscape in Oakland, and asked what work could reduce the reach of policing into Oaklanders' daily lives and take steps toward making policing obsolete. The

Oakland Power Projects (OPP) grew out of these conversations and built on the idea, held by members of the CR Oakland chapter's Anti-Policing Working Group, that people in Oakland had the resources and capacities to create alternatives to police responses.

In OPP, we identify projects through a multistep process. We start by having one-on-one interviews with Oaklanders about their experiences of their city and neighborhoods, their experiences with police, and their dreams and ideas for creating well-being in Oakland. Through collective listening and reflection on the themes, concerns, and ideas that arise in interviews, we map out common threads. From those, we choose a project to develop, working with the people who had the underlying idea and with others who are well-situated to begin building capacity and developing strategies around the project theme. Together, we workshop ideas and needs to arrive at a shape, goals, and next steps for the project, along with a core of people to organize it and carry it out.

## KNOW YOUR OPTIONS

As we developed the first OPP project, CR Oakland organizers spoke with Oakland residents. Health emerged as a broad theme: people needed resources but didn't feel they could access them in Oakland without police involvement. Through bringing together people who shared this concern with healthcare workers from a range of fields, sites, and areas of expertise, we identified and began to develop resources for emergent and preventative health needs. These included medical kits that people can use for first-response emergencies or for everyday use to help prevent calls to 911 and a workshop series combining basic information about the prison-industrial complex (PIC) and policing with critical healthcare information for responding to emergency health, chronic health, opioid overdose prevention, and mental health–related situations. These workshops are called "Know Your Options," and the goals are to increase people's options in the face of medical, mental health, and other kinds of emergencies; to get help and meet people's needs without calling the police; and, if the police are called, to prepare people for their arrival. By the spring of 2018, the OPP healthcare worker cohort together with Critical Resistance had offered over fifty Know Your Options workshops around the Bay Area. In this guide, we share some information from the workshop series and examples of resources made by the health worker cohort.

We encourage you to make your own resource list with specific information for your area! Below, you'll find materials that are, in many instances, specific to Oakland city policies and practices, but we encourage you to use them as a starting point for where you live and work. You can find out more about how your local government addresses 911 dispatch, learn about naloxone access, and find allies in local healthcare sites, including clinics, hospitals, and community-led spaces. Use these to map your local resources, relationships, and needs. We recommend "Standing Up for Our Communities: Why We Need a Police-Free Future," by Rachel Herzing, for a beginning community and self-assessment plan.[1] Also, practicing collective and individual planning with these tools can strengthen your capacity to use them confidently during emergencies.

In the trainings we offer, some of the key components of which are outlined in the rest of this chapter, we say that we have options, not rules. In other words, we can't tell you what to do in every situation, but in the spirit of reducing police involvement we focus on teaching people *options*, which *may* include but are not limited to 911. For example, in most cities there's an alternate ambulance number that goes directly to the fire department. You can consider developing your own local trainings so people can build confidence and knowledge with some of the tools in this chapter!

---

1   Rachel Herzing, "Standing Up for Our Communities: Why We Need a Police-Free Future," *Truthout*, March 7, 2017, https://truthout.org/articles/standing-up-for-our-communities-why-we-need-a-police-free-future/.

## FROM THE OPP HEALTH ACCESS AND ANTIPOLICING WORKSHOP

You can ground yourself and everyone involved in an emergent situation with the following tools, which draw on an abolitionist political framework:

- When approaching the scene, assess your ability/capacity to show up in this situation:
  - What are potential dangers/risks?
  - What are your needs/boundaries?
  - What is appropriate for you to do?
- De-escalate yourself by grounding yourself:
  - Take a deep breath.
  - Feel your feet.
  - Name something around you related to your five senses to get into your body.

## IN ADDITION TO THESE IMMEDIATE QUESTIONS AND TECHNIQUES WHEN A SITUATION EMERGES, IT CAN BE HELPFUL TO FOLLOW THESE COMMUNITY CAREGIVER BASICS:

*Introduce yourself.*

- Humanize the interaction by exchanging a hello.

*Ask for consent.*

- If the person is conscious, ask them what they want.
  - Ask before touching someone!
  - Do you want me to call Emergency Services? Do you have any concerns around calling 911 or if the police show up?

- Continue to check in with the person about their needs throughout the process, and involve the injured person as much as possible.

*Check your assumptions.*

- People and their bodies have different experiences of "normal."

*Stay with the person!*

- You can function as this person's advocate in navigating possible police response and advocate for them with EMTs and so on.

## TAKING CHARGE OF THE SITUATION

*Things to call out:*

- "Does anyone have any medical training?"

- "Is anyone close to this person?"

- If applicable: "We're not calling the cops or 911."

*Roles to assign (if possible):*

- Anchor (Lead)

- Community de-escalator

- Police liaison

- Medical advocate

## NON-RESPONSIVE PERSON

If the injured person does not respond when you arrive at the scene of an accident:

RED FLAG: call for an ambulance; stay with injured person; and, if trained, begin CPR.

ABC (airway, breathing, circulation) or CAB (circulation, airway, breathing).

- Airway: No signs of breathing? Roll onto back and open airway.

- Breathing: If not, start rescue breathing.

- Circulation: If no pulse, start CPR.

- Serious bleeding: Stop the leak with pressure (use gloves!!).

## THINGS YOU CAN DO

- Stay with the injured person (talk with them and keep them calm).

- Be a buffer and advocate when police arrive.

- Give a focused report to EMS.

- Stabilize neck in case of cervical fractures. (We demonstrate this in our workshops.)

- Support airway (head tilt; chin lift; if vomiting, turn on side to protect, then clear obstruction).

- Hold pressure on bleeding wounds (direct pressure and elevation of extremity above heart).

- Keep the person warm.

- RICE (rest, ice, compression, elevation).

- Offer emotional support.

# IF YOU TAKE SOMEONE TO
# THE HOSPITAL OR CLINIC

*Some ways to reduce harm in these places:*

- Give a focused report to EMS.

- Have someone stay with the person as an advocate.

- Ask the person if they would like to do something with their belongings.

*Or, you can do something else!*

- Call a nurse practitioner, medical doctor, wilderness first responder, or health worker in your community.

- Create emergency response teams in your communities.

*Follow-up work:*

- Ask the person if they'd like you to contact any support people in their life and let them know what happened.

- Debrief with community so experiences can be shared and so we can all learn what happens as a result of the risks we engage in.

- Access trainings to cultivate more skills.

*Self-Care:*

- Make sure you're taking care of your own health (drink water, eat food, take deep breaths, engage in activities that relieve stress, and the like).

- Be compassionate toward yourself.

# FROM THE OPIOID AND OVERDOSE WORKSHOP:

## RECOGNIZING AN OPIATE OVERDOSE

*Symptoms include the following:*

- Unresponsive to words or pain.

- Not breathing, or very slow or shallow breathing.

- Turning pale, blue, or ashy (especially in lips or fingernails).

- Becoming limp.

- Throwing up.

- Making snoring or gurgling sounds.

This can look a lot like alcohol poisoning, so try to figure out what they took—if in doubt, give Narcan.

Your response has three steps:

### (1) Check for Responsiveness

- Say, "I'm going to NARCAN you."

- Kick foot, call their name, get their attention.

- Provide a pain stimulus by doing a sternum rub (rub your knuckles firmly on their chest bone), pinching them, or pressing on a nail painfully.

- Continue to watch their chest and feel for breathing.

### (2) Engage in rescue breathing (optional)

- Open airway by tilting the head and lifting the chin, then clear their airway if you see something

- Pinch the nose and breathe into their mouth with your mouth sealed over or use a mask (a breath for them, a breath for yourself).

### (3) Administer naloxone.

- Administer naloxone through an injection into the muscle or in another form (nasal spray, auto injector).

- Monitor, and if they don't begin breathing or responding within two or three minutes, give a second dose.

## ADMINISTERING NALOXONE (AKA NARCAN)

- Naloxone is available as a liquid you administer with a syringe or in a form that allows you to administer it through a person's nose (like a nasal spray).

- If you're using a syringe, draw up 1cc (*all of it*) into a syringe.

- Inject one dose (1cc) into the muscle areas of the upper outer thigh, upper arm, or upper butt.

- Continue rescue breathing.

- If the first dose doesn't work within two or three minutes, give a second dose.

## AFTERCARE

- Anticipate that the person may have a physical reaction. If they use regularly, they are suddenly in acute withdrawal—this can include vomiting or diarrhea, but most likely will include serious irritability or flu-like symptoms.

- Narcan is short-acting; it lasts forty to ninety minutes. You still need to monitor them or get them to a hospital within that time because naloxone will wear off and they could go back into an overdose. Do what's needed to be a buffer if law enforcement arrives. You can give another dose if it seems they're overdosing again.

- If the person is not going to be medically monitored, stay with them or ask someone else to. Inform the person who overdosed and the person staying with them what to expect. Give them an additional dose if you have one in case it is needed.

## BE PROACTIVE
*Do you know what resources are available in the communities where you spend time?*

- Where are the clinics and hospitals near you?

- Are there medical professionals on your block?

- Do you know if the people around you have specific medical needs or people they feel safe with?

## HARM REDUCTION

- Harm reduction is a set of practical strategies and ideas aimed at reducing negative consequences associated with drug use. Harm reduction is also a movement for social justice built on a belief in and respect for the rights of people who use drugs.

- Harm reduction actively challenges narratives that have been told about people who use drugs. Giving people access to tools like naloxone is a way to reduce the harm of both drugs and the War on Drugs.

- Giving naloxone to community members has been done in this way since the mid 1990s and has saved hundreds of thousands of lives.

- It started as an illegal practice of distributing this safe prescription drug without prescriptions. People have since advocated for laws—such as the Good Samaritan Law and the Overdose Treatment Law in California—to protect people who distribute, carry, and administer naloxone.

## SAGE: SELF-CONTROL, ASSESSMENT, GIVE HELP, EMERGENCY SERVICES BUFFER
### RESPONSE TO A PSYCHOSOCIAL CRISIS

### (1) Self-De-Escalation

Encountering a potential emergency situation can engage our bodies' natural stress response, which will move us away from our ability to think clearly. In order to be effective, we can take three quick steps to interrupt this reaction:

- Breathe. Breathing is the easiest way to interrupt the stress response. Because your body is preparing to move quickly, fight, or hide, most people's breathing changes. If you're holding your breath, let it out! If you're breathing too rapidly, slow it down! If you're not getting enough oxygen with each breath, deepen it!

- Grounding. When the stress response kicks in, you may lose the ability to sense where your body ends and the rest of the world begins. To reset this, you can touch something—touch your hand to your leg, touch your fingers together, feel your feet on the ground.

- Self-talk. Have a short phrase you say to yourself in an emergency situation. Make it three to five words. Some examples might be, "I'm OK," "It's going to be alright," or "One, two, three, four, five."

You can also coach the other person through these steps. You can model calm breathing for them. You can ask them to touch something or to notice where one of their body parts is touching something. You can ask what they'd like to be called.

## (2) Assessment

- Now that you're as calm as you can be, you can assess the situation. Here are some things to ask yourself.
  - ○ Is what's happening imminently dangerous? Is someone currently being harmed or about to be harmed? Is there a medical emergency?
  - ○ Is it safe for me to try to help?
  - ○ How can I minimize the threat to the person? Is there something they are afraid of that I can remove? Can I make changes to the environment, such as reducing noise or other stimuli? Can I redirect traffic?
  - ○ What are my resources? Are there people around who can help or who know this person?

- Can I establish a connection with this person? Can I introduce myself and offer help?
- Here are some questions you may ask the person, though it is best not to ask all the questions at once:
  - "Can you tell me what happened/what's going on?"
  - "How can I help you feel safe?"
  - "Is there someone I can call for you?"
  - "What has helped you in the past?" It is important not to assume that you know what is happening for them or what their baseline is.
- Address physical needs and readily available resources: "Do you need water? A blanket? A snack?"
- It may be helpful to ask orienting questions: "What can I call you?" "Do you know where you are?" "Do you know what day it is?"

*(3) Give Help. Assess the environment and try in your own responses and actions not to escalate the situation. You can do the following:*

- Try to keep your body posture open.

- Give the person as much eye contact as they feel comfortable with.

- Keep hands visible.

- Keep a neutral expression. Let go of those furrowed brows. Use a half smile.

- Keep your voice at a steady volume and pace, unless you must raise it to give directions to ensure safety. Think about removing energy from the situation, not adding to it.

### For panic attacks:

- Use the self-control techniques from above.

- Something very cold to the brow bone can help—such as an ice pack or a refrigerated soda or metal bottle.

### For someone in psychological distress (psychosis, "bad trip," manic behavior, trauma reaction, or suicidal thoughts):

- Remember to use basic motivational interviewing techniques for a "patient-centered" approach to communication: Open-ended questions, Affirmations, Reflections, Summarize (OARS).

- Stay with the person. Continue to assess how to make the environment safe for the person or help the person get to a safe environment.

- Create a suicide watch. Find people who can stay with the person in shifts until the person is out of crisis.

### (4) Emergency Services Buffer

- If emergency personnel have been called or you've assessed that the medical emergency or imminent danger is such that you must enact emergency services, take these steps to protect the person from further harm by emergency services personnel.
    - Introduce yourself and your skills for helping. Ask: "Is it OK if I try to help you?"
    - Ask how you can help: "What do you need? What can I do to help?" "Do you have any issues with 911 or the police?" "Can I help you contact someone you trust?"

- Stay with the person and be an advocate if or when police arrive by taking the following steps o  Ask what name they want to use in front of the police.

   o  Observe (or record) police activity.

   o  State to the police (and repeat as needed), "This person needs medical attention." Make sure they get the care or help they need.

These are some of the components of the workshops offered through the first Oakland Power Project. We continue to offer and refine these workshops through the ongoing development of resources, experiences, and skills among organizers, health workers, and other community members.[2]

---

2  Learn more about the Oakland Power Projects, including these resources, our process, and new projects, at www.oaklandpowerprojects.org.

15

# EXCERPTS FROM THE *WHOSE SECURITY IS IT ANYWAY?* TOOLKIT[1]

*Lara Brooks and Mariame Kaba*

THE COPS HAVE YOUTH WORKERS AND HOMELESS YOUTH PUSHED UP *against the front of the community center, legs and arms spread.*

*The security guard in the community center carries a gun and sexually harasses young, Black transgender women who access the job-training program.*

*The cops enter the drop-in center without warrants, intimidating young people and threatening to arrest youth workers for asserting the program's legal rights.*

*The church, which houses an overnight shelter, is forced to install surveillance cameras.*

During the years that both of us were youth workers and advocates for young people, and that one of us directed a youth center, we have repeatedly heard of or witnessed incidents like these and worse. Young people in group homes, at drop-in centers, in

---

1  The complete toolkit is available here: https://www.thepicis.org/whose -security/.

homeless shelters, and at recreational facilities are encountering highly securitized spaces that are quick to punish and expel them. Institutional violence within community centers, healthcare organizations, and social services, in concert with the "helping" industry's increasing collusion with and reliance on law enforcement, fuels the prison pipeline. Working in collaboration with youth workers from across Chicago, this toolkit evolved from practicing violence prevention in complex spaces, holding youth and adult workshops, engaging in thousands of conversations, attending meetings convened from organizational crisis due to the impact of policing and surveillance, learning from strategies used at the Broadway Youth Center (BYC), and drawing on research released by Young Women's Empowerment Project (YWEP) and Project NIA.

Most importantly, this work is informed by the experiences of healthcare and social service consumers, patients, clients, and participants—individuals who filed grievances, reported violence to YWEP's Bad Encounter Line,[2] demanded better services for themselves and their communities, and organized their communities to fight back.

---

2  Before closing its doors in 2013, YWEP was a member-based, social justice organizing project for girls and transgender youth with current or previous experience in the sex trade or street economy. YWEP's 2012 study *Bad Encounter Line* provides critical feedback for those of us working within the social service and health care industries. C. Angel Torres, Paz Naima, and the Young Women's Empowerment Project, *Bad Encounter Line: A Participatory Action Research Project* (Chicago: YWEP, 2012), https://ywepchicago.files .wordpress.com/2012/09/bad-encounter-line-report-2012.pdf.

## VIOLENCE PREVENTION, INTERVENTION, AND TRANSFORMATION STRATEGIES: PRACTICAL STRATEGIES FOR YOUTH MILIEUS, DROP-IN PROGRAMS, OR GROUP WORK

### *Individual/Group Staff Interventions*

- Develop a weekly group that addresses, prevents, and interrupts violence. Discuss concerns, issues, or flags about youth participants, generate opportunities to prevent or interrupt all forms of violence in your space, and develop proactive transformation plans. The most effective transformation plans are created in partnership with young people. Document and centralize this process so that it is available to all staff.

- Develop a communication plan. Regularly communicate updates about youth participants. Who is going to communicate the transformation/accountability plan? How do we collectively welcome a youth participant back into the space?

- Youth workers create individualized plans with young people as a way to prevent violence and reduce harms in chaotic milieus or drop-in spaces.

*This could look like...* An agreement to check in for five minutes at the beginning of a drop-in or before a group starts: "Is there anything that you need from us today?" or "How can I support your self-care today, however you define it?" If the relationship is further along, you can ask, "How are you feeling in your body today?"

- Reminders about the plan: "I just want to remind you of your transformation plan. [Insert brief overview of what has been agreed upon.] Do you have any questions about it?"

- Identifying a quiet space that is always accessible to young people—combinations of quiet group space and one-on-one space provide different options for youth to take care of themselves.

- Using one-on-one time with a young person to talk about trauma, create a list of triggers in the space (for instance, people getting too close to me when they are trying to pass me, people moving my belongings, and so on) and ways to respond to them. Allow youth to practice working through these moments in your space. Affirm when young people are working hard and stretching themselves in group spaces.

- Nonshaming boundary-setting in groups. Create a universal cue that indicates to both youth and youth workers that someone is asserting a boundary—whether it be to not touch me, hug me, touch my belongings, or talk to me that way. For example, "Respect the limit."

- Create intentional and thoughtful responses to verbal violence. For example, a youth worker uses the words "keep it cute" to interrupt moments when we say things that are hurtful or shady. These are words that young people can also use when responding to verbal attacks. Create group and community space to discuss, define, and respond to "shade" or "hurtful reading."

- Create working agreements and connect it back to internalized oppression, which is often the primary root cause.

### Staff Roles and Considerations

Designate a youth worker to watch for vibes. The "vibes" person possesses strong relationships with different young people and has strong skills in mediating conflict and assessing for crisis. This person should be moving throughout the shared community space during the entire program and is responsible for reading vibes and checking in with other youth workers and youth. Responsibilities may include the following:

- Supporting the capacity of the person working reception and/or greeting young people.

- Keeping the team updated when a new person enters the space and requires an orientation or introduction.

- Reminding youth workers to follow up with young people (for instance, following up on an issue, gathering more information about a situation that needs resolution, discussing a transformation plan, and so forth).

- Engaging youth throughout the entire accountability process. Identify a point person to maintain contact with youth participants when they are unable to access the space.

### Space Considerations

The physical space of a program or drop-in space is one of the most important violence prevention elements.
*This could look like...*

- Creating multiple spaces for young people to vent frustrations and release emotions. This could be a space for people to dance or a private space that is always available for emergency mediation.

- Designating a self-care space can look many different ways. Identify a room within your space for resting and quiet.

- Intentionally creating spaces with specific structures, weekly schedules, and purposes. For example, what will our working agreements in the computer room be? What is the individual capacity for each room—six people or sixty people? How many youth workers are needed for each room?

## BUILDING STRUCTURES AND SYSTEMS

- Document and process daily. Create an efficient method to discuss youth participants, areas of concern, and opportunities for growth and learning.

- Facilitate intentional orientations for new youth participants. Create a fifteen-minute, relational orientation that shares messaging around values, mission, services, and expectations.

- Provide youth with a packet of referrals and resources when a consequence—involving time out of the space—has been decided.

- Consider designing ways for young people to have access to basic needs, like hygiene supplies or sack lunches, when they are unable to access services. Just because young people make a mistake doesn't mean they shouldn't have access to human needs, like food and soap.

- Create an intentional process for young people "aging out of your services" (this is language that social workers use to describe young people who are no longer eligible for services because of their age). As expected, this time produces incredible anxiety for young people and often means an exponential decrease in supportive spaces and programs once young people turn twenty-five (in other communities, young people age out of certain services at twenty-one).

- Host weekly community meetings with space for young people to discuss issues related to the space, accessibility, and resources. Receive this feedback with open hearts and minds—it is a great sign of investment when young people take time to offer feedback and critiques to help us evaluate our programs and services.

- Implement an accessible grievance policy. Train youth workers and young people on how to use it as a tool for advocacy and meaningful feedback.

- Create learning spaces for youth that incorporate Theatre of the Oppressed components that ask youth participants and youth workers to experience, play, and share ideas.

- Redefine engagement to include space for resting, self-care, and community care. Let us eliminate this idea that young people are "doing nothing" in our spaces. No young person is doing nothing when they are surviving, 24-7.

- Give youth more control of the space. Train, support, and pay young people for their leadership and expertise as it relates to facilitating community meetings and workshops, running a food pantry or clothing drive, or helping with the daily meal.

- Create and practice a plan to protect safety and privacy when an emergency 911 call is made.

## Investing in Staff and Volunteers

- Training. Provide ongoing in-house trainings to develop staff and youth on issues related to violence, oppression, internalized violence/oppression, violence prevention, harm reduction, and consent.

- Healing. Build practices into the daily work that support youth workers impacted by violence and its devastating impact on our communities.

*Top Ten Ways Staff and Young People Can
Reduce the Harms of Security Guards*

- Advocate for alternatives to on-site security guards. Less expensive ways to keep our community spaces, clinics, and youth programs safe include increasing the presence of youth workers, patient navigators, and greeters in high-traffic areas or shared spaces. Other examples include hosting safety labs, without the presence of security guards, for staff and young people to create and practice strategies to prevent, interrupt, and transform violence specific to the program or organization.

- Learn about the complaint and grievance process before something happens. Ask a staff member to show you the forms and ask questions about how the process works. Some questions to ask include the following:
   ○ Is there a different process for on-site security guards?
   ○ Does the organization have a grievance officer?
   ○ How does this process hold security guards accountable?
   ○ Who supervises and trains the security guards?

- File a complaint or grievance when on-site security harasses, intimidates, threatens, or harms you. If you have a staff person that you trust, this person can also help you complete and file the complaint. If you want to file a complaint anonymously, find out how that process works to protect your confidentiality.

- Safety plan with your friends and chosen family. Share what you have learned about the grievance and complaint process with your friends and family. Some security guards work for a police department and can arrest you. Make sure your friends know your safety plan.

- Safety plan with a staff person. Ask them directly if you can request that they be present if you are ever detained and questioned on site by a security guard or law enforcement. What are the ways that a staff person can support you? This may include asking them to call legal hotlines or providing them with consent, in advance, to notify a friend or family member in the event of your arrest.

- Demand staff presence when you are being detained or arrested on-site. Request that a staff person is present whenever a security guard is detaining you. File a complaint if you are ever detained in a room without the presence of additional staff.

- If you are forced to leave a building or program by staff or on-site security guards, follow up with a staff person that you trust. Do not return to the building. They may try to arrest you when you return.

- Staff can ask for transparency around the number and type of arrests that occur within the building—including the date and time when they occurred. If there is a certain issue occurring frequently, this may be an opportunity to gather staff and young people to create and practice specific interventions that prevent the harm of youth being arrested. Similarly, this is an opportunity to examine staffing patterns and capacity. For example, if most of the arrests of young people occur between 8 p.m. and 10 p.m. on weeknights, it is important to explore creative strategies that may directly respond to this trend. Staff can file complaints when security guards harass, intimidate, undermine, or threaten them. If it is happening to you, it is most certainly happening to young people. Staff may request that security guards leave the spaces where staff and young people are working through conflict or community issues. The presence of security guards often exacerbates violence and conflict and negatively impacts trust and relationship-building between young people and staff. By requesting that security staff leave the space, young people and staff are trusted in their abilities to de-escalate and mediate conflict in ways that are usually more effective and long-term.

# 16

# EXCERPT FROM
# *COMMUNITY DEFENSE*
# *ZONE STARTER GUIDE*

*Georgia Latino Alliance for Human Rights
(GLAHR), Mijente, and Puente Arizona*

## WHY WE NEED COMMUNITY DEFENSE

ACROSS THE COUNTRY WE SEE INCREASED RACISM, INJUSTICE, AND criminalization just days into Trump's presidency. We know these problems didn't start with Trump—but we have real reason to believe these problems will escalate. Whole communities are being targeted and attacked; there are diminishing options to petition government because of the balance of forces and toxic politics that is taking hold at the federal level. Our silence will not stop what's happening. We need to organize. When we say organizing, we are referring to the most classic definition: uniting people to fight back for a common goal.

For communities being targeted by the Trump administration, specifically immigrants and refugees, Muslims, LGBTQ, and Black communities, we must create community-based sanctuary as well as advocate for policies at the local and state levels. To truly build community protection, we must acknowledge and include the ongoing issues of mass incarceration and criminalization that have ravaged communities across the country. Our objective with sanctuary is not to arrive at the status quo; in fact, we need to expand its meaning and its impact.

Because Trump's regime does not even pretend to represent us, we must organize to resist, defend ourselves, and transform our communities: county by county, town by town, city by city. It is imperative that we organize where we live, work, party, and pray in order to attract more people, build leadership, and make change in an arena that is within reach right now. We can bring people together to rekindle our most precious shared values and spark actions to build power and make a real difference in local communities.

We know that many people are doing different kinds of work right now, but we also have heard from many people about the need for templates for where to start under the new reality of the Trump era.

## A FEW THINGS ABOUT THIS GUIDE:

- It is designed to be adaptable for small towns or larger cities, and it recognizes that the pace and approach in building base or waging policy-change campaigns are different across place. We hope it's useful across that spectrum of local context.

- It has framing, ideas, and tools that are adapted from red state organizing veterans: all of the contributing ideas have been tried out by organizers in red states under hostile state and local governments. We believe people who have organized and resisted in hostile conditions (whether because of group identity or local/state government) have very important contributions in this time.

- It emphasizes how we might be able to reach beyond our existing circles and engage nonactivists we encounter in a variety of ways.

- This training is meant to be paired with "Know Your Rights" materials to help facilitate greater understanding and recognition that all communities have inalienable rights, regardless of skin color, religious creed, country of origin, or whether they speak English.

## GOALS

- Identify the needs of communities who are being attacked and targeted by long-standing and emerging policies and practices. The best way to do this is through ensuring both the engagement and leadership of these communities.

- Get local elected and appointed officials to support demands and policy to expand and defend sanctuary and create Community Defense Zones.

- Recruit a base of supporters, with leadership and participation of vulnerable communities, for Community Defense Zones.

- Create various ways for people to engage and support, specifically through activities and commitments from your base of supporters.

- Bring everyday people in local communities into the fight for expanded sanctuary.

- Nurture and support leadership of people targeted by the Trump regime.

- Connect different community leaders and members targeted by the Trump regime to each other.

## ACTIVITIES

One of the main questions that will arise in the formation of a Community Defense Zone is, What do you want me to do? Developing locally relevant and creative responses to this question will be an ongoing task. The list below is meant as a starter list to help spark the process, providing initial answers to how people can participate.

- Reach out to identify supporters, see where people stand, and recruit committee members.

- Distribute posters, yard signs, and window stickers.

- Hold a press conference with supporters, including statements from community leaders (this doesn't solely include elected officials) to demonstrate widespread and growing support.

- Hold a community meeting with people who have signed on to determine local needs and next steps.

- Hold community building events to get more sign-ons. For example, you could hold potlucks, sports, movie screenings, children's activities.

- Hold fundraisers to support directly affected communities. For example, this could include costs associated with legal fees, moving expenses, rapid response, and loss of employment.

## OUTREACH

The main purpose of outreach is to build a base of human beings who support the campaign. This base can then be mobilized into action (to some degree) as needed. Not everyone recruited will be equally involved, and that is fine. But the more people who endorse or align with the campaign, the more people you have to call on locally for support for the work that needs to be done. Another goal is to educate communities around what is needed, what is happening, what their rights are, and that creating Community Defense Zones is possible. Many of us also feel it is an opportunity to remind us all that constitutional protection should exist and we deserve to have it.

The outreach invites different members of a community to take a side and a stand on what is happening. It also creates an opportunity for people to join in and do their part to protect the community from the threats we are under. Many members of communities and groups do not know that we have a constitutional right to not allow ICE, police, or federal agents into our homes, buildings, and spaces unless they file a court order signed by a judge.

The posters, signs, doormats, and placards we create can remind us—every time we enter or exit our homes, place of business, school, or faith community—what we believe in and what we deserve. Organizing can be contagious and give us courage: but only when we reach out to more and more people and do not settle for preaching to the choir. When we do this work, we show our children, families, neighbors, and community who we are and what we believe. We show them that we believe we deserve rights and dignity, and we teach them how to demand the same.

Outreach is a core method to find supporters for the work and to grow your base. Organizers should think of "community leaders" as broadly as possible: who do people in your county, town, or city listen to and respect? That person is a leader that it makes sense to reach out to. Leaders are in neighborhoods, in institutions and outside of them, and in so many other places in every community. Many of the outreach steps are similar for the different outreach targets listed below.

## WHAT'S NEXT?

This is only a starter guide. Many local communities have already been working on these issues, have their own contexts and successes, and are looking to meet this moment with what has come before and what can come after. Also, organizing is about bringing people together, and that process is not one that can be fully predicted—you will learn and iterate your approach and plan as you receive feedback from people. We see this guide as giving local organizing a boost and providing some helpful tools where it makes sense.

# 17

# EXCERPTS FROM *THE SAFER PARTY TOOLKIT*

*Safe OUTside the System Collective, Audre Lorde Project*

THE AUDRE LORDE PROJECT IS A LESBIAN, GAY, BISEXUAL, TWO-Spirit, trans, and gender-nonconforming people of color (LGBTSTGNC POC) center for community organizing, focusing on the New York City area. Through mobilization, education, and capacity-building, we work for community wellness and progressive racial and economic justice. Committed to struggling across differences, we seek to responsibly reflect, represent, and serve our various communities.

The Safe OUTside the System (SOS) Collective is an antiviolence program led by and for LGBTSTGNC POC. We are devoted to challenging violence that targets LGBTSTGNC POC, specifically hate and police violence, in Central Brooklyn by using community-based strategies rather than relying on the police or state systems. The Safe Neighborhood Campaign, a decade-long, multifaceted initiative, generates community-led safety strategies in solidarity with local Brooklyn-rooted and POC-owned small businesses, organizations, faith-based spaces, neighbors, and community to respond to and intervene in increased policing and communal hate violence targeting LGBTSTGNC POC.

*The Safer Party Toolkit* is a collection of strategies generated by three generations of SOS members and staff to build safety in party spaces without relying on the police or state systems. It is based on strategies that we've used to build safety for our communities within Central Brooklyn. This toolkit is for anyone throwing, attending, or working at a party or community event—that is, partygoers, party promoters, bouncers, and community members. It focuses mostly on preventing violence (stopping violence before it happens) and intervening in violence (stopping violence from getting worse).

## GOALS FOR *THE SAFER PARTY TOOLKIT*

- Create a space in which partygoers' self-determination and safety are prioritized.

- Prevent and intervene in violence before it escalates.

- Make a community atmosphere where violence isn't acceptable.

- Encourage others to intervene or prevent violence from happening.

- Support survivors of violence.

## WHAT TYPES OF VIOLENCE CAN HAPPEN AT A PARTY?

Violence can happen anywhere, but it takes on different forms in different situations. Here are different types of violence that can occur in a party:

## Between Individuals

- Sexual violence: unwanted sexual advances, like come-ons or touching; groping in bathroom or door lines; rape; following into a bathroom; being followed; not respecting physical and emotional boundaries.

- Physical violence: pushing, hitting, throwing objects, throwing drinks, stabbing, shooting, or other forms of violence involving physical touch.

- Harassment: direct slurs, insults, or threats.

- Intimidation: hostile looks; attempting to frighten; homophobic and/or transphobic, racist, or sexist jokes and statements; isolating someone from community.

## Between Individuals and Law Enforcement

- Sexual violence: groping or inappropriate touching during a frisk, strip searches, physical gender checks, rape, sexual harassment, coercion.

- Physical abuse: limiting movement, using excessive force, using pepper spray, tasing, shooting.

- Harassment: questioning, interrogating, or accusing; asking questions without reasonable suspicion or probable cause; asking for personal information; following; using slurs, insults, or threats.

- Gender/sex policing: gender checks on gender nonconforming, nonbinary, and trans people; assuming LGBTSTGNC folks are sex workers; questioning gender presentation or legal documentation; and harassing sex workers.

- No response: Refusing or failing to respond to homophobic, transphobic, and all other forms of violence.

## INITIAL QUESTIONS TO CONSIDER

- What skills do people have? What skills could people learn over time?

- What characteristics of the area could contribute to making a violent situation? (For example, a gentrifying neighborhood; gang or turf fights; a history of homophobic violence, transphobic violence, or street harassment; increased police presence; or openly homophobic and transphobic business owners or residents.)

- What is the police presence near your party space, and is the space near public transportation? What is the route like? (For example, are there police watchtowers, cops regularly stopping or harassing people, or parked police cars?)

- Have there been instances of violence in the past between partygoers? What kind of violence? Did these instances involve weapons?

- What types of violence and harassment have you and your friends experienced in your neighborhood? (Such as catcalls; homophobic, racist, or transphobic slurs; physical threats; or violence.)

- What would you do in case of an emergency or crisis? When, if ever, would you deem it necessary to call the police? How would you prevent police violence in that situation?

- What are the characteristics of your parties or your communities that impact violence? (For instance, illegal activity escalating police presence or folks with high consequences for being arrested—such as undocumented people, sex workers, disabled people, and/or people on parole.)

## INTERVENTION STEPS

Intervening in violence can be intimidating for most people; however, there is a lot one person can do without risking personal safety. We know how to intervene and de-escalate because we've done it before. Often, intervention skills are about naming and sharpening the ways we've done this effectively before.

Because most violent situations escalate from verbal harassment to verbal conflict to physical violence, it's important to intervene *before* things turn violent. Here are a few tactics you can try:

### Verbal Harassment

• Avoid sudden movements that may startle or be perceived as an attack.

• Create space between the person causing harm and the person being harmed.

• Clearly explain your purpose or intention to de-escalate; do not respond with threats or verbal attacks.

• Explain potential consequences like police arriving, arrest, and other harms.

• Stay calm. Speak slowly, gently, and clearly. Use a firm voice.

### Verbal Conflict/Argument

• Clearly state your intention to de-escalate the situation. Do not take sides in the argument.
• Do not verbally insult either person.

- Encourage friends to help separate the two people and create physical space.

- Show that you are listening. Avoid arguing and confronting the people before trying to solve the problem.

- Show concern and demonstrate that you are actively listening through nonverbal and verbal responses.

- Speak calmly and clearly.

*Physical Violence*

- Shout or scream to alert the attacker that someone is watching. Make noise. If outside or in a public space, yell "Fire!" or something else to distract those involved and bring attention to the situation.

- Use your camera, cell phone, or digital camera to record the incident. If you do not have access to a camera, write down the place, time, and description of attacker.

- Keep both hands visible; use open arms and minimal body contact with all parties.

- Help all parties get to a safer location. Call ambulance if needed and with the consent of the injured person, but stay at the scene as the ambulance will likely come with police presence. Write down everything police and medics do and say.

## SAFETY FOR PARTY PLANNERS

If you are planning a party or will be working at a party, it's important to have a safety plan. The following are ways you can minimize risk, prevent violence from happening, and be more prepared if it does:

*Safety Team:* Build a team! Create a safety team prior to the party, assign roles, and stick to them.

*Substance Use:* Consider asking all members of the team to refrain from alcohol and other substance use, or to limit their use. These can impact judgment and, if noticeable, can change how police and partygoers interact with you.

## ROLES OF THE TEAM

*Decision Point/Team*: Coordinates the safety team and makes emergency decisions.

Purpose: Lets the people in your safety team know what the purpose of the team is—to ensure self-determination and a safer party space for everyone. Requires the person to leave personal biases against individuals at the door.

Who: Anyone who can make quick decisions, is familiar with the party space and partygoers, and has strong communication skills.

*De-Escalators*: Intervene in potential incidents and incidents as they are occurring. If physically attacked, de-escalators can and should defend themselves.

Who: Anyone who is willing and able to verbally and physically intervene in harassment, attacks, and other types of violence. Requires the person to be a strong communicator, have a good relationship with community members, listen to directions, move quickly, and deal with confrontation.

*Safe Transporters*: Teams of people willing to drive or walk individuals home or to the nearest public transportation.

Who: Anyone who is familiar with the area, has a cell phone, and is able to move to and from public transportation.

*Dispatchers*: Help partygoers connect with the safety team.

Who: Anyone who is familiar with the safety team members.

## CREATING A PLAN

It's important to create scenarios of possible situations with your team and create an action plan prior to the party. The following are a few situations that could come up at a party. Create scenarios of other possible situations with your team and create an action plan prior to the party.

### (1) Situation inside the Party: If two people get into a physical altercation at the party...

*De-Escalators:* Create space between the two individuals. Calmly remind them the party is intended to be a safe space and ask them if they wish to keep the party safe. Calmly ask other partygoers to make space so that the situation can be de-escalated. Do not silence or tone police the people involved. Wait for decision point/ team to arrive in case the situation escalates.

*Decision Point/Team:* Ensure that individuals have been separated and speak to each person separately. Let them know specific ways that their conflict can increase risk to community safety. Determine whether either or both people should be asked to leave party. Offer an opportunity to follow up in the future.

*Safe Transporters:* If either person is asked to leave the party, accompany them to the public transportation they need. Ensure that they are not followed by other partygoers and that they do not re-enter the party. Stay with them until they get on the train or bus, or in a car.

*Dispatchers:* Calmly let other partygoers know that the situation is being de-escalated. Focus on the situation, and avoid being pulled into conversation about what is going on, as this could escalate the situation. Be transparent—if asked, let people know what the intervention and de-escalation processes are.

## (2) Situation outside the Party: If people get into a physical altercation in front of the party...

*Decision Point/Team:* Ensure that individuals have been separated and talk to each separately. Let them know specific ways that their conflict can increase risk to community safety. Explain potential consequences to the people, "There are a lot of cops in this neighborhood. You could get arrested for this. Let's figure out what to do that won't increase yours or anyone else's risk of arrest or harm." Show empathy and concern in calm ways. Be aware of who has the highest risk and consequences for an arrest (such as people who have a record, are trans or gender-nonconforming, or are undocumented). Determine whether either or both people should be asked to leave the party.

If the police arrive, use de-escalators to continue to support the emotional and physical needs of individuals involved. Have one person talk to the police. Do not give the police any information that could increase risk of harm or arrest to anyone involved. Response should also be based on the conditions (that is, is it under control or is it still continuing?) when the police arrive. If it's under control, they are more likely to engage in conversation with decision makers. If it's not, they're more likely to jump in aggressively and begin arresting, pepper spraying, and potentially physically attacking people, etc.

If the cops arrive and things are under control, it's best to ask the officers that arrive to identify the ranking officer on site. Introduce yourself. Once you know who the ranking officer is, you can begin to negotiate with them. If there isn't a ranking officer, you can ask that one be called in. In a calm situation, as soon as the police arrive you should say, "It's over. Everything is OK. We had a small incident but de-escalated/solved it, etc." Do not point out who was involved in the fight. If they seem to want to arrest people, calmly ask for the ranking officer on site. When you're speaking to the ranking officer, say things like, "Can we handle this another way? This isn't necessary. We're separating them and escorting them separately from the party. Everyone is safe." Tell the cops that everything is under control and that the situation has been de-escalated.

It's useful to say this to the ranking officer while negotiating to appease the cops, minimize or avoid arrests, and try to get community control of the situation again. If one person has a high risk of arrest and there are additional decision makers, consider physically putting yourself between the officer and the potential arrestee to try to prevent the person's arrest.

If decision makers, transporters, de-escalators, and other people attempting to prevent violence are arrested, consider canceling the party, going to the precinct to demand their release, and offering jail and court support.

*De-Escalators:* Bring additional folks inside and close and lock the door, if you can. Maintain calm and carefully engage friends and loved ones to support de-escalation until the conflict is over and folks involved are on public transportation. Explain to friends and loved ones, "Can you support us in de-escalating your friend? We're making sure they're as safe as possible. If they're asked to leave would you like to leave as well?"

If the cops arrive, remove all challenging and escalating "situations," such as open containers and drinks outside, illegal substances, and so forth, from immediate view. The police could use the fact that they saw people drinking outside as a reason to ticket, arrest, or raid parties. To reduce risk of police violence, party organizers should ensure that partygoers are not drinking or using substances outside or in front of the entrance. Find ways to calmly show that the community is monitoring the situation (for example, turn on lights, open windows, and record with cell phones). Stop the party and tell partygoers that you're going to monitor the police at a safe distance to help ensure the safety of our folks. Take pictures and video. It would probably be helpful for the person talking to the cops and all team members to know their rights when dealing with law enforcement so they can name and communicate to partygoers when their rights are being violated in or outside the party.

*Safe Transporters:* Once the fight is over, partner safe transporters with the de-escalators that helped de-escalate the fight.

The transporter and de-escalator pairs will accompany involved parties to different places where they can access public transportation. Stay with them until they are safely on transportation. If needed, accompany friends to public transportation once the other group has left. Communicate to decision-making point/team that folks are safe and on their way.

If the police arrest folks, escort family and friends to the precinct.

*Dispatchers:* Other folks in attendance should wait to leave until folks involved in the conflict have gotten on public transportation. Ask partygoers where they live or could be going, and support them in figuring out travel and transportation routes. Check in with involved friends and loved ones about their routes as well, and support them in going in a different direction from the other people involved in the conflict.

If the police arrive, take down badge numbers and identifying information about officers. Have police precinct information ready for friends of potential arrestees. Get transporters to send friends to precinct if an arrest occurs.

### (3) Situation outside the party #2: If a community member is attacked on the way home from a party while with transporter and de-escalator team…

*Decision Point/Team:* Stay on phone with transporters the entire time. Remain calm and give directions to nearest safe space or to transportation if needed. Continue to attempt to separate the individuals. Who is doing the attacking? What are the roles of transporters if the attacker is not a party member? Decide whether it makes sense to go to another location; if so, what location? Did anyone experience injury? Does anyone, including the transporters and de-escalators, need medical attention? Are there other decision makers at the party? Could this situation bring police presence to your party? If necessary, get people medical attention by taking a cab or calling an ambulance, with consent, but be prepared for police presence as well. Consider sending additional de-escalators and transporters to observe, intervene, or de-escalate if necessary. The transporter and de-escalator should consider in advance how they would identify themselves if questioned by police.

*De-Escalators:* If asked go to the location of an altercation, calmly introduce yourself and state you are there to help de-escalate. Take note of the location, time, and descriptive information about folks involved. Be aware that the de-escalators and their notes can be subpoenaed and used as evidence in court if arrests take place.

*Safe Transporters:* If en route, call decision point. If multiple transporters are out, decide ahead if they will all call the same decision person or if dispatch will support. Remain on the phone with decision point until safe location is reached. If unable to get to a safer space, remain calm, get to a more populated well-lit area, and use best judgment. Wait for instructions from decision point. Return to party or other designated safer space as soon as possible.

*Dispatchers:* Send de-escalators to the location. Create instructions and a route for decision team to communicate to de-escalators.

### (4) If the police attempt to enter the party...
*Note:* The police do not have the right to enter or search the premises without a warrant. If the police are coming because of a noise complaint or a fight outside of the party, they still do not have the right to enter the party. They can enter without a warrant if folks are coming in and out with drugs or if there's an underage party attendee drinking outside.

*Decision Point/Team:* Calmly introduce yourself to the police as the coordinator of the party. You do not have to answer their questions, but complete nonresponsiveness can escalate the situation. Use a calm yet firm tone with the police. Do not answer unnecessary, homophobic, racist, or transphobic questions about the nature of the party or partygoers. Do not offer any information about partygoers, organizers, and so on.

In the case of a noise complaint: Offer to lower the noise at the party. You can raise it again once the police have left. (Before 11 p.m. they don't have the right to make you lower the noise, depending on the city you live in. However, this also depends on the regulations in the lease of the party space.)

In case of arrest: Decision point should communicate their contact info to the person being arrested.

*De-Escalators:* Inform the decision point immediately. Do not engage with the cops but say that the party coordinator is on their way. Avoid permitting the police to enter the party by stepping outside and closing the front door (make sure your cell phone is on you). If necessary, have someone get a decision team member. Keep party members calm and make space between the decision point, police, and the crowd.

In case of arrest, try to get the "legal" name and address of the person getting arrested. Note and write down details of the police officer's behaviors, along with their physical description, names, badge numbers, rank, and other identifying information. Find friends of the arrestee and notify them of the arrest.

*Safe Transporters:* Take friends to the precinct.

*Dispatchers:* Inform friends of the local precinct location.

## (5) If you need to call 911...

Every 911 call in NYC goes through the NYPD, and then the medical calls get sent to Emergency Medical Services (EMS). Calls that involve "crimes" send both police and EMS. Calls that involve higher levels of violence are more likely to get police. Police often accompany EMS in heavily policed, rapidly gentrifying neighborhoods.

*Decision Point/Team:* Decide if this is a situation where you should call 911 or get someone medical attention through a cab. Remember that individuals with certain medical conditions should not be moved. If you still decide to call 911, you have the right to not allow the police inside your space. However, if EMS does not feel safe for whatever reason, they can bring them in. EMS can also cancel NYPD if they want to.

*De-Escalators:* Clear space for EMS within the party. Support individuals who are upset, and clear partygoers from the injured person and EMS.

## KNOW YOUR OPTIONS: SAFETY PLANNING

- List names and phone numbers for three people who will be at the party and whom you would trust to help you and other partygoers get away from a violent situation.

- List three people who will not be at the party whom you would trust to support you and other partygoers who experience or witness violence.

- List one easily accessible (that is, open late or twenty-four hours, within walking distance, and open to the public) business or organization where you can go to get away from a violent situation.

- If applicable, list two possible routes to and from public transportation.

- List the closest public hospital.

- It's helpful to know where the local police precincts are, their numbers, and the quickest way to get there.

- Make a list of supportive resources, such as local hospitals, lawyers, or legal organizations you can call, LGBTQ direct service organizations, and local cop-watch groups.

*The Safer Party Toolkit* is an ongoing labor of love and necessity, first imagined and implemented in 2007 by members and staff of the Safe OUTside the System Collective.

Many thanks to the members and staff who came before us, imagined a vision, and built safety outside of state systems.

PART THREE

# WE DIDN'T CALL IT TJ, BUT MAYBE IT WORKED ANYWAY?

MESSY, REAL STORIES

# 18

# WHEN YOUR MONEY COUNTS ON IT

## SEX WORK AND TRANSFORMATIVE JUSTICE

*An Interview with Monica Forrester and
Elene Lam, by Chanelle Gallant*

ALL AROUND THE WORLD, SEX WORKERS ARE PUSHED OUT OF THE charmed circle of respect and protection and must organize their own safety. The most recent attacks on sex workers in the United States came from the introduction of a set of laws called SESTA/FOSTA (Stop Enabling Sex Traffickers Act/Fight Online Sex Trafficking Act) that effectively shut down online escort ad platforms—and with it, one of sex workers' most effective screening tools. The Right *and* the Left like to tell us that these laws are designed to stop trafficking. It's bullshit, and sex workers have fought them tooth and nail. Criminalization has *never* helped sex workers. Instead, it's why cops can get away with committing about a third of all sexual assaults against sex workers.

Many people assume that sex work safety measures are necessary because sex work jobs are intrinsically dangerous. This isn't true, and it blames sex workers for the risks of abuse they face. Taking money doesn't make sex dangerous. (I think most sex workers would agree that money is the best part of the job!) Sex workers face risks of violence because their whole *lives* are at risk of violence. The danger comes from the systems that devalue and isolate sex workers and expose them to unchecked stigma, discrimination, deportation, and interpersonal and state abuse. Caty Simon describes the role of sex workers and the effects of the systems that devalue them:

> Sex work is a low entry-barrier job which functions as a failsafe for many groups marginalized by capitalism: women, people of color, LGBTQ people, disabled people, and poor and criminalized people.... This is why *whorephobia* is actually an intertwined combination of stigmas. The way people loathe sex workers—the way they think of us as dirty, dumb, perverse, amoral agents of infection with no self-respect—is heavily coded with misogyny, racism, classism, transmisogyny, homophobia and ableism.[1]

Millions of others face the same dangers that sex workers do. I interviewed Elene Lam and Monica Forrester, organizers with decades of experience, to ask them how sex workers manage their safety outside of systems that are indifferent to their needs.

## ELENE LAM OF BUTTERFLY AND MSWP

Elene Lam has been involved in the sex workers' movement for almost twenty years. She is a founder of Butterfly: Asian and Migrant Sex Workers Support Network, and cofounder of the Migrant Sex Workers Project (MSWP). Both projects are based in Toronto and include a grassroots group of migrants, sex workers, and allies who demand safety and dignity for all sex workers regardless of immigration status. Butterfly and the MSWP create

---

1 Caty Simon, "'They Want Us Dead': Anti-Trafficking Laws Attack Drug-Using Sex Workers," *Filter*, September 25, 2018.

tools used by migrant sex workers to protect themselves against human rights violations, to educate the public about the dangers of antitrafficking initiatives, and to advocate to change policies that hurt and exploit migrants in the sex trade. Chanelle Gallant interviewed Lam in September 2018.

ELENE: Police are not always the solution for sex workers because of criminalization and discrimination, especially for migrant and sex workers of color. Both are targeted by municipal enforcement, the police, and immigration enforcement. They all bring negative consequences. For example, if a sex worker is robbed, she knows how much she lost. But with police, she never knows how often they'll come to rob her again, if they'll tell her family or attack her. Encounters with police are very dangerous—you never know what will happen when the police have your information in the system. They could criminalize the sex worker, her boyfriend (who they see as a pimp); she could lose her immigration status and lose custody of her children.

Sex workers know the problems of regulation and the law. They live in the gap between the laws. Sex workers live with the complexity of the legal system and navigate it every day as they create alternatives to handle problems like surveillance by social services, discrimination, their own family problems, and policing. So they are very creative and have many ways of handling issues—but most of their solutions are criminalized. For example, sharing information with other coworkers, screening clients, knowing how to negotiate with clients so that they feel like the sex worker is protected (e.g., saying to a client "Say hi to my security guy!"), having another worker stick around when a client comes in, or calling a trusted client if something goes wrong—because the clients often have resources. All these measures that people take to protect themselves are illegal. People think that clients are all dangerous, but only aggressors are dangerous—not clients.

When I first started working with the sex workers' community in Hong Kong, there were lots of serial robbers and sexual assault. Sometimes they'd attack a sex worker three times in a single day or five times a week. People were being tied up during the assaults and sometimes not found for up to forty-eight hours. We had problems with serial rapists, people causing serious injury, and gang rape. The politicians and the police were no help. The politicians would announce a crackdown on sex workers before elections to get votes, so sex workers would be dealing with abusers and increased police harassment. Police would drag sex workers into the station and force them to sign a document saying that they would leave the area. Sometimes they would, or they'd stand right in front of the workers' business to scare away clients. If the cop was extra mean or lazy, he would fuck with the locks to the business doors so sex workers couldn't get back in. If sex workers called the police because of these attacks, they would be strip-searched by the police, told to leave, and threatened with arrest. Because of this hostile situation, no one called the police. It was a very dangerous situation and we needed to respond urgently, so we started to develop solutions.

Instead of getting protection from law enforcement, they developed protective measures in the community. The sex workers I worked with developed an observation network. The Internet was less common at the time, so people depended on the phone for their communication. We set up a phone number where people could report violence to us, and we started to collect the information. We needed to find a way to tell other sex workers and share the information about abusers and police.

We started to train sex workers to take consistent reports on aggressors so they could share accurate information with other sex workers. For example, aggressors often change their pants and shirts but not their shoes and bags (they were always carrying a bag to take things in). We learned how to record someone's height by paying attention to how much taller he is than you. We got volunteers to come in and role-play being aggressors, then train sex workers on how to see someone and remember the critical details about them.

We also learned how to collect evidence for our own or a police investigation. For example, give the client a glass of water so that he leaves his prints on the glass. Empty the rubbish bin so that aggressors can't guess how much money you have based on how many client condoms you have in the trash. If he becomes aggressive at the end of the service and has used a condom, you'll be able to easily identify which condom is his and have his DNA evidence.

We also recommend ways that sex workers can keep their money and minimize their losses. They have to prepare for how to respond when they experience robbery or other kinds of violence. It is important to create the space where they can develop "tips" to educate other community members. We collectively bought surveillance equipment at a discount and loaned it out to sex workers on the condition that they share information about any incidents of violence. At first sex workers didn't trust us because they didn't feel comfortable with surveillance and worried it would scare off clients. But eventually they began to trust us more and preferred to screen out known abusers even if they couldn't call police. Sex workers would let their clients see that they had surveillance to deter problems. If we had video of an aggressor, we'd take a shot of his face and make a poster and share it with everyone. If the aggressor was spotted in the neighborhood, we'd follow the guy, get a picture, and send to others. We wanted them to feel watched and afraid of getting charged with possession of weapons and stolen goods.

We used our position as a "social service organization" to negotiate with police. The sex workers couldn't call police, but we could call and report someone with a weapon. We arranged with police so that sex workers could make a collective complaint without identifying themselves and giving their work addresses. Sex workers would call the organization in front of the client and pretend that they were calling their boss. We would be the workers' safe call. We would wait for their call at the end of the service and if they didn't call us back, we would contact a friend of the workers (pre-arranged) who would go to their workplace to check on them.

Collectively we advocated for changes with police and judges not to disclose personal information of sex workers including in robberies, which was standard practice at the time. The media also follow the police scanner, so we offered identical jackets to women who were charged so they could cover their faces and avoid media after they left the courthouse. We advised sex workers to call the police station if they decided to and not 911, because the police station number was not on the media's radar. In some cases, we convinced police to stop harassing sex workers and other people in the neighborhood and sometimes to even serve as security for sex work businesses. We built this by working with a particular team of cops whose mandate did not include arresting sex workers. The police, you have to guide them. We also did political lobbying against police harassment. We started with small, practical things like negotiating for them not to request ID from sex workers. Our efforts were completely focused on what was practical. The police published a letter agreeing not to harass sex workers, and we printed it out and put it on the walls of sex worker businesses. When police came by to harass workers, we would remind them that they would be going against their boss, the head cop. When police practices or administration changed, though, we would lose everything we'd gained, especially if they decided to target sex workers again. We might spend three years developing an initiative only to see it destroyed in a week.

As we collected information, we began to notice patterns in sexual assaults and began to learn investigation techniques. This helped us to develop better protection strategies. Migrant sex workers were often less organized and less connected but often still connected to local community members. Sometimes when we would do outreach, it was community members on the street (like vendors) who would tell us about the bad guys and point them out. We would explore solutions with non–sex working community members about dangerous people, which can include warning them, or taking a picture and putting it on a poster, or having someone beat them up. Then the sex worker is protected by non–sex worker community members. One guy disappeared after being beaten up.

We focused on restoring agency and sense of power to sex workers. If they can avoid the abuser, they already feel empowered. We learned about how to emotionally manipulate abusers and police to reduce harm. For example, make the police feel like we appreciate their protection and make thieves feel like you understand their story and are on their side. Workers being robbed would say, "I know you're in desperate need. Don't worry. I understand. Here, take the money!" and give him one stash of money. While doing that, she would tell him a sob story about how she hoped he would just leave her enough money to get home and her ID—all while noticing all his features so she could later report him. He thinks it's all your money and sometimes feels bad for you. Sex workers also learned to negotiate with a rapist to use a condom or, if not, to reduce injury, or get him to cum quickly and leave.

The most important thing though isn't how these self-defense strategies affect the aggressor. It's that this makes the sex worker feel powerful. Facing a rapist or thief can be mentally destroying, but this approach gives agency back to the sex worker, gives the sex worker the time to collect evidence, and connects the sex worker to the aggressor's humanity. This is so important for building resilience. *How you manage your agency in crisis really affects how much you are traumatized.* To deal with crisis, you need to manage yourself, manage the situation, manage the aggressor. This is why "trauma-informed" solutions can be problematic. They can reinforce the person as a site of trauma, not agency. We took a resilience-based approach.

We also had four self-defense instructors come in to help us develop a self-defense class that worked for sex workers. It focused on how to move your body so you get injured but not killed by a murderer. We developed collective strategies like how to hide knives and anything that can be used for strangulation, how to deal with hiding money. They developed a system for how to manage the environment, manage the aggressor, and manage oneself.

Sex workers who've been harmed can get justice in many ways without police:

They can share their experiences with others to protect them.

They can train others.

They can work to change the system.

All of these forms of justice can restore agency to the sex worker. Sex workers have to move through sexual trauma—or they can't work or survive. Sex workers are targeted because the perpetrator knows that they are criminalized and they are not protected. So sex workers are forced to develop tools and ways to protect themselves, due to the failures of the justice system. It is important to recognize that sex work is work and sex workers should be respected and be able to work safely.

## MONICA FORRESTER OF MAGGIE'S:
### TORONTO SEX WORKERS ACTION PROJECT

Monica Forrester, a Black and Mohawk Two-Spirit trans organizer and former sex worker, is the program coordinator at Maggie's: Toronto Sex Worker Action Project, a Toronto sex worker drop-in and advocacy center. In the late 1990s, along with Métis trans sex worker organizer Mirha-Soleil Ross, she started almost every grassroots organization for poor and street-involved trans people in Toronto and advocated and won the right for trans women to be in women's homeless shelters. In 2018, she won the Steinert & Ferreiro Award for LGBT leadership. She continues to be a respected leader in Black, trans women of color, and sex-working communities.

MONICA: Sex workers have a number of ways to stay safe without the police, which I will describe here in three categories: prevention, healing, and justice:

*Prevention.* Sex workers share information quickly to protect each other from abusers and from police. We share it in person on the corner or at sex worker–led drop-ins, by texting, we'll post about it on social media, report it to bad-date lists through agencies, or we'll share it on our advertising site if there are sex worker–only forums on it. People always have a safety plan like letting others know where they are working, how, and when. They take precautions like working in groups, in lit areas and seeing the client in areas that we're familiar with where there are people around and we can access help if we need it. Having control over *where* we work is really important. We always have a plan for what to do if things get out of control. We also practice all kinds of self-defense like not wearing anything around your neck that could be used against you, and we carry whatever a weapon looks like to us but won't get us criminalized like a pen or hairspray you can spray in someone's face.

*Healing.* We can heal from violence without going to the cops—a lot of that is through validation and not blaming our work for violence. We need validation that if we smoked crack or worked the corner or looked too sexy, we didn't bring violence on. A lot of sex workers get blamed for being in "risky" work or leading "high-risk lifestyles," and this saying that it's their fault—but they don't say that to people who aren't sex workers or trans or Black/African/Caribbean or people of color. We can heal each other through that validation.

*Justice.* Justice looks like more funding into community-led programs that are centered around sex workers' needs; worker centered, working with policy and legislation that supports sex workers; repealing laws that put sex workers in harm's way; working on policing practices at a municipal level. Justice is allowing sex workers to lead the conversation about their own experiences of sex work and violence. The experience is different for everyone, and we need counseling and resources that make clear that we're not traumatized by our work but by our oppression. We need to be validated as strong communities, not victims. Justice is served when we get to define our own experiences, breaking down the power imbalance in agencies and government, and giving that power back to sex workers. Yes, we need to remember those who have passed, but we need to remember the living too. We need to ask: How can we better the lives of the living?

CHANELLE: *Can you tell me about Alloura Wells's story?*

MONICA: Alloura Wells was a homeless Two-Spirit trans sex worker who disappeared in 2017. She was a regular at Maggie's, and the last time she came in was late July of that year. She was very depressed, suicidal, and traumatized. She was having issues with her boyfriend, and he'd beaten her with a brick. We didn't see her for months after that, and we started asking around in the community. Her sister contacted me and we phoned the jail. They said she was inside, and we figured, OK, she'll be out in a few months. A few months went by and we didn't hear anything, so Maggie's sent a letter to the jail asking about her. We never heard back. We called the jail again, and this time they said that she wasn't there and hadn't been.

We asked Alloura's father and sister to go to the police and file a missing persons report. Her father went to 52 Division (the local police precinct) to report her disappearance—and they refused to even take a report. They said she was homeless and made up all kinds of excuses to dismiss him. So that's when we called the local news. Me and Jen Porter (of Maggie's) gave interviews talking about the police refusal to even take a report and about our fears. Alloura was dealing with trauma and violence and it wasn't like her to not be around—she came to the Indigenous drop-in every week. When that news story broke, the police said, "Oh, that's not our protocol, we take everyone's lives seriously, blah blah blah."

I went online and asked everyone if anyone had seen her. I organized a search party for the ravine where she was living at the time she disappeared. A large crowd supported it and came out. We respected the people that lived in the ravine, *and* we engaged with them. The search was televised, and we postered everywhere to try to find her. Regardless of who she was, as a homeless Two-Spirit trans woman she deserved the same rights as anyone else in our society. We did a rally down at police headquarters to speak out about their lack of integrity and support, dismissing their claims of alliance with LGBTQ2S communities and how the Alloura Wells situation proved to the larger community that the police are not who people think they are.

Then, possibly because of our publicity, a woman came forward. Becky Price had found a body in the ravine, and she knew the person was trans by her clothing. She reported it to the police and to the 519 LGBTQ Community Centre. She asked the 519 and the police to make a public announcement about a person found dead so the person could be identified. They both brushed her off, and she forwarded us those emails. The whole time we were searching for Alloura, her body was with police who failed to even identify her and didn't do any work to reach out to communities to determine if anyone was missing. They just did nothing. This was at the same time that the cases of Bruce McArthur and Tess Richey were in full swing.[2]

At that point, all we knew was that there was a body, but we didn't know if it was Alloura. December was when we finally found out that it was Alloura's body. We had a memorial and tons of people came out. The coroner said that they weren't sure what she died of, but there was major trauma to her body. All her chest bones were broken and there were lacerations to her face—but that wasn't what killed her. Her injuries were not from her death—they were just starting to heal. So she was living in pain. We finally buried Alloura thanks to a private donor. It happened a year after her death, but she is buried with her mother.

The boyfriend is very visible in the community and the police haven't even questioned him. He's in the trans community,

---

2   Between 2010–2017 there were a series of disappearances, mostly of South Asian, Arab, and North African immigrant queer men in Toronto's queer village. Many queer people feared a serial killer was hunting queer men of color, but police brushed off community concerns. After a "respectable" white man was killed, the police finally conducted a full investigation and discovered that the community was right all along. Sixty-eight-year-old Bruce McArthur had been targeting brown men, and in one case, a street-based, white, sex-working man. He was eventually charged with eight counts of murder. Tess Richey was a young woman who was also killed while in the Toronto queer village late one night. Police were so indifferent to her disappearance that they failed to discover that her body was fifty feet away from where she was last seen. Her mother discovered her body during a community-run search party.

he's around. People have spoken to the boyfriend who said he was there when Alloura passed. I have made sure that everyone is aware of who he is and the trauma he inflicted on her. A lot of people knew the violence she endured because their relationship was very public. There have been so many deaths this year of community members from overdoses that people are still mourning. Even today I went to a funeral for another trans woman. So, there hasn't been enough engagement about it.

The next steps are to identify those gaps and discrepancies and those botched investigations and how the community organizations responded. The police always use excuses to claim that they can't get far in their investigations, but it's because they do nothing to protect the community. And then, like in the case of McArthur, they denied that there was a serial killer in the area for years. As far as I'm concerned, police won't give you nothing. That's when I was asked to be part of a committee formed to do an external investigation on police practices like how they report or identify missing and found bodies in the community, like the way they didn't when the first few missing men were killed by Bruce McArthur.

Out of that whole situation, a whole external review of police was put together with representatives from the community, Aboriginal Legal Services—all lawyers except me. I said, "Why am I here?" and they said, "Well you're the one with the biggest mouth in the community" because I'm the only one pushing for police accountability for their misconduct. So, we looked at some of the protocol and why investigations were botched, at their transphobia and homophobia and who they deem as important, you know what I mean? I've been asked to work on another committee to do consultations with trans and sex-work communities and their experiences with police, identifying some of the stuff that came up in the external review and making recommendations in the police force from the top all the way down through different divisions.

The 519 Community Centre also knew that a trans person had been found dead and hadn't notified the community. When a trans person is found dead and you run programs for homeless sex-working trans women, you have a responsibility to notify community about safety and to engage with community and take a role. They make a lot of money campaigning off marginalized communities—well, put that money into those communities. How much of their millions go into trans programs? It's really saddening that a program that I initially started in 1997 with Mirha-Soleil Ross has not progressed over the past twenty years. Because of my activism around the Alloura Wells case, they have taken a more supportive role in the case of Moka, a Black trans woman convicted of manslaughter for defending her life against a client who had attacked her. Maybe they know they are under a microscope and they need to pull up.

I am trying to keep raising awareness about violence. I have also started the Alloura Wells Trans and Nonbinary Support Group for Persons in the Sex Industry with money from SURJ [Showing Up for Racial Justice] and left over from the online fundraiser. It is a support group because so many racialized, sex-working trans women experience violence regularly. So, they can talk about it, find support and tools to support each other through trauma—and have a space centered around them. This could take the form of art work, one-on-one counseling, or homeopathic medicines. We're really getting out there and trying to find people who have the skills who understand trans people and our experiences. We've had two sessions of the group. The first one was a celebration of life for Alloura, and then we had a BBQ to get to know each other. An elder did ceremony to get people moving to a space where people can really be able to engage and talk about their experiences.

## CONCLUSION

These interviews reveal some of the powerful ways that sex workers collectively organize safety. They point to the strategies of turning away from the police, courts, and criminalization while turning toward each other for collective, community-based protection. They show us how important it is for survivors to have safety systems such as comprehensive, reliable information sharing, rather than punishment systems that might create more harm and discourage reporting. They also show us how we can reimagine justice and healing—demonstrating that sometimes we can find both without directly involving the abuser, and that survivors have many kinds of agency, including the power to resist rape culture myths and to believe each other. Lastly, they show the importance of coming together—how political organizing, advocacy, and peer-led training are tools of collective healing and transformation.

# 19

# I WOULD LIKE TO RETURN MY TJ PROCESS, OR DISCARDING TJ LIKE WE DISCARD FEMMES

*Ejeris Dixon*

I WAS HELPING A FRIEND THINK THROUGH A REALLY CHALLENGING transformative justice (TJ) process, and we were talking about how to best support the survivor. The survivor felt betrayed by their support team because they had desired a goal for the process that involved permanently excluding the person who caused harm from a space without giving this person a pathway for re-entering the space. The support team was trying to name their own boundaries, name their politics around the goals that they wouldn't pursue, and negotiate an alternative. This process angered the survivor, and they were directing that fury at my friend. Their anger was personal and cruel. There is a way that survivors navigating recent trauma can process boundaries as rejection. And when this happens, I've witnessed and experienced survivors raising their voices, yelling, seemingly directing the entirety of their pain at the support team. When this has happened to me, I've felt it was impossible to know what piece of this pain I was supposed to hold. And the guilt and self-loathing that this experience can trigger or unearth can feel unbearable.

Through talking with my friend I began to think about the intensity of the rage TJ practitioners hold when the process doesn't go exactly how a survivor expects. And the anger and hatred is not just directed at TJ practitioners, but at TJ as a practice itself. There's a piece of capitalism in it. It feels like a terrible purchase. "I purchased a process, and you were supposed to give me salvation. This is not salvation. I hate you and I curse you and all of your generations." I'm not blaming survivors or support teams at all. It's just that we can't return people to their lives before trauma, or before violence, and that realization can feel devastating.

But there was something in this "cursing of generations," in this "You're supposed to hold my pain forever," that also felt entitled and familiar. It reminded me of the way people would react with anger and sometimes hatred when I named my sexual boundaries as a fat girl. It just kept reminding me of the way cisdudes treat fat girls when they won't have sex with them. It was like these dudes were entitled to my body, or that the survivors I was supporting were entitled to my labor. Somewhere in this experience, there was this familiar loss of agency.

The place where these two experiences intersect is within the expectations. Whether as slutty fat girls or TJ practitioners, we aren't allowed to have boundaries. This expectation is gendered, raced, classed, and so very queer. Folks who hold processes are queer, are trans, are nonbinary, are immigrants, are women of color, have disabilities, are survivors ourselves, are from working-class backgrounds, identify as addicts or former addicts. The majority of people I know who hold TJ processes also identify as women and/or femmes. And of course we are, because we are people who've had the least access to safety, accountability, or "justice." But as people who hold multiple intersecting oppressions, we also hold the expectations of those oppressed identities, and people expect that women and femmes of color are boundaryless sources of emotional labor. TJ is not immune to that.

I'm the type of person who likes a tool, a strategy, a rubric to fix these kinds of issues. I haven't yet encountered a tool that could address this. I still struggle to hold a fully formed conversation about this dynamic. I just know that I am in a community of tough bitches who know how to hold people's pain and know how not to take the anger personally, even when it's cruel, even when it's personal.

I desire that people can critique processes without tearing other people apart. I desire that we have stronger systems and practices that don't involve us quietly swallowing other people's anger, hurt, trauma, and pain. When I first started this writing, I hoped that this piece would create a set of questions for survivors who find themselves hating their TJ process, but then I realized that the only true answer for that is for the survivor to get the healing that they need, and often the trajectory of healing is on a different timeline and trajectory than a process.

So, instead, here is a list of ideas for the person who is holding the anger:

- This is not about you. This is trauma projected on you.

- You do not have to win this process. It is not about winning or losing. And you do not have to make this process perfect, because the criminal legal system is so flawed. Do your best, stay in your integrity, grow, learn, rinse, repeat.

- Be accountable for your mistakes, but don't immediately assume that your mistakes are harmful. We are all learning within this work.

- Water, rest, homies, hugs, good food, good sex, and all the self-care strategies wrapped up together.

- We are doing the work of centuries. You don't have to get it right in one process.

## 20

# VENT DIAGRAMS AS HEALING PRACTICE

## TJ TIPS FROM THE OVERLAP

*Elisabeth Long*

YEARS OF ANTIVIOLENCE MOVEMENT WORK AND STUDY DOES NOT make one invulnerable to intimate partner violence. I knew this intellectually, yet it came to me as a humiliating shock when I found myself trying to leave a sexually and emotionally abusive relationship with a fellow queer woman organizer. Though my antiviolence experience did not shield me from the relationship, it helped me tremendously as I strategized to leave the relationship and lead a transformative justice process, a process that I describe as successful because I met my goals to (1) increase my safety, (2) prevent and reduce future harm by the person who harmed me, and (3) build capacity within white antiracist movement to re-spond to intimate and sexual harm. Despite the process's success and the phenomenal support I had, it was painful to experience our communities' struggles to hold complexity and the nuances of survivorship and harm.

Near the close of my process, E.M./Elana Eisen-Markowitz and Rachel Schragis launched Vent Diagrams, a collaborative social media and art project. They define a "vent diagram" as

> a diagram of the overlap of two statements that appear to be true and appear to be contradictory. We purposefully don't label the overlapping middle.... A good vent draws out a tension that we don't have language for because that non-binary overlap isn't really part of our public discourse (yet). By styling these tensions as unlabeled Venn diagrams, we get to a) actively confront binary thinking and b) imagine what's actually in the overlap every time we see and feel the vent.[1]

Vent Diagrams became an outlet for privately working through my rage, resentment, and grief about the process and publicly sharing lessons. Below are a few of my top vents with accompanying tips for practicing the overlap.

## HOW DO WE PRACTICE BELIEF IN PEOPLE'S CAPACITY TO TRANSFORM WITH THE ABILITY TO SEE THEM AS THEY ARE RIGHT NOW?

Both sides of this vent are oft-conflated with untruths that get in the way of transformative change. On one side, there is a conflation of belief in people's *capacity* to transform with a belief in their transformation, regardless of evidence of behavior change. This often occurs when people (1) have not witnessed the harmful behavior themselves, (2) are struggling to reconcile it with their positive idea of the person who has done harm, and simultaneously are (3) trying not to wholly deny the survivor's truth (or not be perceived as doing so, at least). On the other side is the conflation

---

1   Vent Diagrams, "What Is This About?," https://www.ventdiagrams.com /vision-and-values (accessed April 5, 2019).

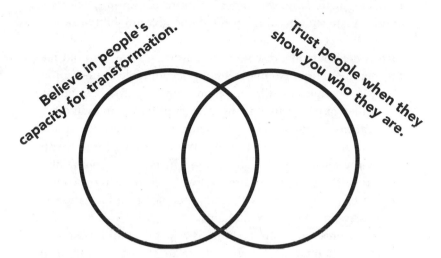

Believe in people's capacity for transformation.

Trust people when they show you who they are.

of present behavior with future behavior, a smart protective strategy and an understandable response when we have invested in people's transformation and repeatedly been disappointed. But neither of these conflations are true.

How do we practice belief in people's capacity to transform with the ability to see them as they are right now? We can do so by building our accountability assessment skills and practicing in relationship with ourselves.

Creative Interventions (CI) describes accountability as a process that can vary in depth and time.[2] Accountability can look many different ways—stopping harmful behavior, naming harmful behavior, giving sincere apologies, stepping down from leadership roles, developing daily healing and reflection practices to address root causes of harmful behavior, building a support pod,[3]

---

2   Creative Interventions, *The Creative Interventions Toolkit: A Practical Guide to Stop Interpersonal Violence*, June 2012, Section 4F, 3–4, June 2012, http://www.creative-interventions.org/wp-content/uploads/2019/05/CI-Toolkit-Complete-FINAL.pdf.

3   Mia Mingus, "Pods and Pod Mapping Worksheet," *Bay Area Transformative Justice Collective*, June 2016, https://batjc.wordpress.com/pods-and-pod-mapping-worksheet/.

providing material repair, contributing to community efforts to end intimate and sexual harm. Dodging accountability can look many different ways—denying, avoiding, minimizing, shifting blame, manipulating, disconnecting, waiting it out without taking genuine action. No one is wholly accountable or unaccountable. We demonstrate different expressions of (un)accountability with different people in different ways at different times in different contexts. We need to be able to discern where people are at in this process in order to increase safety and healing for survivors, honor the change people are making in taking accountability, and provide support and redirection when needed. In the context of transformative justice, discerning people's transformation requires assessing their accountability.

CI's Staircase of Accountability is a helpful tool for assessing levels of accountability.[4] The steps are to (1) stop the immediate violence; (2) recognize the violence; (3) recognize the consequences of violence without excuses, even if unintended; (4) make repairs for the harm; (5) change harmful attitudes and behaviors so that violence is not repeated; and (6) become a healthy member of your community.[5] This tool outlines what each step means and provides examples of how someone may demonstrate it and what action may be needed from community supports.

We can build our accountability assessment muscles in relationship with ourselves. The Northwest Network defines accountability as "taking responsibility for your choices and the consequences of those choices."[6] We all have accountability work to do. Shannon Perez-Darby describes self-accountability as a tool to assess whether the choices we make align with the person we want to be in the world and as a process for making change when they don't. She encourages a daily practice that includes asking

---

4   Creative Interventions, *The Creative Interventions Toolkit*, Section 4F, 3–4.

5   Ibid.

6   Shannon Perez-Darby, "What Is Accountability?," video, Barnard Center for Research on Women Accountable Communities Video Series, October 26, 2018. Video posted on Vimeo by BCRW Videos, September 26, 2018, https://vimeo.com/291929184.

oneself: "Are there things I did today that are outside of my values? Are there things I need to do to clean that up?"[7] When cleanup involves taking responsibility for the impacts of my choices on others, I use CI's Staircase of Accountability to look at what accountability I've taken (or need to take) and how I can deepen it.

Change is incredibly messy and complicated. When caterpillars go into a cocoon and become butterflies, they completely fall apart into a big pile of goo before they turn into a totally different creature that is still them. The process that both survivors and people who've abused go through to transform and take accountability is like that.

It's understandable to assume that people have already transformed, especially if you have not personally witnessed their harmful behavior. It's hard to hold the reality of the harm people have done, or their lack of accountability, especially if they are people we love. It's understandable to make assumptions about our own transformation for the same reasons. But none of us win when we do that. We can demonstrate our belief in people's capacity to transform by building the assessment skills and discernment to see clearly where folks are starting from and understand what behaviors would demonstrate transformation.

## IJ MAKES ME VENGEFUL

Honoring survivor contradictions makes transformative justice possible. Revenge fantasies and transformative justice are not mutually exclusive. In fact, I didn't start having revenge fantasies until the process was in full swing. At the beginning of the process, I was angry but also felt a lot of compassion toward the person who assaulted me. As she denied any harmful behavior while continuing to cause further harm, my revenge fantasies took flight. Honoring and experiencing them dissolved their grip on me, making it more possible to act in alignment with my values throughout the process.

---

7   Ibid.

Despite my understanding of this, I was terrified to share lessons about managing revenge fantasies, scared it would be used to discredit my motivations, my political commitments, my process, me. But when Mariame Kaba and adrienne maree brown acknowledged their revenge fantasies in conversation at the 2018 Allied Media Conference, I was emboldened to share my revenge fantasy vent and accompanying tips.[8] Survivors clearly needed it—it was my most-engaged-with vent.

Expressing revenge fantasies can feel liberatory. Acting on revenge fantasies usually doesn't.

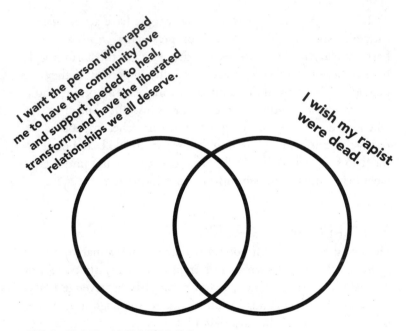

## TIPS FOR SURVIVORS

- Let yourself experience the fantasy completely.

---

8  adrienne maree brown and Mariame Kaba, "Education for Abolition" workshop held at the Allied Media Conference in Detroit, Michigan, June 17, 2018.

- Write it out, as many times and as many ways as you want.

- Do a photo shoot. Check out queer femme photographer Kenzi Crash's revenge fantasy photo series, *Coming for You*.[9]

- Punch a pillow. Kick a pillow. Stab a pillow.

- Vocalize your revenge fantasy to trusted supports (with consent).

- Start a martial arts or weightlifting practice.

- *Scream!*

- Listen to "Goodbye Earl" twenty times a day.

- Watch *Thelma and Louise*.

- Take it to the batting cages.

- Ask beloveds to intervene if you move toward behaving vengefully and to support you in making decisions aligned with your values and safety needs when it comes to sharing any of the above publicly.

## TIPS FOR ALLIES AND SUPPORTERS

- Don't equate vengeful feelings with a move toward vengeful action. If you're concerned or confused about discerning the difference, *ask*.
    - Hold space for rage and grief and messiness. Don't try to fix it or stop the feelings.
    - Affirm that revenge fantasies are OK and that it's brave to name them.

9   Kenzi Crash, *Coming for You*, poster, http://kenzicrash.com/coming-for-you/

ᵒ Ask the survivor where they feel the revenge fantasy in their bodies and use that as a guide for finding a generative expression of it.

ᵒ Find an outlet for *your* revenge fantasies.

## TIPS FOR PEOPLE WHO HAVE DONE HARM

• Accept that a consequence of your behavior is that others may wish you harm.

• Build practices and supports that affirm your dignity in the context of that.

• Be curious about how (unexpressed) revenge fantasies related to your past may have shaped your harmful behavior. Look to the tips for survivors about how to express those. Do not express publicly. Do not share privately without consent.

• Remind yourself that you have a responsibility to heal and change *and* that you deserve to be free from harm. Do not conflate consequences with harm. Ask for support if you are struggling to discern the differences.

## MY SUCCESSFUL, TRAUMATIC TJ PROCESS

When working toward engaging people to stop violence, take responsibility, and make new choices, stay away from making all of your goals reflect how you'd like other people to respond to you and your requests. Avoid thinking of success as only what you get the other person to stop doing or start doing or change. You can never guarantee someone else's response. And you can never monitor someone's every move.[10]

---

10 Creative Interventions, *Creative Interventions Toolkit*, Section 4F, 15.

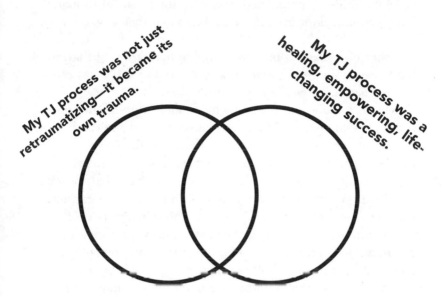

At the close of my process, after a year of TJ work, I was exhausted, resentful, and heavy with grief and shame. I was also proud of myself and grateful for the comrades and beloveds who supported me and pushed change on individual, organizational, and movement levels. But the last thing I wanted to do was write or talk about TJ. When I was finally ready, I shared this vent.

TJ is hard. Coming forward about violence is hard. Investing in the transformation of ourselves, others, our communities, and organizations—it's all hard work. Often, it's beyond hard and becomes its own trauma. I have triggers I did not have before the process. Going into the process, I didn't know how traumatizing it would be, but I knew it would challenge all of me.

And still, all my goals were met. Some were met in different places and ways than I expected at the beginning, but they were all met. I set myself up for success by setting goals that were measurable, flexible enough to be met in more than one way, and not dependent on the actions of the person who did me harm. So, for example, my goal to prevent and reduce future harm by the person who harmed me was met by her removal from a position of leadership and by sharing information about her history of sexual violence with our mutual networks with the intent of supporting others in making informed decisions about their engagement with her. Ideally, this goal would have been met by her taking on the labor of addressing the root causes of her harmful behavior, but I knew from the beginning that to risk the success of my process on that was to give her too much power.

My story about myself and my life changed through this process. I want survivors and allies to know the probability of (re) traumatization going in. I don't want that truth minimized when I center what feels like a much deeper truth for me—the power of the people who protected, defended, held, and cared for me through it. My story of this process is one of further harm, but it is also a story of reducing harm, of connection and care, of receiving profound generosity and patience, persistent compassion, and brave love. I can tell you about the hard shit, none of it exceptional or surprising. But know that it magnified the power of the good. TJ is hard and it may be a new trauma, but it can also be a path to writing ourselves into new stories.

## WANT TO USE VENTS AS A HEALING PRACTICE?

Make a commitment to practice with some form of regularity. Maybe you want to commit to venting thirty minutes a week or having a vent hang with friends every other week. My commitment is to post a TJ vent on Instagram monthly. I usually have a few going in my head, and I work on focusing and refining them throughout the month, especially when tension is high, I'm triggered, or I'm inspired to encapsulate a piece of wisdom from another resource.

Here are some prompts to get you started:

- What do you want people to know?

- Where do you feel closed in?

- Where do you jump to conclusions?

- What nuances do you forget? What nuances does your community forget?

- What complexity do you need to remind yourself of?

- What do you find yourself repeatedly reminding others of?

- Where is the wholeness of your story dishonored? What would make it whole?

21

# FACING SHAME

## FROM SAYING SORRY TO DOING SORRY

*Nathan Shara*

ONE OF THE VERY HARDEST THINGS ABOUT PREVENTING AND ending violence is that most of our work isn't really about getting someone to stop being violent. Most of the time, that's not the heart of the thing. The even-more-rigorous struggle is to cultivate all of the awareness and skills that would have been necessary for the violence not to have happened in the first place.

Which is why, when we talk about violence, we always end up talking about *everything*: slavery, binary gender, the original disconnection of humans from the rest of life on this planet, and so on. Solving violence is rarely as much about the moment at hand as it is about everything else that preceded it.

Which is where shame comes in.

As a therapist who has spent the last decade working with movement folks who are survivors of intimate violence—as well as with many people who have caused harm—I see shame as one of the most pervasive, painful, and insidious barriers to our efforts to fulfill the aspirations of transformative justice.

In order to develop real responses to the myriad harms in our lives—or even the *capacity* to develop real responses—we need to understand shame and develop tools for working with it, individually and collectively.

In 2012, I began working with Zahra, a Pakistani American woman in her late twenties who sought me out to pursue healing from trauma that she said "has ruined everything I love." I knew Zahra peripherally through her organizing work on immigrant rights and her local involvement in blocking the construction of a new detention center. She was a passionate, high-femme flurry of movement who usually showed up out of breath, twenty minutes after the time we'd scheduled, in a bolt of patterns and color that brightened my far-more-subdued therapy office.

As our work began, Zahra shared that she had been sexually abused by an adult male community faith leader when she was in elementary school. When her family learned about the abuse, they acted protectively to immediately cut off her relationship with him, but they never acknowledged the abuse with her again. Zahra had not even remembered until an anti-oppression workshop years later, during one of those "Stand up if you grew up with two parents, stand up if…" activities. The facilitator had said "Stand up if you've ever been sexually assaulted," and Zahra found herself on her feet, crying, saying, "Why am I standing? I don't know why I'm standing," over and over through her tears.

In working with Zahra over time, she shared more about the profoundly confusing messages she had received from her family. While her parents never acknowledged the abuse throughout her childhood, adolescence, or early adulthood, they had pressured her about what she wore, where she went, and whom she spent time with. Even now, her parents were unable to talk about the abuse when she brought it up with them, which she attributed to her father's overwhelming shame at having "failed" to protect her. Despite political values that affirmed that the sexual abuse was not her fault, Zahra moved through her life with a belief that she was tainted. *Shame.*

# WHAT IS SHAME?

*Shame is different than guilt.* While guilt focuses on our behavior ("I did something bad"), shame creates an identity: "I am bad." Shame keeps us stuck, isolated, and hiding. With no way to escape from the totality of our belief ("I just *am* wrong"), we may do some of the following:

- *hide* what we feel is bad about ourselves and try hard to pass as "good."

- *overcompensate* in other parts of life through overwork, caretaking, or perfectionism to make up for whatever is "wrong" about us.

- *defend* ourselves from any insinuation that we might have done wrong, attempt to rationalize, or justify our actions.

- *blame* someone else, try to divert responsibility, or shift the focus onto another.

- *attack* anyone who draws attention toward the source of our shame, try to have power by dominating or shaming others.

- *numb* through self-harming use of alcohol, substances, food, sex, technology, and so on.

Most of us use all of these strategies in different moments. Overaccountability and underaccountability are two sides of the same coin: "I can't stand how bad I feel and can't imagine making it right (overaccountability) so I'm going to hide that it (whatever it is) even happened, or lie about it or blame someone else (underaccountability)."[1]

---

1   Folks within community accountability work have described this dynamic in a variety of ways and have developed tools to tease out responsibility and fault. Communities United Against Violence's (CUAV) "Gems of Change"

224 • Beyond Survival

Early on in my relationship with Zahra, she described the crushing self-doubt that she lived with and her struggle to trust anything that seemed to be going well. "It feels like if someone is into me, it's because they're objectifying me and if they really got to know me, they wouldn't like what they'd find. If someone tells me I did a good job at work, I don't feel happy about it, I just feel all this pressure, like what if I can't do it as well the next time?" Zahra had changed job, partner, or city (or all three) at least once every six months for the last seven years and said that in many cases she found herself leaving a decent situation for a worse option. "At least if it's shitty, I know what to expect. Sometimes it feels like I'm just moving as fast as I can to try and stay ahead of the feelings."

Our work initially focused on Zahra learning to tolerate the sensations in her own body without running away from them. As she stayed with her feelings for longer and longer moments, she began to acknowledge how much she had been running from and the depth of hurt that she was carrying. The fear and anger that she discovered were certainly about the abuse, but also about her parents' inability to support her. She realized that she had learned years ago that not feeling allowed her to stay connected with her family. By denying her own emotions, she had been able to protect herself from some of their shame-filled (and shaming) reactions to her.

In order to move from shame toward accountability and healing, we need to believe that safety, connection, and dignity are possible. If we know or believe that our physical, sexual, or material safety will be violated if we disclose either the harm that was done to us or the harm we have caused), then concealing these

---

Pendulum offers a "middle path" between retaliation and minimization. The NW Network of Bi, Trans, Lesbian and Gay Survivors of Abuse's "Find Your 6" tool supports users in finding the "six" on a scale of responsibility from one to ten rather than flip-flopping between "zero fault" and "one thousand percent responsible." This language for describing shame, "overaccountability, underaccountability, and centered accountability" comes from the work of Generative Somatics and generationFIVE.

things is an understandable and fundamentally adaptive way to maintain our safety. If we experience social rejection, ostracism, and isolation by disclosing our experiences of harm (whether surviving harm, causing harm, or both), then concealing, minimizing, and denying these experiences are logical and fundamentally life-affirming strategies (albeit with huge costs).

If we cannot reveal what we have done or what was done to us without being seen as inferior, damaged, tainted, broken, monstrous, irreparable, and so on, then, out of a core human drive toward dignity, we will not do it. Therapist and author Harriet Lerner writes: "If identity—who you *are*—is equated with your worst behaviors, you will not accept responsibility or access genuine feelings of sorrow—because to do so would invite feelings of worthlessness. How can we apologize for something we are, rather than something we did?"

One day, just over a year into working with Zahra, she came in for one of our sessions visibly upset. She sat on the small couch in my office folded in on herself with her fingers digging into the front of the cushion behind her knees. She said, "There's something I haven't told you, and I understand if you can't work with me anymore." Sobbing throughout the session, she shared that when she was in her early teens, she had sexually abused her younger sister. She had never shared this with anyone, nor had she ever acknowledged it with her sister.

Though my work with Zahra wasn't initially connected to any type of TJ or community accountability process, I routinely found myself reflecting on what a transformative process would look like around Zahra, her family, and their communities. What had Zahra needed as a nine-year-old girl? What resources would her parents have needed to have been more supportive after the abuse? What ever happened to the man who sexually abused Zahra? Did he sexually abuse other children? As I learned more about her family, I also came to see greater nuance and complexity; how Islamophobia, class privilege, assimilation, and patriarchy had intersected to shape the context within which Zahra was sexually abused.

After this huge disclosure, I also found myself wondering: What if Zahra had started working with me because her sister had called her into an accountability process? How might she have showed up in that process in the first six months of our work together? How would that have looked different if she was asked into a TJ process during or after this moment in her healing process?

## ASSESSING FOR SHAME AND CAPACITY WHEN CHOOSING WHAT KIND OF TJ PROCESS TO ENGAGE

Working these last years with folks who have been abusive, I see a consistent paradox: people who have done harm often need to share their experiences of *being harmed themselves* before they're able to feel or acknowledge the impact of their own actions. And yet, what many survivors need *first* from the person who caused them harm is acknowledgment of the abuse. How do we develop responses to harm and TJ processes that anticipate and account for this ongoing tension?

I think at least one part of the answer is for us to significantly widen our view of what transformative processes can look like. A community accountability process involving all parties together in a room can't be the gold standard for every situation.

From my view, the impulse toward engaging in a community-based process that includes a person who caused harm and an impacted party is sometimes based more in reactivity and hope than in a grounded assessment of current-time reality. "I just need her to know that I didn't mean to…" or "I just want to see it in her eyes that she's sorry, that she understands what she did to me."

Any of us choosing to engage in a process or supporting another individual within a process need to maintain a big enough view of the situation to assess the capacity of the person who has caused harm for accountability before putting parties together. One of the most critical questions for us to engage with is the capacity and motivation of the person who caused harm to face the impact of their actions.

# SAYING SORRY, FEELING SORRY, DOING SORRY, BEING SORRY

Most of us have plenty of examples of how easy it is to say the word "sorry" without meaning it. And we also probably have at least a few examples that reveal how radically different that is from when we say "I'm sorry" and mean it wholeheartedly. Saying sorry can definitely be a starting point for accountability, but it can also be a way to avoid facing consequences.

*Feeling sorry* can mean a lot of different things—and it is another place where unpacking shame can be very relevant to TJ. Feeling bad is not the same as feeling sorry. And feeling bad doesn't inherently make us more capable of stopping our harmful behavior, nor does it magically provide us with the skills to be able to do something different when presented with a similar scenario. Feeling remorse—the pain of regret for actions we've taken that violate our own values—can be an important part of the work of becoming accountable. It usually requires some level of "un-numbing," or developing our compassion for the experience of the person or people we've harmed.

*Doing sorry* means that we are taking specific actions toward repair—even if these occur largely separately from the person we've harmed. For example, one person with whom I worked made monthly financial contributions to two women he had abused while in relationships with each of them. Another person eventually was able to ask two members of their broader network of friends to support them in understanding the impact of their violence toward their ex-boyfriend.

Transformative accountability means that when we apologize, there is congruence between our words, emotions, and actions. We're not just saying the words, but we can also name what it is that we're sorry for—recognizing the harm we've caused and being able to acknowledge its impacts. Feeling remorse. Taking action toward repair and restitution and demonstrating a commitment to stopping the harm and to changing.

*Being sorry.* As folks involved in convening, supporting, and facilitating accountability processes, we need to ask ourselves and

one another: Is direct engagement among parties at this time likely to be transformative, neutral, or harmful? "Transformative" is
a high standard. It means investing in everyone's transformation
over time—which rarely aligns as neatly between parties as our
theory and dreams would suggest.

Complex as it is, this assessment also has to include our capacity to register or receive accountability. Sometimes we are so eager
to believe that someone has changed that we may rush toward
forgiveness, extending trust long before they have demonstrated
any real shift toward new action. Other times, the volume of our
own pain and anger about the hurt or the betrayal is so loud
that we can't actually hear anything but our own story, including anything the other person might say or do that indicates real
remorse, apology, or amends. Where we have experienced harm,
we may sometimes need help in assessing our own capacity to
*perceive* centered accountability. As folks supporting TJ processes,
we may also be in the position of supporting someone who has
experienced harm in their assessment of readiness or willingness
to engage with the person who harmed them.

Different stages of accountability and shame healing may need
different community processes.

## SOME ASSESSMENT QUESTIONS FOR FOLKS WHO HAVE EXPERIENCED HARM

1.  What would it mean/look like/feel like if X were able
    to take accountability for the harms they caused? How
    would you know?

2.  What specific requests do you have of them?

3.  What are your boundaries?

4. How do you think about or understand what caused X to become harmful?

We can be listening for whether the person who experienced the harm wants the person who caused them harm to be punished, to leave them alone, to be forgiven by their friends and family, to apologize to them, or to behave differently so they can re-engage with them—or something else. While there isn't any clear, if-this-then-that formula, someone's responses to these questions can offer us a lot of information about whether direct engagement is likely to produce positive movement.

## SOME ASSESSMENT QUESTIONS FOR FOLKS WHO HAVE CAUSED HARM

- How are you relating to this situation?

- How would you describe your behavior with A?

- How do you think it impacted A when you _____?

- How do you feel about telling people in your life "I caused harm to A"?

- How do you think about or understand what caused you to harm A?

Here, we can begin to get some sense of how much shame, numbness, blame, and avoidance may be running the show. We can also listen for indications about whether the person is able to acknowledge their behavior as harmful, the extent to which they are able to consider the person or people they've harmed enough to consider the impacts of their behavior, how much they are or aren't able to feel remorse, as well as their will and motivation toward change and repair.

In many cases, we may conclude that more healing and accountability support are needed with one or more parties before it will be useful to bring a group together to address the impacts.

My work with Zahra did not end with her telling me about her sister, though she struggled—transparently—over the next several months to stay in. The intensity of the feelings that came rushing forward once she disclosed made her want to unsay it, to move even faster, to put it away again, and to just keep running. She was simultaneously relieved to have finally told someone, angry with me for knowing her secret, devastated that she could have hurt her sister whom she loved so much, and livid that she was sexually abused in the first place.

When we are able to face it, shame lets go to reveal pain. This includes both the pain of being hurt as well as the pain of remorse. Where we have been hurt, this pain can include terror, agony, rage, despair, and helplessness, all of which are natural responses to having our integrity violated or our consent stolen from us. We may also experience intense pain in having to grieve the life we might have had if the harm had not occurred.

Where we have caused harm, we may experience pain at recognizing that we did something that violates our own integrity or humanity. We may feel grief or regret at having hurt someone, or at the recognition that we could not see our actions as harmful at the time. This pain and remorse often signal the return of feeling and empathy after having been numb, like the pain of feeling returning to a limb that's fallen asleep. For people who have caused harm, some of this emotional work may be necessary for transformative accountability to be possible.

As people living within oppressive social conditions, we have all been shaped by the lies of capitalist, eco-murdering, settler-colonial, ableist, white-supremacist heteropatriarchy. This ideology of who is valuable and who is expendable can leave us with shame across the board: both where we have been targeted and denied our full humanity and where we have benefited from unearned privilege.

When we start digging into the conditions around an incident of harm, we usually discover that there were other harms that preceded this one. As we follow the thread back through time, it splits and splits again, tangling and weaving into other stories and histories, until we find ourselves asking still deeper questions about love, fear, scarcity, and the origins of harm. In doing TJ work, most of us are forced, at some point, to confront our own contradictions about who deserves connection, compassion, and forgiveness—and what those things include.

By facing our shame, we can begin to free ourselves from the inferiority we have internalized, reclaiming our agency and taking bolder actions for social justice and right relationship with our planet. Confronting our shame can also unstick us from the immobilization of privilege, allowing us to join in the solidarity and interdependence our spirits long for. What mistakes might you need to face in order to trust yourself? What hurts are you carrying that remain unmourned?

For many of us, transformative justice becomes a set of guiding principles toward lifelong personal, moral, political, and spiritual development. How do I love someone even when I'm angry? How do I make boundaries that protect me and still respect the other person? How do I forgive myself for the things that were never my fault? TJ requires that we stretch our capacity for love and dignity wider and wider, until we are able—individually and collectively—to include nothing less than all of life.

# 22

# CRIPPING TJ

*Leah Lakshmi Piepzna-Samarasinha*

IN MY EXPERIENCE, MOST PEOPLE DOING TRANSFORMATIVE JUS-
tice work didn't get into it because we thought it would be a random, fun thing to do. (Like, hey, I could go for a walk, or I could listen to some of the most harrowing shit imaginable, let's go for door #2!) We do it because we're survivors, or the people closest to us are. We care about survivors; we know what it's like to survive brutal shit, often alone. We want to change the world so this stuff never happens again. We are also mostly Black and brown women, queers, trans, and nonbinary people.

Many folks doing TJ work are also disabled. Some of us have physical disabilities or chronic illnesses, some of us are Deaf, some are neurodivergent. Many of us have Madness, psychiatric disabilities or mental health issues (whatever your favorite word is). We are people who experience anxiety, complex PTSD, dissociation, and depression. Some of us have "the bigger guns" of psychiatrization—schizophrenia, bipolar, BPD—and have various takes on how those diagnoses work for us. Some of us might have been Mad/had mental health disabilities even if we weren't survivors.[1] But for many of us, our survivorhood and our neuro-

---

1   There is a huge diversity of opinion within Mad communities about what

233

divergence are pretty damn intertwined. As disabled TJ workers, we know what it's like to inhabit secret bodymind stories that many turn away from, as "too much," and that knowledge helps us in our TJ work—people trust us with their survivor stories because they can tell we've seen some shit.[2]

Yet, even though there's a vast number of Mad, sick, and disabled survivor babes out there doing TJ work, there's very little writing out there about the places where disability, survivorhood, and doing TJ work come together. In writing this essay, I wanted to start to change that.

There are a million subjects I could write about when it comes to disability and TJ. I focused on three: (1) how many people doing TJ work, including myself, are survivors with anxiety and CPTSD, and how this confluence of disabled and survivor identities both aids us in our work and exposes us to a ton of vicarious trauma; (2) some specific abuse dynamics I see disabled folks facing; and (3) how "cripping TJ"—centralizing disability and anti-ableism in how we do the work—can and does open up new

---

words we like to use to refer to ourselves, and which we find oppressive. As a person with psych disabilities, I use "crazy" and "Mad" as loving and respectful, sometimes rueful, reclaimed language, not an insult, to refer to those of us who experience psychiatric/mental disabilities from depression, anxiety, CPTSD, DID/plurality bipolar, schizophrenia, psychosis, borderline, altered or extreme states, and more. My use of "crazy" as insider language sometimes gets me lectures from abled people about how inappropriate it is, but I've found it often brings knowing laughter from other folks who've been there.

2   In this article, I am using my definition of disability, which includes all people with non-normative body/minds. This is a broad, cross-disability understanding of disability, used by many people in disability justice movements. Some people who identify as Mad or mentally ill don't identify as disabled, something that can stem from many places, including a history of narrow definitions of disability, cross-community ableism, or thinking of disability as negative. However, I believe in the strength of a definition of disability that includes all of us.

possibilities, fueled by disability justice organizing strategies, for how we can hold the work well and for the long haul.

## PART 1: ANXIOUS AF AND TRYING TO MAKE THE REV: I ALREADY HAVE PTSD, WHY AM I DOING THIS TJ SHIT THAT MAKES IT WORSE?

I've lived with panic attacks and debilitating anxiety since I was eighteen, when I accidentally smoked a joint dosed with angel dust at a high school graduation party. Up until then, my experiences with psychiatric disability were clustered around deep depression, dissociation, and suicidality, linked to the sexual, physical, and emotional abuse that I was surviving. At the party, I hallucinated my ass off; my friends took all the sharps out of the bathroom and locked me in it until I came down. For the rest of that summer, I had week-long panic attacks mixed with depersonalization—the world looked like a TV screen, unreal. I would intermittently feel like the world was ending, not be able to breathe, have intrusive thoughts and rapid heartbeat. If there had been a safe place to get care or information about what was happening, that would've been great, but talking about any of it didn't feel safe. I was waiting to escape my family on a long-fought-for scholarship, and I was terrified that if I talked honestly about how nuts I was feeling, I would be stuck in their house forever.

I danced with panic and altered states for the next twenty years, and with the impact of the ways ableism impacts Mad people. A lot of people know I left the United States at age twenty-one to live in Toronto/T"karonto, Canada; fewer people know that I did so because when I confronted my parents about my incest memories, they responded by saying I was "sick and needed help" and threatening to institutionalize me. Their threat was terrifying; it's also a place where their ableism (manifesting as threatened forced psychiatric institutionalization) intersects with survivor-hatred—telling me that "nothing happened, you're crazy and made it all up and need help."

In my early twenties, as a very young, poor, feral survivor of color, a large part of how I healed was finding the psychiatric survivor movement and other movement spaces that talked about Madness and ableism as political. These spaces, led by Mad and disabled people, often Black and brown, were rare places where it was OK to be "nuts in public"—to be crying, experiencing panic or altered states, in a meeting or just in life. They allowed me to be my survivor, neurodivergent self in public, with other Mad and neurodivergent people, who, far from shaming me for being "too much," welcomed my experiences and self as a community member and organizer. As Mad people organizing for human rights and autonomous control of our bodies, we created Psychiatric Survivor Pride Day and other activist work, and shared our experience living with trauma and altered states of consciousness. Being in these spaces in and of itself was healing, and I never forget how lucky I was to be able to access them. Many social justice communities are unaware that Mad/psychiatric survivor communities and movements exist.

However, much of my late twenties and early thirties were spent trying to pass as "normal." During my early twenties, while I was connected with Mad movement space, I was also surviving two violent relationships that involved death threats and physical violence, the second of which came in the midst of being the sickest I've ever been with chronic fatigue immune deficiency syndrome and fibromyalgia. My communities for the most part had no idea what to do about either the abuse or my disabilities, and mostly shrugged, called me "too much," and looked the other way. When I got free of my relationship and started to get a little less sick, I needed to access work and community to survive. I was worried I would lose out on both if I was honest about my neurodivergence. I was not wrong. Today the community-building and activist work of disabled and neurodivergent BIPOC people (Black, Indigenous, people of color), from Autistic Hoya to the Fireweed Collective have created space where I am able to be out about my neurodivergence—allowing me to respect and learn from my mental difference, not living a closeted, compartmentalized life, hiding my crazy and only showing most people the shiny parts. But I didn't have that then. I don't know anyone who did.

As I emerged from the latter of these two violent relationships, people would hear I'd had a "situation" and come to me with their own "you're the only one I can tell this to" abuse stories. I did a lot of listening and safety planning late at night on the phone, with little to no mentoring. Like many people thrown into TJ out of our own survivorhood in the late 1990s, we just made it up as we went along. In the late 1990s and early 2000s, I knew hardly anyone else talking about the realities of abuse within activist communities—and community accountability or dealing with abuse without the cops? That was an even wilder "crazy talk" idea. Because of this scarcity, I was "the only one" a lot of people could talk to, and as a result I held a lot of intense stories of abuse in my head that I couldn't tell anyone.

As I got older, I worked as a counselor at a partner abuse and rape crisis line run by feminists of color, ran TJ workshops, and coedited a zine that became a book of survivors' stories. As my work got more public, many more people, most of them strangers, came to me asking for support—on email and Facebook messages they sent at two o'clock in the morning. Like many people doing this work, I had a hard time figuring out how to set boundaries around these asks. I knew how desperate people have to be to write a stranger their abuse story at 2 AM. I also helped out with a lot of hair-raising TJ circles—death threats to survivors and their supporters, doxing, people bringing a weapon to an intervention, incredibly complicated intracommunity processes that took years to work through, trying to make things work out within tiny communities where survivors weren't ready to talk about what happened but my friend was now dating their rapist and wanted to invite them to my house.

All of this just felt normal, like, what else would I be doing? I had been alone when I survived the worst of my abuse, and I had promised myself that I would never say no to anyone who came to me. But my commitment to leaving no one behind didn't stop me from getting vicarious trauma from all the stories of abuse I was hearing. My panic attacks increased in both frequency and length, as did my free-floating anxiety. The "survivor focused/anti-nonprofit" rhetoric of much feminist antiviolence and early

TJ work did didn't leave me or other TJ organizers much room to talk about the vicarious trauma we were experiencing, or to articulate that me might have limits. I absolutely believed that the work we were doing outside of institutions was saving lives, but there was no supervision, no sick days, breaks, or employee assistance programs—the forms of built-in worker support I might have been able to access if I were doing this work as a paid worker. This was an unpaid job where you never punched out.

There's rarely been space for us as people doing transformative justice work to talk about how being the bitches listening to everyone's hard stories and carrying their secrets affected us. Our small community of TJ activists was barely keeping up with the ever-increasing load of requests landing on the small number of people seen as "people who actually know how to do this shit." Building structures for support, reflection, and breaks often felt like a luxury, so our trauma and burnout came out sideways. I know I'm not alone in watching people who had been key organizers suddenly stop answering their email or quitting TJ to become massage therapists or tax accountants. Burnout dynamics occur on a larger scale when organizations shut down abruptly or don't renew their websites. Finally, doing this work often replicated our roles as the secret keepers and fix-it people in our families of origin, but we weren't talking about it.

A common practice I've witnessed in TJ work has been to not share any details about a TJ process with anyone, because of security and privacy concerns—which makes sense. But as the work went on, I know I have not been alone in needing a place to debrief. However, other than my therapist, I didn't know anyplace I could get support. Sometimes, exhausted, I let out a story to a friend, and felt instantly guilty. There was rarely understanding in the communities I lived in that someone holding a lot of support work or coordination in a TJ process who shared a story one night might not be a gossip, but an overwhelmed survivor who needed someplace to process. And there were certain questions no one was asking: When do you get to tap out? Is it OK to have a limit? Are you a bad person if you don't answer a frantic email because you're on vacation?

As TJ has grown in popularity, I sit with these questions. Sometimes I see people scoff at the idea of TJ, saying, "Why the hell would I want to do that?" Their statements are often met by people rushing in to tell them how community, transformation and love are wonderful things, but I understand the first statement's hesitant cynicism. Sometimes when I witness people talking idealistically about TJ, I want to roll my eyes and ask if anyone's ever brought a gun to their house.

If we want TJ to continue to grow and thrive as a movement, if we want people to be able to come in and stick around without being destroyed—and, just as importantly, if we want longtime organizers to be able to stick around instead of burning out—we need to talk about all of this stuff from a disability justice perspective that believes that our exhaustion, vicarious trauma, and triggers are not sidelines to the struggle. We need to take a breath and dare to imagine models for doing this work that are actually sustainable. This could look like planning for breaks, having different roles for folks, allowing folks who have been doing the work for years to move into mentorship and advisor roles, or just understanding that the only way to do TJ isn't to hold fifteen intense processes at once. Instead of being surprised by crises, collapse, and triggers, what if we planned for them? And most of all: What would our transformative justice work look like if we put everyone's access needs at the center?

## PART 2: MAPPING DISABLED SURVIVOR STORIES

It's an understatement to say there's not a ton of writing out there about disability and abuse. While disabled writers like Eli Clare, billie rain, and Peggy Munson have written crucial work about their personal experiences as disabled survivors, Google searching "disabled survivors" will mostly turn up links to mainstream sites like the "Violence against Women with Disabilities" page of the U.S. federal government's Office on Women's Health website. The sites all cite the same statistic that chirps, "Research suggests that women with disabilities are more likely to experience domestic violence, emotional abuse, and sexual assault than women without disabilities (62% of disabled women have been abused, in the most common study)"[3] and that "women with disabilities may also feel more isolated and feel they are unable to report the abuse, or they may be dependent on the abuser for their care."[4]

These reports are a start, but leave out a lot, and they flatten disabled survivorhood stories. When I read them as a younger disabled survivor, I related to the stats, but I didn't see the complexities of my own or other disabled survivor stories in there. We're not present as full, complicated beings—as the diabetic trans Latina whose depends on her sometimes emotionally abusive partner for access, or your disabled brown friend who's one of a million disabled sex workers navigating potential violence from the cops, or the abusive dynamics within a local disability justice community, or your Black family member who got tracked into special ed and raped by a teacher there.

Disabled survivors who are other than cis women—who are men, trans, non-binary, intersex, and/or Two-Spirit—are never included in these discussions. There's rarely any discussion of the sexual, physical, and emotional abuse that *is* ableism—from medical stripping in hospitals to medical experimentation to the genital mutilation of intersex people; from forced treatment, restraints, and chemical or psychiatric surgery to forced sterilization, or to simply never being asked before being touched by a medical provider. The abuse issues of many disabled Black and brown people that happen in jails and residential schools and

---

3   U.S. Department of Health and Human Services, Office on Women's Health, "Violence against Women with Disabilities," September 13, 2018, https://www.womenshealth.gov/relationships-and-safety/other-types/violence-against-women-disabilities.

4   Ibid. U.S. Department of Women's Health & Human Services, Office on Women's Health, "How Common Is Violence or Abuse against Women with Disabilities?" September 13, 2018. Accessed April 5, 2019. https://www.womenshealth.gov/relationships-and-safety/other-types/violence-against-women-disabilities#4.

special ed classrooms don't always get mentioned. Neither do our stories of individual and collective resistance to abuse.

Disability is a part of many abuse stories, but in TJ, it's often been an afterthought, something that surprises us rather than something we think about from the very beginning of the work. There are a million different stories of what abuse and survivorhood look like in disabled lives, and how ableism and disability play out in abuse stories, and there's no way I can do them justice. But here are some made-up stories, based on dynamics I've observed in my own life and my own communities over the years. (All of these are composites.)

1. Maritza and Yecelica are two disabled Latinx partners who live together: Maritza uses a powerchair, Yecelica is a "walkie," using forearm crutches. They are looked up to as role models, as a "dream disabled brown queer couple" in their local crip and queer/trans people of color community. Yecelica has a wider social circle because she can go to spaces that are inaccessible to Maritza. They do a lot of care for each other and share a politic of "collective access" where they believe they and the community can and should provide for each other's needs without government support.

Maritza needs more daily physical care that Yecelica does, but Yecelica discourages Maritza from getting a personal care attendant, saying that "community should be enough." Yecelica also sometimes snaps when Maritza needs help transferring, or refuses to do care tasks when she's angry at Maritza. Maritza feels afraid of Yecelica but has fewer IRL friends because she can't go to inaccessible events. Being honest that they're struggling, and disrupting the image of the "perfect crip of color couple" people want to believe in feels overwhelmingly hard to Maritza, and like she'll lose social currency that might help her leave her relationship. She's also scared about whether she can find another accessible apartment if they break up—it took almost a year for them to find a home with a ramp the last time they looked.

2. Ravinder is a South Asian trans guy who is plural/has disassociation/DID. Sometimes, when he's in a part, he yells when triggered. After he comes back from being triggered, he is

panicked that he might have hurt someone by yelling, and shame spirals, hating his disassociation. He's afraid that if he's honest about what's going on, he will lose community because of the deep stigma against DID. He needs somebody who gets neuro-divergence who can talk him through what's happening, without judging him but also helping them figure out accessible ways of being accountable and changing behaviors. The only local counselor who is queer positive and has some knowledge of DID has a one-year-long waiting list.

3. The local Disability Justice Action Collective has been meeting for a year. One person starts showing up uninvited at other members' houses late at night, as well as making sexual comments and staring at members in ways that make them feel uncomfortable. When people try to talk with them about it, they respond by saying that the way they are is just their neurodivergence and asking them to stop is ableist. After all, doesn't disability justice mean we're supposed to accept each other as we are?

4. Mollena is a Black femme with lupus. In her last relationship, her partner used ableism to gaslight her, telling her that the abusive things she remembered her partner doing weren't true and that, she was just mis-remembering them because of brain fog.

5. Lisa is a developmentally disabled Indigenous butch active in local self-advocacy and independent living groups. She has been repeatedly screamed at and sexually harassed by white disabled men in both organizations. When she tries to talk about it, the abuse is brushed off—people don't believe she could be abused because she is butch, and they stress "disability solidarity."

6. Ronald and Lisa are two of the many autistic youth locked up at the Judge Rotenberg Center in Canton, Massachusetts. Since 2012, the Center has come under scrutiny and faced lawsuits because of its use of electroshock during "applied behavioral analysis"—a common "treatment" for autism, where youth who stim or don't make eye contact get electric shocks from packs strapped to their bodies to punish them for "acting autistic." Despite multiple lawsuits, shock "behavior modification" continues, and autistic youth institutionalized in the center continue to face medical violence and abuse. What would TJ look like for them?

I want to talk about how ableism pushes us into isolation, strips us of social capital, and thus so many of us stay in abusive relationships of all kinds—or sometimes act in ways that cause harm—because finding love, sex, and companionship as a disabled person is so goddamned hard, and we feel like we have to take what we can get, or because we haven't had any role models of other disabled people loving and dating well. I want to write about how disabled people of all kinds are targeted by abusers, not because we are disabled, but because abusers target people who are seen as less credible because of ableism, knowing we are less likely to be believed—for reasons ranging from "that person's crazy" to "who would rape you?" I want to write about how survivors being dismissed as "crazy" *is* ableism.

I want more disabled people to write our real stories of just how fucking hard it is to find love, sex, and friendships that are not violent, where you're not closeting all of your weird body/mind secrets—and the deep triumphs and complexities of crip love when we make it happen.[5] I also want there to be space to talk about the specific challenges even the sweetest disabled love faces. I want us to talk about the ways we blow open/crip what sex and love can look like, talk about the ways we negotiate consent and bodily autonomy nonverbally and through every cripped-out means of communication.

Finally, I want to start to dream about what transformative justice looks like when someone who causes harm is disabled, I

---

5   "Crip" is a term used by many disabled activists, scholars, organizers, and just plain folks for at least the past fifty years, as "insider language" for disabled people and community; we also use it as a verb, talking about the ways we "crip" (bring disabled knowledge and experience and genius to) our homes, lives, communities, organizing, hangouts, et cetera and so on. It's a similar reclaiming of a despised word that's been used against us that is similar to as the way many LGBTS2SA+ people use "queer." Ubiquitous in many disabled communities, its use often makes abled people very confused—how could we possibly be calling ourselves that terrible word? Black disabled writer and organizer Leroy Moore coined the term "krip" to differentiate the word in the disabled sense from the Crips underground street organization.

want there to be something—anything—that isn't ableist written about the intersections of neurodivergence or psych disabilities and being someone who's caused harm. Right now, if someone talks about how our psych disabilities or neurodiversity are intertwined in some way with how we've caused harm, either people fall into apologism: "they have psych disabilities, you can't blame them," or we're seen as monsters: "they have *that* disorder, they're toxic, stay away from them." Mostly, it's the latter, and the ableist demonization of people with psych disabilities as killers and monsters leaves no room for us to really talk about what happens when we are Mad and might cause harm. I want something else. I want anti-ableist forms of accountability that don't throw disabled people who cause harm under the bus, into every stereotype about "crazed autistic"/"psychotic"/"multiple personalities abusive killers." Instead, I want us to create accountability recommendations that are accessible to our disabilities and neurodivergence.

I want to start to think about what TJ might look like by and for disabled people harmed in hospitals, institutions, schools, special ed, and jails. I want to explore how TJ might work in our disabled Black and brown queer circles, which are so small and precious, where we know all too well the killing implications of being shunned—and yet abuse can and does happen here too.

## PART 3. TJ ON CRIP TIME: THE SLOWEST PROCESS IN THE WORLD

For the past four years, I've been part of a transformative justice process some of us have laughingly and lovingly called "the longest process in the world." It's also been one of the most successful, hope-giving processes that I've been a part of. The person who caused harm went from total denial that they had sexually violated someone to believing what the survivor was telling them and respecting and following the survivor's wishes. It's a scenario that everyone who tries TJ hopes for and often doesn't get.

Everyone involved in this process—the survivor, the members of their support circle, the person who caused harm, their support and accountability circle—are sick and disabled queer and trans people, mostly of color. Sometimes we went six months between answering an email. We got sick, we had mental health hard times, we had access challenges like losing affordable housing. Often in this process, one or more of us has repeatedly apologized for how long it was taking.

But how long is a process *supposed* to take?

In many TJ/CA processes I've witnessed over the years, it's been common for people to operate on adrenaline and panic. We hear about a rape or an assault; our cortisol spikes, and people rush in to confront an abuser and "deal with it." There's a flurry of texts, emails, meetings, actions. When the adrenaline crashes, processes unravel, and people stop answering emails or the phone.

What we realized over time was that we were making a process happen on "crip time." We relaxed some. Maybe we weren't failing. Maybe this was one way of doing it right.

Writer Ellen Samuels defines "crip time" thusly:

> When disabled folks talk about crip time, sometimes we just mean that we're late all the time—maybe because we need more sleep than nondisabled people, maybe because the accessible gate in the train station was locked. But other times, when we talk about crip time, we mean something more beautiful and forgiving. We mean, as my friend Margaret Price explains, we live our lives with a "flexible approach to normative time frames" like work schedules, deadlines, or even just waking and sleeping. My friend Alison Kafer says that "rather than bend disabled bodies and minds to meet the clock, crip time bends the clock to meet disabled bodies and minds." I have embraced this beautiful notion for many years, living within the embrace of a crip time that lets me define my own "normal."[6]

---

6   Ellen Samuels, "Six Ways of Looking at Crip Time," *Disability Studies Quarterly* 37, No. 3 (2017), http://dsq-sds.org/article/view/5824/4684.

Everyone in the process shared an overlapping disabled knowledge that shit happens: disability happens, panic attacks happen, SSDI failing to deposit checks in our banks account happens. What our bodyminds can do shifts unpredictably—sometimes slower, which lets things simmer and sink in, sometimes incredibly, wildly fast.

The most substantial changes that we hope for when we work on a transformative justice process—for someone who has caused harm to actually admit they've hurt someone and do the brick-by-brick work of change—will always take more than two weeks. Often, survivors, disabled and not, need time off between big moments in a process to take a breath or a break, come down from triggers, or ground into what they need. The changes we long for often happen in crip-time moments when we are supposed to be doing something else. It's a disabled knowledge that sometimes things are happening when nothing seems like it's happening. In working from a disabled space, we are doing something right and piloting new ways of making TJ work for everyone.

## DISABILITY JUSTICE SKILLS FOR TRANSFORMATIVE JUSTICE

Disabled survivors bring crucial disabled wisdom to transformative justice work. We have rich histories of organizing against individual and collective forms of violence in institutional and community settings where we often have very little institutional power—as self advocates, as members of patients' councils in psych wards, and as everyday disabled people having each others' backs, believing each other's stories of abuse from families, partners, and in institutions. We have rich histories of refusing to obey and protecting each other from abuse even when the space we have is incredibly limited. We know how to lie, scheme, and hustle the law to get each other out of institutions and bad situations. When we organize to support survivors, we bring that crip innovation to our work, figuring out ways of getting survivors' needs met and getting people who have caused harm to change their behvior, and do it in ways that those who have not lived at our margins may never have thought of. A gift I have cherished in many disabled communities is how, out of our experiences being disposed of easily, we are skilled at not throwing people away when they cause harm, and still asking them to change their ways.

We often have more lived skills in the delicate art of interdependence than abled people do, at the vulnerable, risky, and often life-saving work of asking for and receiving help with dignity. Because of this, when we're designing TJ interventions, we can follow a disability justice practice of "for real" interdependence—where there are many roles for people in a TJ process, instead of everyone having to take leadership in the same way, and where people can move back when they're tired.

And we know about tired. We know people are going to get tired doing this work. We are real about how long things really take. We also know that you can do things really well slowly in slow time, in ten-minutes-of-spoons time in slow time, ten-minutes-of-spoons/energy time. We also know that sometimes doing an intervention quickly and efficiently with limited spoons can be a disability justice way of doing something. We can do TJ in a way where we anticipate curve balls, U-turns, breakdowns, and things not working out according to plan—because those are things living disabled is filled with all the time. We often know, and are not afraid of, the big emotions of grief, anger, pain, suicidality, and anxiety. Further, we often know how to witness and honor those feelings without trying to "fix" them.

We know how to kick ass. And we know how to rest. Often, we do both at the same time.

# 23

# WHAT IS/ISN'T TRANSFORMATIVE JUSTICE?

*adrienne maree brown*

I'VE BEEN THINKING A LOT ABOUT TRANSFORMATIVE JUSTICE LATELY.

In the past few months I've been to a couple of gatherings that I was really excited about, and then found myself disappointed, not because drama kicked up, which is inevitable, but because of how we as participants and organizers and people handled those dramas.

Simultaneously, I've watched several public takedowns, callouts, and other grievances take place on social and mainstream media.

And I'm wondering if those of us with an intention of transforming the world have a common understanding of the kind of justice we want to practice, now and in the future.

What we do now is find out someone or some group has done (or may have done) something out of alignment with our values. Some of the transgressions are small—saying something fucked-up. Some are massive—false identity, sexual assault. We then tear that person or group to shreds in a way that reaffirms our values.

When we are satisfied that that person or group is destroyed, we move on.

Or sometimes we just move on because the next scandal has arrived.

I'm not above this behavior—I laugh at the memes and "like" the apoplectic statuses. I feel better about myself because I'm on the right side of history ... or at least the news cycle.

But I also wonder: Is this what we're here for? To cultivate a fear-based adherence to reductive common values?

What can this lead to in an imperfect world full of sloppy, complex humans? Is it possible we will call each other out until there's no one left beside us?

I've had tons of conversations with people who, in these moments of public flaying, avoid stepping up on the side of complexity or curiosity because in the back of our minds is the shared unspoken question: When will y'all come for me?

The places I'm drawn to in movement espouse a desire for transformative justice—justice practices that go all the way to the root of the problem and generate solutions and healing there, such that the conditions that create injustice are transformed.

And yet ... we don't really know how to do it.

We call it transformative justice when we're throwing knives and insults, exposing each other's worst mistakes, reducing each other to moments of failure. We call it holding each other accountable. I'm tired of it.

I see it everywhere I turn. When the response to mistakes, failures, and misunderstandings is emotional, psychological, economic, and physical punishment, we breed a culture of fear, secrecy, and isolation.

So, I'm wondering, in a real way: How can we pivot toward practicing transformative justice? How do we shift from individual, interpersonal, and interorganizational anger toward viable generative sustainable systemic change?

In my facilitation and meditation work, I've seen three questions that can help us grow. I offer them here with real longing to hear more responses, to get in deep practice that helps us create conditions conducive to life in our movements and communities.

## LISTEN WITH "WHY?" AS A FRAMEWORK

People mess up. We lie, exaggerate, betray, hurt, and abandon each other. When we hear that this has happened, it makes sense to feel anger, pain, confusion, and sadness. But to move immediately to punishment means that we stay on the surface of what has happened.

To transform the conditions of the "wrongdoing," we have to ask ourselves and each other, "Why?"

Even—especially—when we are scared of the answer.

It's easy to decide a person or group is shady, evil, psychopathic. The hard truth (hard because there's no quick fix) is that long-term injustice creates most evil behavior. The percentage of psychopaths in the world is just not high enough to justify the ease with which we assign that condition to others.

In my mediations, "why?" is often the game changing, possibility-opening question. That's because the answers rehumanize those we feel are perpetuating against us. "Why?" often leads us to grief, abuse, trauma, mental illness, difference, socialization, childhood, scarcity, loneliness.

Also, "Why?" makes it impossible to ignore that we might be capable of a similar transgression in similar circumstances.

We don't want to see that.

Demonizing is more efficient than relinquishing our worldviews, which is why we have slavery, holocausts, lynchings, and witch trials in our short human history.

"Why?" can be an evolutionary question.


## ASK YOURSELF/SELVES
### WHAT CAN I/WE LEARN FROM THIS?

I love the pop star Rihanna, not just because she smokes blunts in ballgowns but also because one of her earliest tattoos is "Never a failure, always a lesson."

If the only thing I can learn from a situation is that some humans do bad things, it's a waste of my precious time—I already know that.

What I want to know is: What can this teach me/us about how to improve our humanity?

For instance, Bill Cosby's mass rape history is not a lesson in him being a horrible isolated mass rapist. It's a lesson in listening to women who identify perpetrators, making sure those perpetrators are not able to continue their violence but instead experience interventions that transform them, make that injustice impossible. If the first woman raped by Cosby had been listened to, over forty other women could have been spared.

What can we learn? In every situation there are lessons that lead to transformation.

## HOW CAN MY REAL-TIME ACTIONS CONTRIBUTE TO TRANSFORMING THIS SITUATION (VERSUS MAKING IT WORSE)?

This question feels particularly important in the age of social media, where we can make our pain viral before we have even had a chance to feel it.

Often we are well down a path of public shaming and punishment before we have any facts about what's happening. That's true of mainstream takedowns, and it's true of interpersonal grievances.

We air our dirt not to each other but with each other, with hashtags or in specific but nameless rants, to the public, and to those who feed on our weakness and divisions.

We make it less likely to find room for mediation and transformation.

We make less of ourselves.

Again, there are times when that kind of calling out is the only option—particularly with those of great privilege who are not within our reach.

But if you have each other's phone numbers, or are within two degrees of social media connection, and particularly if you are in the small, small percentage of humans trying to change the world—you actually have access to transformative justice in real time. Get mediation support, think of the community, move toward justice.

Real time is slower than social media time, where everything feels urgent. Real time often includes periods of silence, reflection, growth, space, self-forgiveness, processing with loved ones, rest, and responsibility.

Real-time transformation requires stating your needs and setting functional boundaries.

Transformative justice requires us at minimum to ask ourselves questions like these before we jump, teeth bared, for the jugular.

I think this is some of the hardest work. It's not about pack hunting an external enemy, it's about deep shifts in our own ways of being.

But if we want to create a world in which conflict and trauma aren't the center of our collective existence, we have to practice something new, ask different questions, access again our curiosity about each other as a species.

And so much more.

I want us to do better. I want to feel like we are responsible for each other's transformation. Not the transformation from vibrant flawed humans to bits of ash, but rather the transformation from broken people and communities to whole ones.

I believe transformative justice could yield deeper trust, resilience, and interdependence. All these mass and intimate punishments keep us small and fragile. And right now, our movements and the people within them need to be massive and complex and strong.

I want to hear what y'all think and what you're practicing in the spirit of transformative justice.

Toward wholeness and evolution, loves.

PART FOUR

# WHAT DID WE DREAM THEN, WHAT DO WE KNOW NOW?

## MOVEMENT HISTORIES AND FUTURES

## 24

# OUR HEARTS ARE
# BEATING TOGETHER

## A CONVERSATION WITH
## SOME TJ OLD HEADS

*Adrian Cole, YaliniDream, Alexis Pauline
Gumbs, and Jenna Peters-Golden, Ejeris Dixon
and Leah Lakshmi Piepzna-Samarasinha*

WHEN WE FIRST STARTED ENVISIONING THIS ANTHOLOGY, ONE OF the most important things we wanted to include was interviews with people who'd been involved in transformative justice "back in the day"—in the late 1990s and early to mid-2000s. There were so many foundational community accountability projects from those days that were disappearing from common knowledge because they were from the "MySpace generation"—a lot of their Web 1.0 websites had gone offline, or they were never online in the first place.

In the course of putting this book together, the "old heads convo" kept getting shoved to the bottom of our agenda. When we finally finished editing our email and sent it out, we realized that the proper archiving of community accountability work done from the late 1990s to 2010 is a huge project, one that deserves an archive of its own. Instead, we present to you the learning we received from four people in an hour-and-half-long conversation. Speaking from their experiences in transformative justice collective work in the early 2000s in Durham, Philadelphia, and Brooklyn, their words map some of what we dreamed then, how far we've come today, and the future we are creating out of our biggest hopes, mistakes, and learning by doing.

EJERIS: TJ is in a really different place now than when a lot of us were doing it—in ways that can be awesome, in ways that can be, from my perspective, challenging. I would love for y'all to talk about the projects you have been involved in, some of which are still continuing, some of which are not. If you have any major lessons or takeaways when you look back to that time, what are they?

YALINI: I worked with the Safe OUTside the System Collective of the Audre Lorde Project in Brooklyn, New York. We were looking at community safety and responsibility, as well as community defense, which necessitated us to also be engaged in transformative justice practices. I've been informally a part of several different TJ processes within political and artistic communities—in some of which the person doing harm was not able to take accountability, and other processes they were able to transform.

JENNA: I was part of a group called the Philly Stands Up Collective from around 2007 until around 2015. Our collective also sometimes worked with a sibling collective, Philly's Pissed, who supports survivors. Philly Stands Up worked with people who perpetrated harm, mostly sexual assault and intimate partner abuse in queer and radical and kind of like punk communities.

That took the shape of us facilitating accountability processes, and also doing some writing and resource development, and some popular education stuff, and, especially around 2010 to 2011, getting a lot more connected to prison abolition work happening in Philadelphia and the United States. Since Philly Stands

Up wound down by 2015, we're still kind of a loose collective of comrades who meet and work on projects together.

All of us individually are called on pretty regularly to participate in processes, working with survivors and/or people who perpetrate harm to seek accountability and transformation, steadily since then. As well as getting, I'm sure many of you experience this too, getting a lot of calls and asks from people all over the country, or Canada and beyond, around how do we build our own local TJ projects. Which is always like an interesting little scan of what are some of the things happening.

And yeah, my takeaways are like, I don't know, a million-fold. Maybe one or two kind of bubbling up for me right now are, like, we talk a lot about survivor-centered, healing-focused accountability processes. And what does it look like for there to be healing for people who are harmed in accountability processes that are working to transform behaviors of a perpetrator as well as a community. And, you know, infinite microscopic questions of trying that, and moments feeling like it works, and a ton of moments feeling like it doesn't work, or like those things don't fit together, and feeling stuck, and sometimes motivated around that question.

Another takeaway that's maybe more uplifting is that in the moments that I, or our collectives or communities, have felt the most alive is when there's different sectoral antiviolence work or transformative justice work linked up in a kind of coordinated way. And so in Philadelphia right now, based on a Supreme Court ruling from a couple years ago, where they found it unconstitutional for people in Pennsylvania who were sentenced to die incarcerated—yeah, life without parole sentences as juveniles—as unconstitutional.

So, right now in Philadelphia, we're experiencing this incredible moment where people who have been in prison for twenty, thirty, forty years, since they were teenagers, are quickly getting resentenced, and coming home, like, weeks or months later. And that's amazing, and creating so many moments of also working with a lot of groups that identify as victim support groups, in communities where people who were harmed by the acts of violence that people went to prison for are still in community, or attend the same place of worship with each other's families.

And I think that we're unlocking lots of new moments and places of stuckness and opportunity and questions, and it's like, when things cannot just be in a, like, "only when intimate partner violence happens," or "only when street-based harm happens," or only when this other piece of violence happens—that we can all really figure out what are we networking, cause every little sector and every little community has a different perspective and major wisdom working on this. That's definitely when I see the strength spreading. Even in moments of major stuckness and confusion and pain. So, that's definitely a lot of big stuff happening.

ADRIAN: I was involved in this work in Philadelphia, through Philly's Pissed. I was a member from the very start in 2005 until about 2009. But for the last decade, I've been doing work organizing with incarcerated trans people, as part of an inside/outside collective. And working on HIV criminalization as an issue.

Certainly, the way that I think about the work I'm involved in now has been profoundly affected by the things that I learned through organizing around community responses to harm.

ALEXIS: I moved to Durham, North Carolina, in 2004, and became part of an organization called SpiritHouse. And, in 2006, in response to the Duke lacrosse rape case, SpiritHouse was one of the founding organizations, and I was one of the founding individuals, of UBUNTU, which was a women of color survivor-led coalition to end gendered violence through sustaining transformative love. With Ebony Noelle Golden, I was initial cochair of the artistic response team.

And that is a defining, incredible experience of my life, and one way that I would describe it from here is that it was a time when—in response to a really public crisis in our community, and repetitive crisis in the media that criminalizes us, and a crisis via social media and the Internet where those of us speaking out individually were getting death threats—many organizations and people realized how much our unresolved trauma from living in a society that perpetuates gendered and sexual violence intersected with everything that we cared about, our overt work for racial justice, environmental and economic justice was underlaid with this unresolved trauma of the impact of sexual violence on all of us. It was a powerful moment of organizing and recognition.

There were some beautiful awareness-raising campaigns and public direct actions and political education curricula and organizational transformations that happened, and then—I'm not really great at remembering years, except like, years leading up to 1982 in regards to Black feminist publications. [*laughs*] So, I don't know exactly what year, but I know it was after the National Day of Truthtelling, the most visible direct action of our coalition, there was a transition of UBUNTU to really focus on the harm-free zone as a concept and really, especially inspired by work that Kai Lumumba Barrow had been involved in, in Brooklyn, in terms of generating the concept of what is a harm-free zone. Kai had moved to Durham and was central to the creation of UBUNTU (it was, in fact, founded at her house), and she played a major role in sharing the concept of the harm-free zone with all of us and creating a structure where we could define it for the needs of our community.

And that is work that has continued, and is held mostly by SpiritHouse, the same organization that has been my first and lasting movement home since I moved to Durham fourteen years ago. So, the harm-free zone, now, is ongoing. It has structure. There's organizational commitment and a community of participants beyond SpiritHouse. There's a growing community investment. With the police violence and the police infrastructure building going on in Durham right now, the existence of a working alternative to police responses to community harm is crucial. There's also lots of stuff around climate and the hurricanes that are going on right now and the concept of building communities of care that can respond to crises, interpersonal harm, and state violence is also key for that work.

My role in relationship to SpiritHouse really isn't directly on the harm-free zone team right now, even though I'm part of that extended community and I'm available as a resource. But, day-to-day it's really held by other people who I'm hoping will write something for this book. [*laughs*] I'm trying to encourage that and make that connection, and, you know, I just know that my folks are doing so many things, and I'm grateful for all of it.

So, some of the takeaways that I have from my vantage point … and I hope I'm making it clear that I have some more distance now from what I would see as the direct TJ work that's happening than I did earlier in the decade when I was more directly involved. I think there's something that I have seen about just how much we want to live in the world that transformative justice teaches us is possible. Time has come up a couple times in the conversation, and I would say that in relationship to time, early on we may have rushed towards that future in ways that were harmful for us and challenging organizationally.

As in we were not, as our loved one adrienne maree brown would say, "moving at the speed of trust," but instead moving at the speed of lust for the world that we deserve. And I'm 100 percent implicated in that. And it's also a result of the urgency we feel in our community. There's so much ongoing police harassment, and so much in-our-face state impact and detainment, that it's—we just could never get away from how harmful those state systems are, and we really want to have something else, and other ways to hold each other.

And sometimes I think we've moved faster than we can, and that has caused other harms or caused us to drop each other when we really want to hold each other. And so, part of what that has looked like is seeing the survival skills that we've had to cultivate used against each other, in ways that have been hard, and that has been heartbreaking for me, at times, and not only for me, but I'm the one here, so I can speak about it, I can speak about my heart.

And, yeah, and I would say that there's something that I don't quite have fully articulated yet, but I'm thinking about it right now because I'm looking at what the hurricane response is like right now in North Carolina, and who's participating in it, and I'm like, oh, it's the same people. The same people, and there's something about survivors, and those of us who have and are attuned to survival skills, and maybe because of some of the things that we've survived, that really move very fast when it comes to something that's an agreed-upon disaster that we're surviving together.

And then all of the smaller things that we're surviving and also putting each other through can sometimes get skipped over, because there is always a disaster to respond to, even if it's not a hurricane. As people have shared in our check-ins, there's always something happening. So, I'm thinking about that, too, like, what would it really—what does it really take to move at the speed of trust in the midst of compounding disasters?

And also just how much a difference it makes, from my own vantage point, to see the harm-free zone, as it functions in our community, as something that's long-term and really held, and that is something that people are engaging on regular basis, not just in response to different crises, but are engaging as an ongoing collective practice of retraining ourselves, and then having it expand. How that actually can allow folks to slow down in a number of ways. Allow folks to slow down who are holding it on a daily basis, acknowledging that we are not gonna learn this in one day. Or, even through our response to one conflict.

This is something that we're committed to for our whole lives, and that we're committed to intergenerationally. But also, I'm learning what it means for people to be able to also have different roles. So, for me, for example, as a person who knows that there is a harm-free zone happening, and that there are harm-free zone gatherings that are regular, and that there's a way for me to participate in that, that's not in the drop-everything way that I once was relating to this work. At the beginning for me it was always a response to emergency, and I wasn't as aware of my specific skills and gifts in relationship to the gifts of those around me. It was not necessarily something that I knew that I could be playing different roles in building for the rest of my life. It felt very all or nothing. I was either working on this all day or abandoning my community. Now I see it in a more expansive way and I trust my community more. So, yeah, that's something that occurs to me from this vantage point, too.

LEAH: What were your hopes when you started doing this work, and how did that shift over time? As an example, I totally thought ten years ago that by now we would have transformative justice councils in every community, in a North America–wide network. I was wrong about that. Very wrong. [*laughs*]

ALEXIS: I can say that at the beginning of the process for me, I hoped that the kids who were part of the families who were involved with us, like, the children of my fellow cofounders, would not experience interpersonal or state violence, and would not be impacted by that in their families, and some of them have. Which is something that has been really hard. Just how pervasive it is. Not just in the world we live in, but just for even those of us who are directly convening to transform. The intergenerational time scale is different than what I thought it would be.

And I will say that in thinking about our families, and the intergenerational scale of this work as I've seen it over the past ten years, I do think that I've seen the generation that I've seen grow up have different resources, have different skills and options around dealing with that harm, and that makes a difference for me. But I did have a hope that, like, OK, we had to go through all this stuff, but at least we can have this set of children that we can see from here, this set of children that we are raising in this context and they will not have to go through things that are very similar.

And they have gone through things that are very similar, and that is something that—you know, intellectually, we understand that these things are intergenerational cycles of violence, and it's really hard to accept that it will be incrementally different, but not totally gone within the span of a decade or two.

ADRIAN: The thing that I was thinking of when Alexis was talking just now that early on, Philly's Pissed was nicknamed "The Two-Year Plan," and I think that all of us—
[*laughter*]
Like, the way that you do make change is you have some workshops, and you have some conversations, and then we're not

as fucked-up anymore, right? But, in fact change happens really slowly over time, and we have to have compassion for ourselves and each other in the long term, and that there's painful, painful setbacks. I went into this—I mean, I don't think we really thought it was "Two-Year Plan, and there won't be any more sexual assault," but that was, like—there was an optimism that was maybe, well, you know, it was optimistic.

LEAH: Thank you. I hope you heard me laughing.

JENNA: Oh man, the Two-Year Plan, that's amazing and heartbreaking. Yeah, actually really similarly to that, Adrian, when I got connected to Philly Stands Up, I was nineteen, and when I joined the collective I was like twenty, twenty-one. And so, I definitely had a sharp vision of how prisons would be, like, totally unnecessary within maybe ten years, you know, like in long term. [*laughter*]

I think, in a more specific way, I really thought that once people got wind of stuff, maybe by like drenching the streets in zines or something, about how freeing it was to actually do the work to heal wounds, especially wounds around toxic masculinity and patriarchy, that folks would understand that this was such a gifted opportunity that we all had, like that it was a gift to get to be accountable and not a punishment.

And that kind of core heart sense of, I can get closer to my humanness, and my own connection would be so alluring that it would not only stop violence in its tracks but kinda also just shift the shape of how people wanted to move through it after violence had happened, and people had enacted harm. Yeah. Oh yeah, I love the Virgo dream. I was on more of a Leo tip, but I like that. I was there.

YALINI: Yeah, it's interesting. I think, maybe because I spent my adolescence in Texas, I had normalized this sense of radical obscurity. I expected that obscurity around transformative justice, abolition during my lifetime. So, strangely enough, I actually feel like I was more cynical when I was younger, even though in general, I was very idealistic. I was thinking about things in terms of hundreds of years, so, and beyond my own lifetime.

I saw that in order to—and I still agree with this—that in order to really radically transform the way in which our societies function, and to have true sovereignty and liberation, that it would require deep, deep healing. I do see transformative justice work as necessary for sovereignty and liberation. In order to be able to govern ourselves, we have to be able to hold ourselves accountable in loving and ways that are not harmful or create more violence.

I saw abolition and transformative justice as a project that was beyond my lifetime. And, I think when we were doing the work with Safe OUTside the System Collective, out of the Audre Lorde Project, I was really just hoping that we could provide another option for folks who had been completely dropped by the system, folks who could not rely on police enforcement, and who we knew would not go to the cops—because of the trauma that they had experienced, or the distrust, or the ways in which cops were really violent to trans and queer people of color in Central Brooklyn at that time.

My hope was that we could at least provide another option for folks who are experiencing this kind of violence, racialized transphobic and homophobic violence. I do think that we were able to provide another option. Not for everyone, necessarily, but we were able to open that space. I was really stressed-out when I first engaged in this work, and pretty critical and frustrated—there was a lot of theoretical and not enough implementation, praxis, practice, humanness, care and love and healing. Contemplative or spiritual work, depending on how you engage.

I actually have gotten more hopeful over the last twenty years, because I feel that now there's more folks who do this work—TJ is not as obscure as I expected it to remain, you know? And I'm so grateful for all the folks, especially the Black and Indigenous women, trans, queer folks, and gender-nonconforming folks, who really accelerated these movements and broadened how many people are engaged in these ideas now.

People know more of the basics, like, when somebody brings up that they've been harmed, more people listen to them. More people do that now. They didn't used to do that. Everybody would reject it, you know? Somebody would bring up an incident in which they've been harmed and everybody's questioning them, they want to know the details, they're extracting information from them. It was so painful to witness and be a part of, and I feel like now, at least, folks know to shut up and listen, you know?

And to me that's a huge difference from fifteen or twenty years ago. That gives it a little bit of breath to do this kind of work. Just the fact that people, yeah, believe in it. Believe that it's possible. That it's more than just an intellectual exercise. That it has actually become a practice amongst our progressive communities is something that I feel really joyful and hopeful about.

The biggest change for me between then and now is every time one of these incidences came up, I used to get really, really, really stressed-out. Because I was anticipating everybody just being horrible. [*laughs*] And now, I don't get really stressed-out. Because people actually have more tools and skills available.

[*a few people thank Yalini at once*]

LEAH: That's a really good reminder. Especially when we're still so fucked, and then I remember back when a lot of people I knew were like, "Is domestic violence really that bad?"

EJERIS: I've been in a lot of spaces and doing a lot of work where it feels like the language of TJ is being weaponized between people. "You're not TJ enough, you're not abolitionist enough," and you know, the twenty-five-year-old self who started this work in 2005, who talked to people over and over again and no one understood it, doesn't understand how it's become that, right?

And so, I get really curious about the passage of time, and how y'all think about it connected to TJ. Like, what changed? Would the work that you started work during these times? Opportunities? Challenges? Like, we're in a different time, and I'm trying to touch it, feel it, get it. And I need y'all's help.

YALINI: I think it's kind of like the way I talk about some yoga, which is the residue of the residue of the residue of what people stole from the ancestors. I feel like that sometimes with TJ, because I think people are just getting glimpses of it on social media, and haven't necessarily been in deep practice. We get the residue of the core ideas that end up being, as you framed, Ejeris, weaponized against folks.

So, I definitely have heard the critiques of TJ work being this almost Christian forgiveness, what's it called, apologist, frame. And I think that's because folks are engaging with the residue of what people understand as transformative justice, versus the idea of it being survivor-centered healing, as Jenna articulated earlier.

ALEXIS: Yeah, I was just inspired by that. I was thinking also about the role of social media, and I was thinking to myself, like, would we have been as hungry to gather in person around these things if it had been a time period where we could have had some proxy of that on the Internet. I don't know. And then I wonder, because so much of how our practice grew had to do with transforming our homes specifically, being in our homes together and thinking about our homes as sites of transformation.

I mean, specifically, our practice looked like bringing people who we didn't even know into our homes, brainstorming with them around supporting them when they had just literally survived something in our neighborhood. I just wonder about that because a lot of the character of our early steps was, legit, so kitchen table. And I'm trying to even imagine it. I'm trying to imagine, what if we had this different Internet structure at that time.

Even though the Internet still did play a really big role in what we were doing. Especially the network of women of color bloggers who supported our work and participated in the National Day of Truthtelling in their own communities around the United States. We were vigilant about sharing all the publications (like "How to Support a Survivor") and worksheets we made as PDFs online. And we were able to look at the Harm-Free Zone Wiki. We certainly felt inspired and affirmed by people elsewhere who were connected to us only through the Internet. So, I wouldn't say I know what would it look like now. But I do feel like the inundation of #MeToo, and that you can see it every day, and the many hashtags that also have been created where you can see survivor stories and feel part of a virtual community is significant.

And that is different than how we felt. For us, creating community of survivors was something that we were specifically doing over food, and that we were really doing in person, and if we were sharing things publicly, it was with so many people literally standing with us physically in space, in this community that we wanted to reclaim and transform. Yeah, so, it's hard to be, like, would that work now? Or, if it was now, what would be the different things that we would do? How would now not look like now, if it hadn't been for the things that all of us had been involved in over the past fifteen years or so.

JENNA: I would just love to listen to y'all talk about this forever. As someone who's never used social media before, like in my personal life, I think I sometimes get the residue of the residue of the residue of conversations that are happening, based on the residue of work that's happened. But I do have the chance to facilitate a lot of groups of people, especially younger people, in the last ten years. So, my perspective is slightly analog maybe, of what are the conversations that come up, and then folding.

Ejeris, when you asked the question, I really was picturing, like, a spiral, kind of. Of, right, we have these ideas that start here, kind of, and then they move and change and then they get deeply critiqued and cut up, and then a new thing emerges, and then we move from there, and then that gets cut up, and then at a certain point we're like, well, this looks a lot like what we were talking about five years ago, or ten years ago, or something.

But I have come to really like that. And to be like, cool, this is a conversation that I'm getting to hear folks who are really early on their journey of thinking about this together. And it sounds really similar to conversations I got to be a part of ten years ago, and kind of, Alexis, how I think you were saying it, like, with these kind of—the conditions are a little different. And so, the building blocks that people are using to fabricate a really similar logic have these different assumptions behind them, or something.

And I'll try to think of some more specific examples and then write it down, or something. But, you know, some of the vacillation, and all of y'all have kind of touched on this, of just, I think there's this really tough binary that's been created of a thing, of a process that's centering the person who perpetrated harm, or centering the survivor, and we—I always have been a part of a lot of processes and conversations where we're doing this dance of, like, trading places.

Either within one process, or within a five-year period of, like, what our beliefs and practices are, to match who goes in the center. And then these sometimes really beautiful moments, where it does feel like the binary has been broken, or something like that. And we're figuring out room for a bigger community to be in that center. Yeah, but, y'all know what I mean by those conversations? I'm just doing spiral motions with my hand, over and over again.

ADRIAN: So, Philly's Pissed started as a response to a really specific set of situations that happened in a really specific community. I think there were other conversations like that starting around the country, in different communities. But we certainly didn't know the concept of "transformative justice." I'm not sure it existed yet. It was a little bit of restorative justice. There was a vague sense of, using the police is wrong.

So, I think what was said earlier about how this stuff has crept into the language, and the language has changed, was really profound for me to hear, because there was no model. We were making it up. And we made a lot of really clumsy mistakes where now I look back and I'm like, wow, that was embarrassing. [*laughs*] But there are models now, and the language has changed, or become something accessible, and that's partially the Internet a little bit.

And I was thinking also, I do most of my organizing with people who are in prison, so it's completely analog. Like, people who are in prison are not allowed to have access to the Internet. I'm part of publishing a newsletter to facilitate communication among trans people who are incarcerated, and we got a submission from someone that had, like, a content warning—even in those very slow conversations that take place through the mail, this awareness that we want to center and pay attention to the impact of trauma.

But my own trajectory is that we started Philly's Pissed as a response to specific situations, and then there were more situations that were brought to us. And I didn't want to keep doing the work of directly facilitating. I wanted to be doing work training different communities. Cause, like, actually we're onto something kind of useful. And so, that group, I think, fell apart because of tension between let's keep centering ourselves in this work versus let's center these useful ideas and share with other people how to do this instead of inserting ourselves into communities that aren't ours, if that makes any sense.

EJERIS: I have two final questions. What would you like people to learn from your work? And what was hard? What was great?

YALINI: I'd like people to learn/know that another way of being is possible. That we can—as SOS Collective would articulate— prevent, intervene, and address the harm committed against our communities.

What is hard? When folks who have committed harm refuse to take accountability and threaten survivors and their support network with defamation lawsuits or worse. What are survivors' legal recourses in these situations? We still see a lot of backlash by people in power and the outing of survivors who wish to remain anonymous.

What is great: When you are in a community that practices consistent loving feedback, generative conflict, and consistent accountability—accountability, feedback, and conflict can actually be pleasurable as it helps us to become sharper, more loving, magical, and caring people. It also strengthens trust and it feels really good to trust and be trusted.

ALEXIS: I would like people to learn from UBUNTU and the Durham Harm-Free Zone process that we can create structures of change from the vulnerable place of how we harm and have been harmed. I want people to know that the love we find there is so full of insight and energy that it can change the way an entire city organizes. Today, on Election Day, I am thinking about the fact that one of the outcomes of our organizing this past decade plus is that we have an attorney general and district judge and multiple city council members who have actually come out of our movement and are actively moving our city towards abolition, which is something I could have never imagined. A Black lesbian abolitionist attorney general running unopposed today? What? I see this as a direct outcome of us supporting each other to live the words of Audre Lorde and not to allow our fear to silence us. Articulating justice on new terms is having direct impact on the people most impacted by state violence in our communities right now.

What was hard? It was hard to stay with each other when we acted out our harmful survival skills on each other. It was hard to navigate violence and harm in relationships that had been core building blocks of our movement towards each other. When the households that housed our movements harmed each other and fell apart (including mine).

What was great? It was great to open our homes and our arms to each other. It is great to see the generational impact and to be in each other's lives in meaningful ways. It is great to be part of a place so committed to love and so f-ing brave. #durhamforever

JENNA: From the work that Philly Stands Up Collective did, I want people to learn that when harm is perpetrated, people need holding, structures, resources, creativity, process, and ideas. So many of these things have been lovingly created by incredible collectives and community organizations all around North America (and beyond). It can feel overwhelming to respond to harm that happens interpersonally and in community, but linking up with friends, comrades, and neighbors; breaking things into small and digestible steps; and creatively utilizing these resources can really make complex action feel possible. Remember that when we can figure out how to respond to harm, we are moving closer to building worlds outside of violence that we so desperately crave—let's do this with rigor, not dogma; with joy, not rigidity; in community, not in isolation.

What was hard: Sometimes at the end of an accountability process, people don't feel much better. That is painful, confusing, and sometimes heartbreaking to see and witness. Accountability processes don't delete the harm and violence that has been done and the echoes of past acts of violence and repression that ring throughout the bodies of survivors and communities. How can accountability processes effectively make behavioral and institutional change while still centering healing?

What was great: The love our collective had and has for each other. When you do this work in community you are family for life. This love, support, and connection ripples out of just our small collective and connects us to comrades all over the world doing this work—our hearts are beating together.

25

# EVERY MISTAKE I'VE EVER MADE

## AN INTERVIEW WITH SHIRA HASSAN

*Leah Lakshmi Piepzna-Samarasinha*

SHIRA HASSAN IS A NOTORIOUS BADASS IN TRANSFORMATIVE justice work. A former adult ally and codirector of the Young Women's Empowerment Project, Shira got involved in 2002 and remained in leadership alongside the young people who ran the project until 2014, when YWEP closed. (YWEP is, to this day one of the only nonprofit organizations lead by sex-working and street-economy-involved youth that has ever existed.) Shira has been thinking about and practicing TJ for decades. In 2014, she founded Just Practice, a training collaboration inviting people to learn about transformative justice by practicing it. Shira has a huge amount of on-the-ground experience and good sense. In October 2018, over a lush Taurus meal, I asked her some questions about the current and future state of transformative justice.

SHIRA: We have a lot of good politics around TJ right now. What we need now is good practice, and we need people to feel safe to make mistakes. We've created a politics of purity around transformative justice that's making it really difficult for people to just try things. It's setting up this feeling that we can't make mistakes.

But the truth is that every single mistake moves us forward, and that all the conflict that we have is a resource for our next spot, and we have to really figure out how to give ourselves the space to make mistakes. We've created a culture where we're so afraid to make mistakes that we can't practice, because—who would want to?

A purity politic happens when we think that transformative justice has a formula that you're supposed to follow every single time. And when people hear about processes that are happening that don't mirror what they think is the right way, they have the privilege of critiquing that practice, even if that practice is working for people.

Even if that practice really does match the broader philosophy and goals of transformative justice, it just may not—you may just be hung up on a detail that really doesn't have to work in that moment. I feel a lot like it's suggested ingredients in a recipe. There's a lot of components that are part of transformative justice practice. And there are definitely things that should not be. But each time we sit down to do the work, we're going to pull different things from our toolbox. It's not always going to be a circle. It's not always gonna be a freaking three-year-long community accountability process.

LEAH: *Thank God.*

SHIRA: Thank God. But, you know, it can be something else that uses similar ingredients. And then what we have is purity politics coming in and saying, no, it's supposed to be this plus this plus this plus that, or it's *not* transformative justice. It's not the right way to do things. You hear people calling out processes that are going well to the people who are involved with them.

I saw something play out maybe a year and a half ago, where someone who I happened to know had no experience practicing community accountability heard about a process that a friend of mine was doing, where everyone had agreed to do a circle with someone who had caused sexual violence. It was a completely transparent and agreed-upon process that everyone wanted.

This person with zero experience, who had a really amazing analysis around TJ, and talked about TJ all the time on the Internet, had tons and tons of followers, went hard to be like, "you can't have an accountability circle with a sexual predator in the space with the survivor! That is 101, TJ 101! The survivor and the predator should not be in the same space." And like, seriously ranted at the process, which was working, to the point where the survivor then started to question, am I being harmed? Like, are the people who are holding my process harming me?

And then, after multiple check-ins with the survivor and all involved the survivor said, "No, I want to be a part of this process, this is actually what I want." So, the process kept moving forward. And then, the person on the Internet coming back in again to be like, just critiquing from the side with this idea in mind that it wasn't supposed to happen that way, when that was absolutely what was needed for that process.

And thankfully, ultimately, they made an agreement to stay off social media, and keep the process off social media, and everyone agreed to, if they saw anything about the process, to flag it up to the facilitator, but to not, like, jump on it. And that's how they contained it. But it was very painful and sad, because it wound up being a really large thread that impacted lots of people, and the survivor was actually really solid with the process that she was a part of designing.

I started Just Practice because I wanted us to be able to fucking have space to talk about mistakes. I keep saying I'm gonna do this workshop, but I haven't yet, called "Every Mistake I've Ever Made."

LEAH: *Oh God, please do that workshop.*

SHIRA: Yeah, and just bring your mistakes. I share my mistakes all the time, but I feel like some mistakes are mistakes in the moment, but actually work in other situations, and that can be really difficult. Because there is no rulebook. And then, I think, the other thing around mistakes is we need to admit that we're in learning, and if we can stay students, that we can get so much further than saying we're experts. The truth is, there are no experts in this. It doesn't matter how long you've been practicing. The reason we say it's a practice is because you have to keep fucking practicing, and you're gonna make mistakes. There is no expert level, like, you don't get there.

LEAH: *You work with radical social work students around how to bring TJ principles into that work when you're supposed to be a mandated reporter, if somebody discloses abuse?*

SHIRA: Harm reduction has created an opportunity for social workers to stay radical in their practice of social work. So many radical people get into social work because they're already doing the work of being a resource or a support in their community and the letters from the social work degree makes the work sustainable. So, how do we have the conversations about holding to our radical politic when social work makes us complicit with the state so often?

I don't actually think TJ can be practiced in social work, because so much social work is inherently complicit with the state. And that is the difference between TJ and restorative justice, that TJ is inherently outside the state. I think we can use the values of TJ to guide our practice. And, we can turn to RJ [restorative justice] practices, which can be really useful for social workers, who are already complicit with the state. So there's no risk of co-opting the TJ movement—because we can reach for RJ.

A lot of what we talk about is when to reach for RJ because it reduces harm in that system. And then how do we hold our larger values so that we are not in conflict with the radical practice that brought us to social work, but instead like trying to figure out how to stay sustainable in the work, while holding the value of not being complicit with the state.

The dilemma with mandated reporting is that we have mass sexual abuse, and we have mass childhood sexual abuse. And what makes sense is a mass system to address it. And the truth of that mass system is that it doubles down on the violence. And it doubles down on the harm. And the other truth is that we don't have an alternative to it. And so, the problem is that we want to stop what's happening to children, and we want to stop sexual violence. And we're in these roles where the solution is supposed to be making a report. And that report is supposed to make a change that's measurable in someone's life, towards safety. And so much of what we see is that does not happen, or it increases the risk.

So then you have this tension of like, I don't believe in activating the state, but I'm witnessing horrific violence, and I need to take an action that doesn't lead to violence against me as the worker, and that doesn't increase the violence against the people who are being harmed, and so now I'm in this conflict because I don't believe in being complicit with the state, and this is the only solution that I have going, and I need to sit with how I resolve this effectively, but the truth is that there is no effective resolution for that tension.

That tension exists because it's a giant-ass problem that we need more creativity around, and we need that tension to keep us creative. If we were looking at that from just a purity politic point, it would just be "Never participate in mandated reporting." And that keeps people practicing underground the solutions, because it keeps them at higher risk for losing their jobs, because if they're not reporting, then they're very high risk for losing their jobs. And if they are reporting, then they're at very high risk for losing their community, and really what they're trying to figure out how to do is end sexual violence.

LEAH: *And the beat goes on.*

SHIRA: [*laughs*] And the beat goes on.

LEAH: *Thank you for breaking that down, Shira! There are a lot of armchair anarchists who would be like "Don't report, man!" But that leaves out the massive numbers of kids who are being sexually abused, and the person who's just like "I can't not make the fucking call, so how do I harm reduce that, and if they stay here, they could die?"*

*And the People's Court of INCITE: Women of Color Against Violence is not gonna roll up in a bloodmobile and fix things and have a guillotine, it's not gonna happen.*

SHIRA: One thing I'd like us to do more of is have realistic conversations with survivors about what a TJ process can and can't do. I think that another place that this politic has led us is to the idea that TJ can somehow undo a harm, or that the harm can somehow be healed, and that really, unfortunately, those of us who are survivors know that it's an ongoing lifelong process, and what I want a community accountability process to do is set everyone up for the best possible healing, and set everyone up for the best possible transformation. But what I think we do is sell it as something that undoes harm.

LEAH: *It's like if you can go back to before colonialism through TJ.*

SHIRA: Yeah, and this idea, I think, really sells survivors a bill of goods, and it also sets practitioners up to hold, "Can you undo my experience of sexual violence? Can you help me reverse the clock so it feels like this never happened?" And I don't—I wouldn't say it that way. I'd actually like not to say it that way. But this idea of like, for practitioners, but that practitioners can somehow cure it. That practitioners can somehow cure the harm, and really, it's actually about setting us up for the best possible healing that we can give you, so that you have more than we had, to try to get to your next place with a little bit more ease, and a little bit more nourishment, and a little bit more holding. It's like that quote I've seen on the Internet lately: "Trauma creates change you don't choose. Healing is about creating change you do choose." That's, I feel like, what we can offer in a community accountability process: the beginning of healing and a feeling of the power being back in your hands.

And, also, I feel like we can offer people who have caused harm the opportunity to truly be in transformation, and to truly sit with that, and the gift of being accountable. And that is a gift that we deserve, all of us deserve. So, that's one piece.

LEAH: *What are some things you want people to stop doing in TJ?*

SHIRA: There's the thing of everyone thinking all forms of violence are the same, therefore all solutions to violence are the same. And that all the tools that we have are also the same. And they're actually really different, for lots of reasons.

The harm that comes from thinking that stalking is the same as trafficking, or that sex work is the same as trafficking, or that everything is fucking trafficking. Or that sexual harassment and rape are the same. And, like, I think where it gets real tricky, and I think where we're afraid to have these conversations, is that it's so important that everyone is validated in their experience of survival, and that my experience of sexual harassment can dislocate me for years, and that is still different than someone else's experience of childhood sexual abuse.

And just because the healing process is hard doesn't mean that all the violence is the same, and that we need to address that violence differently. There is not a hierarchy in violence, it's just very important that everyone knows that each thing is not the same. I hear a lot of lumping all sexual violence, or all gender-based violence, and that all of it needs a transformative justice process, and I don't know. There are different things that work for different things. A community accountability process is not the same as a transformative justice practice. A transformative justice practice is how we have our own movement security at demos, marches, and rallies. And how we have a bad dates sheet in the sex trade to track fucked-up johns. And how we have what you brilliantly talked about, that was world-changing for me, around community restraining orders.

Those are so different than a community accountability process, which is a long-term transformative piece that involves lots of people working specifically on one thing that happened between two people. And then we have circles, which, now we're like, circling for everything, and circles are really ineffective for certain things.

LEAH: *Like with organized crime, I don't know if a CA process is gonna work.*

SHIRA: A CA process not only would not work, but would increase danger. Like, when the power differential is—you can't have a community accountability process with your abusive boss in a nonprofit. The power differential is too wide. We can use transformative justice practices in those examples. And, we can think about restorative justice, and the ways it is helpfully complicit with the state in order to reduce harm from the state in certain instances.

And then there's mediation, which, everyone thinks a community accountability process is mediation. Or, not everyone, but it's a common misconception that we can somehow mediate an experience of sexual violence. Like, actually, mediation may never have anything to do with it. Mediation is a very specific skill set that I don't have. I do know lots of great mediators. And that's really great for interpersonal conflict. That can be really useful with your abusive boss in a nonprofit.

LEAH: *Where do you want the movement to go? What do you want us to be doing at this moment in time and over the next four years?*

SHIRA: I really want us to move into deep practice. I want us to be students of each other and students of the movement, and students of violence, and students of healing. And I want us to come humble with all of our shit. And figure out what we've tried that works, what we know we can offer, where each of us have a place in this, and where we don't. Where do we need to step back? Are you someone who jumps in at every fight? Are you someone who's completely conflict-avoidant? Maybe that's not community accountability facilitation. Maybe that's another, really valuable style of transformative justice practice that you can help us get to. Who are you in this movement? I want us to be students of ourselves, and to really just sit with all of the possibilities around how we can participate that don't require us to be in the center. Like, people feel like they need to be holding a five-year process, or they don't have enough experience and they're on the sidelines.

LEAH: [*laughs*] *Ten five-year processes.*

SHIRA: Yeah, and I feel pretty sure that most of us have something to contribute, and that we need to be students of what that contribution is. Because we need so many more brains, and so many more minds, and so many more hands on this. There's probably a less ableist way to say that. [*laughs*] Everyone's labor, we need everyone's labor. Not just femme labor, not just women of color labor, not just trans people of color labor, we need everyone's hard work, and we need everyone to be students in this moment. So, that's where I want us to go. And I want us to document those things. Not document them for political analysis purposes, but like, give me your top ten.

Like, what is your top ten most useful things that you've tried? And, tell me, was it specific to your city or your neighborhood? So that we could just start having compilations of the best ten that worked in whatever intersection. Because this has to stay organic. Someone asked me recently about scaling this work, and I don't want it scaled.

And I think that's another politic critique, is that transformative justice can't be scaled. We know that TJ can't be scaled because we know what scaling looks like. It looks like RJ, we've got that. And so, what we need is for as many organic pockets of people who are practicing the work to start documenting it. So that we can understand all the different kinds of intersections. And learn from all those intersections to create a better practice together.

LEAH: *We are in a period of heightened state repression, and we're also in a time where some people are like "OK, this is it, this is really the revolution, let's make the systems we need!" We're already seeing with SESTA [Stop Enabling Sex Traffickers Act] and FOSTA [Fight Online Sex Trafficking Act] the ways in which sex workers have kept themselves safe becoming criminalized. Do you have thoughts about how we continue to be in those organic pockets of people doing TJ in a time where so much of the work we're doing is being repressed?*

SHIRA: Well, I think that's part of why I don't want it to scale. Because I want us to keep a close conversation around it, and I want what works in our community to be smooth enough and practiced enough that even if they repress me, they can't repress what we built. So, I think, part of it is that. And I think, you know, another part of it is like, we need all the practices.

LEAH: *You come from a strong harm-reduction background, which I don't think is true of everybody who does TJ/CA work, and you bring that to your TJ work. Can you speak more about that connection and how it works for you?*

SHIRA: Harm reduction, for me, is such an organic part of my work, that of course it's a part of TJ, and an organic part of me and staying alive. For me, harm reduction is about surviving, and about figuring out how I can—the moment where I can have the most self-determination over whatever the circumstance is that I'm in. And the moment where I can have the most impact in whatever my situation is. I can look for the best possible outcome for something really horrific that happened, and to try to figure out what are—how do I stay self-determined through the whole piece.

The gift that harm reduction has given me has been to be able to really mean self-determination, and to view things on a spectrum and a continuum, and to think about how to hold all of the truths of all of the things that are happening, and to be able to sit with the beautiful mess. TJ is nothing if not sitting with the beautiful mess. And that's what harm reduction is. That's what harm reduction taught me.

I say this a lot in my workshops, if I wasn't the originator of "Kill your rapist" as a slogan, I certainly tried damn hard to act like I was. I put that shit on everything that I had. I sharpied it on my backpack, on my T-shirts, on the bathroom wall. I chalked it everywhere I could. I am a firm believer in the sentiment kill your rapist. And I think that you can be a firm believer in kill your rapist, and still practice transformative justice and community accountability. And that's another tension that has to exist.

And, I think the other truth is like, who's doing the killing, in terms of, you know, this is why Survived and Punished is so necessary. Because like—

LEAH: *Those are people who actually killed their rapists.*

SHIRA: These are people who have fought back, and when women of color fight back, the targeting increases and the state violence increases, and what TJ is trying to do is reduce the harm from state violence and to come up with other solutions.

LEAH: *Is there anything else that you want future generations to know?*

SHIRA: All any one of us who started trying to do TJ was ever talking about was the reality of our lives. And like, transformative justice has to embrace all the intersections of who we are in a real way, and that's why we need so many people to try shit.

I just want people to try shit. Just try something. Write down what worked. Write down what didn't work. And let's just keep moving on. Let's just keep going and collecting it.

## 26

# BE HUMBLE

## AN INTERVIEW WITH MARIAME KABA

*By Ejeris Dixon and Leah Piepzna-Samarasinha*

IT IS CHALLENGING TO DESCRIBE MARIAME KABA'S IMPACT ON transformative justice in a way that does justice to her work and intellect, which are both genius and foundational. Mariame is the founder and director of Project NIA, a grassroots organization with a vision to end youth incarceration, and has cofounded more organizations than can be easily counted—including the Chicago Freedom School, the Chicago Taskforce on Violence against Girls and Young Women, the Chicago Alliance to Free Marissa Alexander, and the Rogers Park Young Women's Action Team (YWAT), as well as Survived and Punished. She is a constant force for innovative, rigorous, and lifesaving transformative justice thought and practice. Ejeris and Leah interviewed her in October 2018.

EJERIS: *How did you get involved with transformative justice work?*

MARIAME: Really, I fell into the work. I was called into the work because of one particular situation that occurred about fifteen years ago. A friend of mine was assaulted by an acquaintance.

My friend wanted to figure out a way to address the assault without bringing in the police or going through the system. It wasn't something I was calling transformative justice. I was just like, how are we gonna resolve this problem? And I just basically created a small team around her, brought in other friends, and we began to talk with her. Like, what's possible here? What would you like? What's the outcome you want to reach? And actually, we were able to come to a resolution that was a good one for her.

So, my first kind of foray into doing this work was actually a good one. It worked out, you know? And I didn't know what I was doing, and I didn't have a plan or any sort of map to guide me at all. I just had my common sense, and my experiences. I had already been doing antiviolence work for a decade before that. So, I had already been doing work on the crisis line, I'd already been doing work on both an antirape and domestic violence line. I had been forty-hour trained, I had other things that I could rely on, to kind of try to figure out how to intervene in violence, not just from an interpersonal sense but a structural sense as well.

When that happened, other people who were in my community heard what happened in my friend's case, and then began to ask me to help other people within our broader community when some things happened. I have never advertised that I do processes. It wasn't until later that I had language that what I was doing was even a transformative justice process.

EJERIS: *People have the benefit of the experience that a lot of us have put in, and many of us—we didn't have the opportunity to go to the Just Practice three-day training when we started, right? So, what's your opinion on training? I'd love to hear your thoughts on that, as someone who's doing a lot of training right now.*

MARIAME: I'm actually hoping not to do more training. One of the reasons we decided to do training was because it was born out of necessity. I was going to move back to New York. I had been living in Chicago for over twenty years. When I was in Chicago, me and Shira were basically two of the people who got called for almost every potential issue that arose that people thought need-ed a process.

When I knew I was leaving, I started talking to Shira about a year before the time that I was moving, and I said to her, you know, when shit goes down, you refer people to me, I refer people to you, but now that I'm leaving the city, you'll be the only one here, and you're going to get many more referrals.

So, we were like, we've gotta have more people. How are we going to do that? Shira already had Just Practice as her consul-tancy. So, we then created the Just Practice collaborative, which had two layers to it. One layer was to actually build a group of folks as a cohort that would be trained to be able to at least have the skills, and more importantly, to have each other, but to be Chicago-specific on that.

And the second layer was that we would work more togeth-er, Shira and myself, to do more intensive mentorship of a small group of people who would basically run the Just Practice collab-orative in Chicago. So, that's how Rachel, and Deana and Keisa, and Ana came on board. To work with us, to do the training, but also so they could be people who could potentially mentor people in order to be able to move this forward.

And again, we were thinking about this as a very intentional, specific geographical intervention. There was never any interest in training beyond Chicago. That was not the goal. We were also, very much at the beginning, saying, this is gonna be a time-lim-ited thing. I'm doing it for a year or two, and then that's gonna be it. Then I'm leaving. That's the point. To leave something be-hind, to leave some capacity. Allow people to take some of this on themselves.

And when we started, Shira and I were like, if we could train enough people to where we have five people we could refer peo-ple to, this would be a massive success. And we've done that. But what happened when we put out the call for training—this is like an Internet age. Shit, we posted on our Facebook pages. We didn't even do a big marketing push. We literally posted it on Twitter and on my Facebook page, because Shira was not even on Facebook any more.

From there, we got people who wanted to come from literally all around the country, and Canada. And we were like, wait a minute. That wasn't what we were trying to do, but given that there's hunger and desire for people who need a workshop and training space, then we'll open it up on a limited basis to more people. We ended up doing these miniseries to try to build a local base of folks. And I just want to add one more thing that Shira would add, which is that part of this was that we had prepped for years before that, before doing the Just Practice collaborative. We were doing one-off trainings in Chicago, so we had a group of people in mind to invite to this new, second 202-level stuff. They'd already gone to like, a CA-101. They'd already gone to the Carceral Feminism 101 and Abolition 101 workshops we'd been running.

I just wanted to put that out on the table because, again, it was not at all—we did not do this to be able to be like, yes, we are TJ experts, and now come to our training so you can learn everything you need to know in order to do this. We are both organizers. We had an organizing strategy for what we wanted to do in Chicago with this work.

LEAH: *I appreciate you laying out both what you did as an organizing strategy and the specific dynamic of "Those are the two people who know what they're doing! Let's work them to death!" [laughter] I'm really intrigued by you saying, "I want to stop doing trainings," and I'm curious what you think should be happening instead.*

MARIAME: I don't think this is a work that is about experts. I want this work to be work that anyone and everyone who wants to try to do it does. And I don't want people to feel like this is work that you have to get some certification in, in order to be able to do. I don't want to contribute to that. To the extent that it's useful for people to have political education together, that's what we are hoping the trainings we've been doing are. That they're in part political education, in part skill building, and also in part base building, so that we actually organize to be able to end these systems that are based in oppression. That oppress us.

So, that's why. I don't want to do, like, the RJ thing, where everybody is now taking circle training, and, as a result of that, they think they know everything they need to know about RJ because they went to the circle training. I don't want to be part of making that for CA [community accountability]. And so, at our trainings, Shira and I consistently say that we are not the experts here. We are gonna share what we've learned from hard-earned actual experience. And we really hope that you remember that this is so context-specific. If there's anything that's true about CA, it is that it's so specific to where you are, who you're working with, what is the harm, all that stuff.

EJERIS: *I think a lot of us started doing TJ before social media was a thing, [laughs] and now we see social media—whether we see TJ being applied to violence that happens online, or we just see social media impacts of it, I would love to hear your thoughts about the place and role of TJ in online communities because I think you know those worlds well, and you've had some guidelines about what you know doesn't work.*

MARIAME: I pretty much hate a lot of social media. I use it as a tool, but I'm not a fan of the way it can flatten people and can flatten issues, and sometimes allows people to remain anonymous in very harmful ways. That said, I've actually tried to think through with other people what are some potential guidelines that we might agree to, some rules of the road around engagement on social media if you're doing community accountability work and transformative justice work. It's a tool for disseminating information about harm, for sure. It's become that. You see people who've posted about their experiences in open letters. You see people posting about their experiences on their Facebook pages. Some of those interactions have thousands of people responding and commenting and putting in their two cents.

Whether those people know anybody involved or not, it allows people to have an opinion. And so, in that way, it is like the interactive equivalent of the bathroom wall. You know, where people put, like, "So-and-so is a rapist," and then you'd come to the bathroom and then there'd be a bunch of comments under that, like, you know, "What is this about?" or "Girl, I see you." This is the equivalent. Except that the bathroom wall was seen by ten people, and now millions of people could see your bathroom.

LEAH: *And the FBI.*

MARIAME: Yes! And the state, and everybody else can see all the stuff happening in real time. And that can be empowering for some people, because it allows them to exert some power to maybe try to force or coerce somebody to respond to what has happened, in a way that they probably couldn't before, especially if there was a power differential there. And, so, all that stuff is going on and is true, and on its face, I think it appears that it could be a positive development in leveling the power differential, because now you have a way to speak back to somebody you don't have access to in other ways. So, that appears that it could be a positive thing.

But sometimes social media also has become a tool to actually harm people. Like, an actual way to get at people, and also sometimes a way to avoid taking accountability for harms that you cause. So, it's a mix of things. And I've been wrestling with how to manage the impacts of social media, both positive and negative, in the processes I've facilitated. So, I want to ask early on, what is our communications plan when we are working together? Do we have agreements as to how and when we're going to use social media and when we might not?

I've been inviting people who are facilitating CA processes to have very intentional communications plans that include what are the actual consequences if people violate these particular things that we've agreed to. Like, what happens if you're somebody who decides, I'm actually not going to abide by these agreements anymore, I'm going to do my own thing and be like a lone ranger or free agent, what does that mean for the whole entire process? Because it is a matter of trust. CA processes at their most basic are about trust. And if you don't have that, if somebody violates that trust, then the whole thing can just collapse upon itself.

I also tell people, especially those of us who are older and didn't come of age in social media land, that people should not be talking about social media and "real life" as though they're distinct. They are not. What is happening online is happening offline, and what is happening offline is happening online. What happens offline bleeds into the online world, and vice versa. I also tell people, don't minimize the effects of social media. Just cause you're not on it doesn't mean shit's not happening that you're just not aware of. And if you're a facilitator, you not knowing information is the death knell of your facilitation ability! If a whole bunch of mess is happening outside of your knowledge, and you're not paying any attention to it, and you're the key coordinator for a process, then you're gonna get blindsided, literally on all sides, when shit is hitting the fan and you are not in touch with that. So, it's just not an option to pretend that there's nothing happening out there.

A few months ago, I posted a series of suggestions on Facebook around how bystanders and/or people who are directly involved in CA processes can be constructive when they see stuff happening online. It was a set of guidelines or suggestions for how they might react, in a way that would be healthier, kinder. Some of the things I talked about there were: Slow down before you post. Take time to think about what justice would actually look like. When you get information, check it out. Don't feel pressured to intervene. Just because something's happening, you don't have to be part of it.

Almost no one asks what the person who's been harmed actually wants, usually they just go off on their own rants about XYZ—but, like, how about the person who was harmed? Like, what do they actually want from this interaction? Do they want you out there slandering people, or yelling at people, or doing whatever? Or do they have other things in mind?

I just always want to remind people that we're all just human. And we're not perfect. And we need to be able to hold ourselves in all our contradictions, and also I do think it's important to be kind. I really do. To me, kindness is a very important value of transformative justice and community accountability work. I want to see how people can operationalize kindness online. It would be good for people to take that as a value from which to work, before launching into things that are about destruction and about vilification, and, you know—the word disposability has been, to me, bastardized, but—all that.

EJERIS: *What are three things or more that you want people to know about TJ. Or, three things you want people to stop doing.*

MARIAME: One thing I would like people to stop doing, is stop thinking that everything needs a process. [*laughs*] There are so many practices that are steeped in restorative justice, that are steeped in conflict mediation and conflict resolution, that are steeped in other modalities for addressing harm. CA processes are specific. They are time-consuming. They take a lot of emotion. They take a lot of resources, energy, and you don't need to be calling for a process for everything.

Sometimes, you need to pick up the phone and call that person and have it out. Sometimes that's what it takes. Sometimes it's a long email apology. Sometimes it's a circle that's a one-off. We need to be able to think through what demands an actual TJ process versus what are interventions that need to be had because of conflict, right? Abuse, conflict. These things need to be really clearly laid out for folks.

We also have to stop acting like saying that somebody can't be in a space is disposing of them. First and foremost, asking someone who has caused harm not to be in a space, particularly where the survivor would be, is actually a consequence of the action that they took that was harmful. It's a consequence. It is not a punishment. A punishment would be taking this person's liberty and locking them in a cage for three years, or a month, or ten days, because of the actions that they took. We are not taking people's liberty through CA. We are just not.

The idea of disposability in my mind is an idea that applies to the *prison-industrial complex.* OK? That's it. It is not boundaries. It is not a sense of *you are not allowed to do this here.* It is not, you know, people say things like, "You can't ban people." Well, yes we can. If folks do the same thing over and over and over again, and refuse to take accountability for that, and don't want to learn, they can actually be banned from a particular space.

We do have to figure out the other side of that. Which is, somebody does take accountability, and does what people asked them to do. When are they allowed to rejoin community in good standing? That is something we have yet to figure out how to do in consistent fashion. Because you're not gonna be able to say to somebody, "You can never come back to society," and expect those people to join accountability processes. Why would anybody do that?

What currently exists in our culture that makes it possible for people to take accountability and think they actually will be able to—not clear their name, because that's not what we're in the business of trying to do—but, to actually be able to be in a position where they can rejoin our community in good standing, because they have done XYZ that people have asked of them?

LEAH: *You've been doing this for over fifteen years. What are some of your most valuable lessons that you'd want to share?*

MARIAME: Every time I take on a new process, I feel like I'm starting anew. I feel like, while I have a crutch that is years of work, and some things I've learned through that, I do always feel a sense of, like, this is new again. I don't know what I'm doing. Now I'm not so confused about how to start. I know how to start, you know what I mean? And I know how to end. [*laughs*] And I think that the middle part is the one that I'm always negotiating what all that looks like.

Some of the other things I've learned are that we have to embrace the messiness of process. The messiness is inherent. It will always be there. And by messy, I mean that there are multiple U-turns that are happening all the time, that people are sometimes their best selves and sometimes not, that we move forward in some places and backwards in another, and that all this stuff is actually part of the work.

For years, I've heard people say things like, "TJ didn't work!" And I don't understand what that means. Because, even in worst processes I've ever heard of people being a part of, something was learned in that process. Something got taken away, even if it was, these people don't know what the hell they're doing, and I don't like it, and I don't want this. Right? Bench Ansfield and, I think it was Jenna Peters-Golden, wrote a piece years ago in *make/shift* that was all about the failure. Embracing failure and eschewing success in TJ processes. I love that. I use that in training. It just tells you, breathe.

We get caught up in trying to succeed in the nonprofit-industrial complex version of it. And what we did was actually lose sight of the small shifts and the small changes that were occurring that we should still document and hold onto. I think I learned about messiness of processes and eschewing a success/failure binary, and embracing more of the gray.

I've never posited TJ as, quote, "the antidote" to the PIC [prison-industrial complex]. For me, TJ is a way to do the work that needs to happen to make sure that we're transforming our relationships with each other because, ultimately, I hope that this helps foster the conditions necessary for a world without these horrific death-making institutions that I want to see dismantled. I see it as a framework that allows for the transformation of relationships between us when we cause harm. I know for a fact that we can't heal or hurt alone. We must heal or hurt in relationship with other people.

Every time you want to talk about the why, and you want to talk about the reason we need to do it is for all these things, right? The how is always that thing that we get stuck on. Over the years, I've gotten really distressed about the attempt to say that RJ is the alternative to the PIC or TJ is the alternative to the PIC. No, it's not actually *the* alternative. It isn't at all. It is an ideology, a framework, a political vision, a practice. All those things are true, and it's simply a way to shift and transform our relationships to allow us to build the conditions under which we will no longer need prisons and surveillance and policing, and all these other things that are part of the PIC that we, as abolitionists, want to dismantle.

Part of the problem of positing a, quote, "alternative" to the PIC is that it is impossible. What is the alternative to oppression? Do you know what I mean? Like, think about that, as an institution. What is the alternative to exploitation? Like, yes, we don't want to exploit people! That's the alternative. But that's not an institution. Plus, the other thing about the alternative language is that it sets up this weird binary, whereby you now have the PIC as it stands, this horrific set of forces, institutions, etcetera. Ideas that are death-making. And now I have to come up with the alternative to that system. Part of the problem with the prison, for example, is that it treats harms uniformly. We want to get away from that.

So we get trapped in the notion of holding onto all these things and saying, "Now we gotta have something else." Well, something different or the opposite of. That's not how this shit works at all. So I would like people to stop thinking and offering and positing IJ as, quote, "the alternative" to the PIC. It is not. That is not what it is. And we would all be better off if we just did not think about it in that way.

EJERIS: *What have you noticed that's changed in your practice over time?*

MARIAME: One thing is that more people want to do processes. It's the popularization of the work we've done. That people now— they think they know what TJ/CA is, and they want it. In terms of changes in the landscape, I've seen that.

I started off thinking I would get better, that I would become expert at the work if I practiced enough. I would, like, have some shit down pat. And it turns out, no, I'm still making mistakes. I'm still having to clean up my own messes. I'm still having to clean up messes that other people have made. I've stopped trying to achieve mastery. And, if you know me as a person, people will know that that's very hard for me.

EJERIS: *I've been thinking a lot about how this work changes us. And I think I was noticing it in the ways that I connect to other people who've been in TJ for a while. Like, there's a tenderness that I connect with folks with. So, how has the work transformed you? What has happened inside of you in doing this work?*

MARIAME: It is absolutely true that I am more empathetic as a result of doing this work. I'm more empathetic and I'm much more patient. Before I started doing this work, I would say that I, you know, I had empathy for various people, but I don't think I was an empathetic person. I've also gotten much less judgmental. It is absolutely true that people who harm people were also harmed. I know people sometimes don't want to hear that. I know that makes people mad, people feel like that's an excuse, whatever. But I, with every fiber of my being, the both/and harm and survivorship really sits with me all the time.

Cause there's not one person I've worked with who harmed other people that was not also deeply and profoundly harmed themselves in some other context. So, it just makes me much more patient, it makes me much more empathetic, and it just gives me the real understanding that we have to live with the complexity of how harm plays itself out in ourselves, in our community, and in our world.

EJERIS: *There's a lot of folks who hate their process. Or, you know, the process fails. When a process has, quote-unquote, "failed," are there things that you think about if people are asking you to help them with their process that is not going well?*

MARIAME: Well, I'm surprised at how few people actually have goals set before they launched into anything. Like, I don't understand how you cannot have goals. [*laughs*] I see so much of the problem of "failed processes" having to do with not actually having any goals, or that the goals themselves were set in a way that was absolutely unachievable from the beginning. Like, you would not be able to actually meet the goals. And it should be limited goals, because that's all you can do. For example, like, transformation is not a realistic goal within a process. It *is* a realistic goal within a lifetime. I also think a lot about timing as a major contributor to failure. When are you having this process? Are you having this process while the crisis is actually still ongoing in a very severe way? This is not a good time. Crisis intervention is its own thing, OK? It is not process time when you're in crisis intervention mode.

Another thing is people who never ever assess their own capacity to hold this shit down. I mean, if you're gonna do this, it's gonna take a while. You're going to be putting in a lot of energy. You aren't going to get paid. Critically important. [*laughs*] There will be no money coming to you. It's not a job. Those are things that I see happening in the processes that I'm getting called into last-minute to fix. And I'm like, this can't be fixed, y'all have so much water under the bridge, don't call me now. It's way, way too late.

LEAH: *If someone is brand new to attempting any kind of CA/TJ thing, what are some hot tips, where you're just like, don't do that, or know this will happen?*

MARIAME: I think it goes back to the point that I made which is, you know, self-assessment is key. Ask yourself a few questions before you jump in. Critically important. I think that people should figure out what the end is before you start. Things are gonna change all along the way, but I like to know, when I take on a process, what I think the end is gonna look like. Cause the thing that I think I got lost in early on was the endless time. And I think that isn't helpful.

Leah, your work does suggest doing slow work. It's important, and it is also much more in line with disability justice. But there can be a contradiction in slow work too because I think the longer processes go, the more likely it is that there's gonna be no end that people will be satisfied with. So, it's a tension like everything else is, but it's like, can you see the end of this, as the person who's holding it down as the main facilitator? If you can't, it's good to try to figure that out, before you jump in or early in the process at least, so you're not taking something on for seven years. Sometimes, seven years might be needed, but I don't think so. [*laughs*] I think we've gotta start thinking about timing in that way as well. Like, where does this stuff end?

And finally, just, you know, be humble as hell. Get your ego out of it. Be humble.

# 27

# EXCERPT FROM "MOVING BEYOND CRITIQUE"

*Mimi Kim*

IN THE SUMMER OF 2006, A DRUMMING TEACHER FROM SOUTH Korea was invited to teach a week-long intensive drumming workshop at a Korean cultural community center in Oakland, California.[1] He was a teacher within a well-respected tradition of drumming associated with village life and radical antistate politics in Korea. Trusted ties with this Korean institution had been woven through Korean American pilgrimages to the Korean village home and invitations to teachers to visit various drum groups throughout the United States.

After an evening of singing, storytelling, and drinking—the usual festivities accompanying a full day of intensive drumming instruction—several students stayed the night to rest and recover for the next day. For over two decades, the cultural center had developed a safe, multigender, and intergenerational space and haven for the teaching of Korean drumming and dance, community performance, and ongoing cultural and political exchange

---

1   Excerpted from Mimi E. Kim, "Community Accountability: Emerging Movements to Transform Violence" *Social Justice* vol. 37, no. 4, 2010.

between the home country and the diaspora. That night, this safety was shattered when the drumming teacher sexually assaulted one of his students.

The violation was immediately communicated throughout the small building, and center leaders quickly pulled together a direct confrontation involving the members and their community-led board. The next day, members gathered at the center to denounce the violation and support the victim of violence. In this situation, the victim steadfastly refused to name herself as a "survivor," finding the former term a closer match to her experience of sexual violence.

Liz, the president of the Oakland cultural center at the time of the assault, recollects the next day's encounter:

> When we got there, the teacher got on his knees and knelt in front of us, which is the deepest sign of respect. And then he asked us, begged us, not to tell his organization back home. We said we couldn't do that. "We're not here for your apology. We're here to tell you what happened, what we're going to do, and that's it." He made a big sign of remorse, taking his drumming stick and breaking it. He put it on the ground like "I'll give up drumming for this." Most of us were disgusted.

What followed was a set of sexual assault awareness workshops for center members and members of other affiliated drumming groups. An immediate telephone call to the head of the Korean drumming institution elicited the leader's profound shock and unconditional apology. Then a letter with a list of demands was sent. The Oakland organization demanded that the Korean institution establish sexual assault awareness trainings for its entire membership, which ranged from college students to elder farmers in the village, and commit to sending at least one woman teacher in future exchanges to the United States. They requested that the teacher who had committed the assault step down from his leadership position for an initial period of six months and attend feminist therapy sessions that directly addressed the assault. The traditional relationship of deference to esteemed teachers and the teaching institution shifted as the Oakland organization challenged the familiar practice of sexual harassment and violation. The organization also contacted a sister progressive drumming group in Seoul.

The group in Seoul had dealt with sexual assault in a manner that reflected its deeply democratic values. Its one hundred members were collectively organized to address a sexual assault that had occurred among the membership. The person who had committed the violation went through an extensive process with the group's leaders and members. After leaving the organization, he posted a public apology on its website and retained relationships with drumming group members.

Inspired by this story of collective action and its concrete results, the Oakland organization implemented measures that reversed the usual silence and victim-blaming that accompany sexual assault. The annual October festival was dedicated to the theme of healing from sexual violence.

Facts regarding the incident were published in the program and shared as a part of the evening's festival. This was not intended as a shaming act, although the teacher may have been shamed by it. Rather, it was a challenge to the community to take collective responsibility for ending the conditions that perpetuate violence, including collusion through silence.

This story reveals painful lessons about community violence and the limitations of our community-led processes. The Korean cultural center came together with a unified response to violence, but grew divided as the process continued. During the drawn-out period of institutional reflection and engagement, the energy and spirit of the organization, as well as the friendships that had held it together, were sapped. The victim never returned. Korean American visitors who participated in drumming events in South Korea viewed the continued presence of the teacher with resentment and suspicion. His eventual removal from the institution did not necessarily lead to the sense of justice that people desired.

Liz, the center's president, reflected further on this set of events and on the uncertainties accompanying the process of community accountability:

Some people asked us later why we didn't call the police. It was not even a thought in anybody's mind. I know that a couple of folks—her close friends—tried to break in, to kick his ass, but they couldn't find him. Luckily they didn't. Luckily for him and the organization, too, because I think if they had, [it] would have been a … mess. Well, I don't want to say luckily because the victim even felt at some point, "maybe we should've just kicked his ass. Now, I feel like I've got nothing. I don't have the police report. We didn't throw him into jail. We didn't do nothing."

We talked to her and said, "We didn't move forward on anything without your consent." We asked, "What else can we offer you?" We offered her to go to counseling and therapy. We offered her whatever we could do at the time. In retrospect, I wish we could have spent more time to just embrace her and bring her in closer.

This story explores the role of force and violence, as well as our response to violence. Despair over a long and complex process of accountability spurred discussions among the members of the Oakland organization about the potential benefits of violent retribution. Liz reflected on a member's insightful remark as they pondered the expedience of violence: "That's what the teacher wanted. He wanted that. When he was making that apology, he wasn't necessarily saying 'beat me up.' But he was saying, 'do anything you want to me, I deserve it.' That way, once you do, he can walk away and say, 'Okay, now I'm done, wipe my hands and walk away. They've done everything they can already.'" Some may fear a violent response most, but some could also welcome a quick but dramatically symbolic payback. "Kicking ass," a familiar symbol of community rage, can also be a substitute for a process of repair and change.

# CREATIVE INTERVENTIONS
## MOVING BEYOND CRITIQUE

While this story was unfolding, Creative Interventions (CI) was already underway. Inspired by a social movement that challenged gender-based violence—and that had been infused with new life at the historic 2000 Color of Violence Conference in Santa Cruz and the 1998 Critical Resistance Conference in Berkeley—many of us fashioned a critique of institutional responses to violence and then moved beyond it to establish new institutional spaces for creating and promoting community-based responses to interpersonal violence.

These conferences critiqued the network of remedies to domestic violence and sexual assault. Made up of crisis lines, counseling centers, legal advocacy programs, and a system of criminal-legal responses to gender-based violence, it took an individualized, social service approach toward survivor support and a policing response to people who perpetrate violence.

The establishment of Creative Interventions in 2004 was driven as much by disappointment in the failure of progressive communities to challenge violence within our own networks as by the positive mandates of a newly energized antiviolence movement. To populate the void of alternatives with more thoughtful and pragmatic models, tools, and examples of what might constitute community-based responses to violence, CI organized its activities around projects that aimed to build knowledge and practices in what appeared to be a vast unknown.

# REDISCOVERING COMMUNITY
# ACCOUNTABILITY THROUGH STORYTELLING

CI hoped to fill that void through two projects. Liz's story of sexual violence in the Korean community was collected and shared through the StoryTelling and Organizing Project (STOP), or what was originally known as the National Story Collecting Project.[2]

---

2   Rachel Herzing and Isaac Ontiveros, "Making Our Stories Matter: The

This project collects and documents community accountability stories, presenting them as alternative sources of knowledge to inform communities about what people did, how they carried out interventions, and the lessons they provided. The process of story collection, documentation, and listening is also a vehicle for organizing communities to generate action and stories that build upon each other and strengthen their capacity to challenge interpersonal and state violence.

Liz's story inspired others to imagine what a community effort could look like and showed that communities could overcome traditions of silent acceptance of gender-based violence, form a public response, and demand institutional change. This story, and many others published by STOP, clarified promises and quandaries that would later characterize CI's on-the-ground efforts to develop a model and tools capable of supporting community-based interventions to violence through its pilot project, the Community-Based Interventions Project. This story inspired others to move beyond rhetoric. Communities could transcend silent acceptance, build on connections across diaspora to offer solidarity, and learn from the concrete lessons of other organizations. This is one story among many that fueled the second project of CI.

## RECONSTRUCTING COMMUNITY ACCOUNTABILITY PRACTICES

The Community-Based Interventions Project is a pilot study that set out to develop a model and set of tools to be used by family, friends, coworkers, and community members to intervene in interpersonal violence.[3] Although it focused on gender-based vi-

StoryTelling and Organizing Project," in *The Revolution Starts at Home: Confronting Intimate Violence within Activist Communities*, ed. Ching-in Chen, Jai Dulani, and Leah Lakshmi Piepzna-Samarasinha (Brooklyn: South End, 2011), 207–16.

3   Mimi Kim, "Alternative Interventions to Intimate Violence: Defining Political and Pragmatic Challenges," in *Restorative Justice and Violence against Women*, ed. J. Ptacek (New York: Oxford University Press, 2010), 193–217.

olence, including domestic violence and sexual assault, the application was germane to other forms of interpersonal violence. CI and four other primarily immigrant-based domestic violence and sexual assault programs in the San Francisco Bay Area designed it as a collaborative project.[4] Intervention team members met regarding twenty-three situations of violence and worked directly with over one hundred people engaged in violence intervention. The team was made up of seven regular members and one additional evaluator who was a long-time antiviolence advocate committed to progressive politics. All members are people of color. Unlike many conventional violence intervention teams, this group consists of people with extensive experience with survivors of gender-based violence and others who were working with people doing harm (two of them had done harm themselves).

It was critical for an organization established by people who identified with survivors to include others who had substantial experience with and commitment to working with those who had done harm. The project valued and openly discussed the inclusion of intervention team members who identified as having done harm and were actively practicing accountability through their personal and work lives. This mix of experience and orientations contributed to the creation of a multidimensional approach to violence intervention that was committed to "holism"—the consideration of multiple perspectives, including those of survivors, community allies, and people doing harm, in the process.

---

4   The four Bay Area organizations include Asian Women's Shelter, a battered women's shelter targeting Asian immigrant and refugee women and children; Shimtuh, a Korean domestic violence and sexual assault program that is a project of the Korean Community Center of the East Bay; Narika, a domestic violence advocacy organization serving the South Asian community; and La Clinica de la Raza, a Latino health organization that offers domestic violence services and organizing. Intervention team members include Sutapa Balaji, Leo Bruenn, Juan Cuba, Rachel Herzing, Isabel Kang, Mimi Kim, and Orchid Pusey.

## THE CONSTRAINTS OF THE 5Ø1(C)(3)

The tensions between the nonprofit organizational form and a project promoting nonreliance on professionalized institutions led to innovations and contradictions. During the pilot period and beyond, community members and organizational partners viewed CI as an institution with "expertise." As people in crisis turned to CI for support, the personnel who developed the facilitated model inevitably played an active, central role in interventions as facilitators. Since the model and tools never became available in an external form to supplement the questions developed by intervention teams, we were never able to fully test the viability of the approach outside CI.

As an intervention team, we regularly questioned whether our role could be replicated outside our organization. Could a person who is simply a particularly skilled and sensitive member of one's own family, friendship network, or community assume the position of facilitator, supported by a CI toolkit and other resources? Was the toolkit sufficiently accessible and informative to lead to successful interventions on the scale we intended? Would facilitators need additional orientations, training, and ongoing support? If so, how could this be provided without the existence of CI or a similar institution? And how could we offer lessons and guidance without reproducing the errors of prescription and continued reliance on professionalized experts?

## THE PROBLEM OF SUSTAINABILITY

Many people came to CI after their own interventions had faltered. Burnout was a common problem for groups that after many hours and mounting disagreements appeared to have accomplished little. Perhaps a more fully developed model and tools could have prevented that result or generated a sufficient degree of success. Groups lacking full unity concerning goals and bottom lines tended to blame each other because of differing and unstated assumptions regarding what was to be done and how it was to be done. People often felt compelled to follow the lead of the survivor. Survivors, however, were reluctant at times to assume the burden of this role, while others sensed they had insufficient information about the details of violence to make appropriate decisions. Fear of disappointing or betraying a survivor could lead to group paralysis.

Sometimes groups that had been organized by a survivor of violence came to differ with that person's wishes or became frustrated by changes the survivor underwent during a course of action. For survivors still actively engaged with those who had caused them harm, emotions could be confusing as they experienced fear, guilt, and anger. Consequently, antiviolence interventions could produce unstable results and even disintegrate.

## ENGAGING THE PERSON DOING HARM

Relationships with the person doing harm and that person's willingness to engage in an intervention varied greatly. Some survivors did want to confront that person directly. But this model relies on leveraging relationships and community connections as a context for change for the person doing harm. CI therefore endeavored not to make the survivor solely responsible for changing the person who had caused harm, nor to individualize the burden and threat to safety. Beyond the limited options available in the community, CI did not offer substantial support to change people doing harm. Adequate resources for engaging the person doing harm were thus difficult to marshal.

Collective members who were willing to intervene with a person doing harm faced a number of challenges. Awkwardness with friends emerged as relationships of support or shared interests were overtaken by what could feel like the burdens of violence intervention.

Sometimes, those supporting the person doing harm developed a growing sympathy as they witnessed the distress accompanying an intervention or heard "their side of the story." Other friendships or alliances became strained, for they did not wish to remain engaged with a person who had committed harm or to be associated with someone who was publicly known as having done harm. This was rooted in their disappointment with that person and the desire to distance themselves from the responsibilities of intervention. Such engagement with the person doing harm, in CI's experience, never led to violence or serious acts of retaliation. But that certainly could happen. A person doing harm with access to more resources than the survivor—including popularity or standing in the community—could gain considerable sympathy as compared to the survivor of violence.

Many people involved with CI explored various ways in which they and their allies could approach the person doing harm. Often, however, they declined. Fear, lack of adequate leverage with the person doing harm, and the absence of the planning and strategizing needed to sustain a long-term engagement prevented many people from pursuing these options. Those who did become engaged were banned from community events and received requests for public apologies, along with expectations that disclosure of past harms would be broadcast for interminable periods. Indeed, the terms under which the slippery notion of accountability would be satisfied remain an open question.

## EXPLORING ALL OPTIONS, ENGAGING ALL STAKEHOLDERS

During the pilot period, CI did provide an alternative space for violence intervention. Some participants disclosed during evaluation interviews that they were satisfied to find an option that was not otherwise available. For survivors of violence, it offered a space to fully consider a range of options that neither condemned nor questioned their desire to remain in relationships with people who had harmed them. It also encouraged them to bring allies into a supportive space, which cannot be underestimated. For others, the ability to explore and work through goals that might include fantasies of retribution or redemption helped to distinguish realistic objectives from hopes. Indeed, this exercise proved to be an important step in goal setting. CI's approach differed from the way in which intervention team members with considerable experience had previously led sessions in conventional antiviolence settings.

Ambivalence over intimate relationships that were also harmful was held within the space and entered into different goals and strategies. This also provided a rare space for allies to fully explore the impact of violence on their lives, to identify appropriate roles in confronting violence, and to break the sense of isolation as they recruited others to play active roles. Allies could express their ambivalence and mixed loyalties toward the survivor and the person doing harm, and move toward greater clarity. When groups working on interventions experienced tensions among themselves, a facilitated space made it possible to name and resolve those tensions.

Disagreements among allies leading to breakdowns in the intervention were not uncommon. Mediation was necessary in these cases, and it also took place between survivors and allies to reduce tensions and conflicts. The CI model, however, did not mediate between survivors and the person or people doing harm. CI's approach was consistent with other critiques of the role of mediation in violence interventions, such as that of some "restorative justice" models. As such, mediation assumes an equal level of power among parties and is not used whenever there is risk of retaliation or some other form of harm if the process goes awry.[5] An exchange of information during mediation could potentially be used to inflict further harm on the survivor. Thus, CI accepted the conventional dichotomous view of the survivor and the person doing harm as a caution against the use of mediation.

Among those in pilot interventions were people involved in various intimate relationships: heterosexual, same-gender, and gender-nonconforming. Some came from situations of family or community violence. In CI's experience, violence within heterosexual relationships followed the pattern of a male inflicting harm on a female survivor. Within CI intervention teams, tensions

---

5   Ruth Busch and Stephen Hooper, "Domestic Violence and Restorative Justice Practices: The Risk of a New Panacea," *Waikato Law Journal* 4, no. 1 (1996): 101–30.

arose regarding the centrality and expression of gender analysis during an intervention. I normally assumed a gender binary and embraced the doctrine of "believing the victim," particularly when that person was a woman within a heterosexual dynamic of violence. My inability to suspend these assumptions revealed my own internal challenges, as well as those within the intervention team. Should we fundamentally question rather than assume the ways in which gender will play out in a dynamic of violence? Questioning the validity of this form of gender analysis, among other concerns, created discomfort. Some CI facilitators considered analysis to be less important to their role than helping participants explore their own perceptions about the dynamics of violence and intervention. In this pilot project, the organization's personnel, rather than people more organically linked to a community, occupied the role of facilitator. This exacerbated dilemmas regarding how gender analysis, or any other analysis of power based on race, class, sexuality, age, ability/disability, or immigrant status, applied to the intervention.

At times, CI interventions involved people with whom we share community. Our own personal situations of violence were brought to the team to facilitate our own interventions. These situations were personally useful and tested the validity of the model. They answered the underlying question driving the CI project of whether the model would be a helpful alternative in our own lives. Thus, the model and tools derived from our personal experiences.

## THE GENDER BINARY AND THE VICTIM-PERPETRATOR DICHOTOMY

Accepting a gender binary or even a conventional dichotomy between the survivor and the person doing harm did not preclude us from understanding and supporting processes that had the potential to challenge survivors, particularly as they concerned allies involved in violence intervention. The intervention team discussed the possibility of creating more opportunities to challenge survivors to articulate how they may have contributed to the dynamics of violence within their relationships. We sought to understand how people could be challenged regarding the ways in which they carry out an intervention. Of course, creating such opportunities can easily cross the line into victim-blaming or become a dangerous distraction from the process of accountability. Indeed, these dynamics are disturbingly common. CI was not particularly successful in proposing constructive ways to challenge survivors. The resulting model and tools build in more opportunities for identifying and negotiating difference and for increasing trust within the group. They should guide interventions that are aligned with more liberatory values and principles, thereby reducing the possibility that the intervention itself might produce further harm.

In CI's approach, the person doing harm might initiate an intervention or eventually join one as a partner, as opposed to merely being its target. During the pilot period, this idealized vision was rarely achieved. Indeed, internal struggles constrained our advances and limited our capacity regarding the extent to which CI would work directly with these individuals. Some members of CI, faced with an internal plan specifically geared to establishing a group for people doing harm, raised objections since it could clash with the widespread, community-based interventions we envisioned. A separate component for people doing harm was thought to violate our principle of holism because it would artificially focus on people doing harm rather than provide a more integrated model of change. CI was split over these issues. Given the inability to reach a consensus on this aspect of the project, it was never carried out. By the end of the pilot period, therefore, we did not gain adequate information to assess how a community-based model could shift the people doing harm from being targets of intervention to being partners.

## UNPACKING THE ACCOUNTABILITY PROCESS

CI's experiences offer a better understanding of how variations in relationships within which violence occurs and differences in desired outcomes can lead to better-defined intervention strategies. Clarifying whether violence occurred in close and intimate relationships, among acquaintances, or among strangers can help to determine what leverage toward change is available in the community. A better articulation of goals is possible if it is known whether desired outcomes include hopes for ongoing closeness or intimacy, coexistence within overlapping community spaces, or complete separation.

Finally, CI envisioned accountability as a series of steps or stages that could help to guide goals and next steps. These markers are useful even if they are not ultimately reached. Since we always anticipate resistance to challenges to violence, particularly from the person or people doing harm, accountability is best considered as a process of change. No matter how open those doing harm might be when first confronted with demands for change, resistance soon follows.

Understanding the commonality of this dynamic flowed from our own reactions when being confronted about our harmful attitudes and actions. The usual tactics of denial, minimization, and blaming others, including a focus on perceived injustices in the act of intervention, seemed likely. How can community processes embrace resistance as part of an intervention rather than as evidence of failure?

## THE LEGITIMACY OF AUTHORITY, FORCE, COERCION, AND VIOLENCE

Fundamental to a process of accountability is the reduction of violence or threats of retaliation to the point that deeper levels of change can be considered. Given that some form of "confrontation" and a tendency to resist change are inevitable in situations of accountability, CI had to contend with questions regarding the ethics and efficacy of community-based authority, force, coercion, and even violence or the threat of violence.

Members of the antiviolence movement understandably had a weak grasp of the violent dimension of power, but were open to grappling with its complexities. CI's open stance on the issue was indicated by its self-description as an anti-oppression (rather than explicitly antiviolence) organization. There was keen interest in STOP project stories for what they could impart regarding the use of force or violence in community accountability.

We set a low threshold for authority, force, and coercion. Those undertaking community accountability processes often claimed to disavow these forms of power, but exercised them nonetheless. Asserting righteousness or the moral high ground often obscured the fact that some level of force was being used. Elements of coercion reside even in requests for someone to listen to our account of violence, come to a meeting, or read a list of demands—no matter how gently or civilly they are made. Transparency over the assertive use of power and the potential consequences of noncompliance were important first steps in articulating principles and practices regarding their legitimate use.

We also challenged a problematic position within the conventional antiviolence movement that tends to value and profess nonhierarchical or nonauthoritarian structures of power, survivor-centeredness as a reversal of survivor disempowerment and victimization, and nonviolent tactics. Yet authoritarian relationships are often embedded within the rules, regulations, and decision-making structures of antiviolence institutions; survivor-centeredness is often trumped by the assumptions and narrow array of options offered by the antiviolence advocate; and a disavowal of violence ultimately cedes it to the criminal justice system, which the movement upholds by relying on criminal legal remedies.

By shifting the site of intervention from the criminal justice system and conventional antiviolence institutions back to community spaces, CI turned to reclaiming authority within these locations. Community resources can include newly mobilized sites of authority among those formerly denied access to power.

A group of women friends, for example, can decide to organize on behalf of an abused peer. Community-based interventions also rely on traditional authorities such as patriarchal leaders, from fathers, uncles, and clergy to community elders. Although it was preferable to mobilize formerly marginalized sites of authority, it was often practical and effective to rely on preexisting forms of authority. Ultimately, these community resources, especially active participants in education or prevention campaigns, or in direct interventions against violence, offer an alternative to conventional antiviolence remedies.

Finally, the use of force, coercion, or violence as part of the accountability process became an open question. Deception is also closely aligned with these tactics. STOP's stories provided examples of how these tactics were actively used in community-based interventions to violence. A liberatory process, however, questions the legitimacy of subterfuge and force.

Institutional concerns also existed. As the opening story suggests, organizations like CI may consider liability, public reputation, and organizational sustainability when formulating tactics that may establish an institutional precedent that promotes violence and could easily lead to civil or criminal charges. Informal community formations may tend to threaten or actually resort to violence. Ethical concerns and risks did not escape these locations of intervention, but their operations tended to be less public. Some participants sought assistance to prevent friends or family from engaging in violent retaliation, for that course of action could lead to their arrest. They sought community accountability strategies that would avoid further violence and the possible involvement of law enforcement.

CI's community accountability practices relied less on coercion and punishment and more on compassionate engagement. Our liberatory community accountability process sought to mobilize all parties, including the person doing harm, with the view that such processes served their interests. Instead of appealing to a fear of consequences, community accountability appeals to higher values and aligns self-interest with the collective good. In CI's limited experience, liberatory goals were required to guide the process, since pragmatism could lead to the use of coercion or threatened or real violence as temporary measures for assuring the stability and safety needed to make further steps possible. However, the pervasiveness of punishment as a model for accountability and the association of the term "accountability" with retribution contributed to difficulties in moving beyond this mode of engagement. Thus, a practice such as banning, which makes a modicum of safety possible while mobilizing for a more engaged process, can become an end rather than a means.

Even the unintended assumption of a criminalization paradigm can cause those doing harm and those protecting them to resist the process. Banning, even for temporary safety, may be resisted. In response, those initiating an accountability process may strengthen their resolve to make enforcement of a ban the goal rather than one measure within a more engaged process.

## PUBLIC DISCLOSURE AND NAVIGATION BEYOND SHAME AND PUNISHMENT

Another aspect of community accountability is its collective public nature. Participants in conventional antiviolence remedies regularly disclose information to staff or others working within the antiviolence institution, but strict protocols regarding confidentiality beyond organizational walls reinforce public silence. CI's organizational interests unwittingly led to a somewhat contradictory position toward public disclosure. Its STOP project promoted public openness regarding violence and violence intervention. During the formative stages of STOP, we developed a protocol to balance safety and privacy considerations with the public's need to be informed. In its Community-Based Interventions Project, CI protected confidentiality while encouraging thoughtful public disclosure on the part of participants. Perhaps impeding the disclosure process was CI's institutional position as an intervention's facilitator, rather than an organic participant.

CI's liberatory stance concerning public disclosure was complicated by the fact that violence in the community context remains associated with shame. Disclosure can assume the form of gossip, and public information can reveal large, misleading gaps as those involved in the violence tire of sharing details. Survivors and those doing harm can easily confuse disclosure with punishment in communities that view interpersonal violence through the lens of denial and shame.

Communities contending with pervasive violence may resort to a process of public disclosure to curb it. For people doing harm, it can help to compel compliance with processes of accountability. Survivors and communities often expect people doing harm to engage in public disclosure as part of the process of being accountable. Yet how much to disclose, for how long, and to whom were questions not easily answered.

## CREATING CONDITIONS TO SUPPORT COMMUNITY ACCOUNTABILITY

Community accountability rests on a shaky foundation if it fails to support compassionate and collective responses to violence and if it associates accountability with the logic of criminalization. The principles of community accountability, community-based responses, and transformative justice can quickly slide into paralysis, collusion, or vengeance as the conditions for healthy, functioning communities weaken under the stresses of daily living and the systemic strains of neoliberalism, with its multiple forms of violence. Thus, the small and large successes of new social movement forces in articulating guiding principles, viable processes, and practices leading to lasting outcomes may interrupt violence and create the conditions necessary for strengthening liberatory community spaces.

## WHERE DO WE GO FROM HERE?

CI's efforts are part of a larger social movement project to challenge the persistence of heteropatriarchy and white supremacy in our communities and to displace the criminalization paradigm that emerged in response to interpersonal violence over the last forty years. The community-based approach to violence intervention—more familiarly known as community accountability or transformative justice—looks forward and backward to the institutions of the family, friends, neighbors, coworkers, and community. Hence, the reimagining and reconstruction of community accountability practices have required the excavation and reclamation of community "traditions," as well as profound transformations in our assumptions about the roots of, and remedies to, violence.

Abundant perils and paradoxes stand in the way of recentering community spaces that have been fragmented by individualism and competition, organized through persistently unequal power relations, and increasingly plagued by the material realities of poverty, surveillance, and pervasive violence. Thus, side by side with stories of successful community-based interventions to various forms of violence we find ample illustrations of challenges, limitations, and newly unfolding contradictions.

Efforts to document these complex dimensions of community accountability late in CI's institutional life cycle (but at an early stage in the social movement's formation) were intended to strengthen political analysis and practice. Yet public exposure can amplify the multiple threats to the social movement project.

CI experienced external pressures that affect other 501(c)(3) organizations in today's environment. They are pressured to commodify concepts and practices, to adapt to funder-driven appeals to create institutionally identified or "trademarked" approaches and best practices, and to incorporate their efforts into the state institutions they have been resisting. These inescapable conditions of institutional survival increase with each success, as well as with efforts to stave off failure. CI's deliberate strategy was to begin with a limited institutional life cycle. It sought to gain sufficient resources to create and publicly disseminate a rudimentary set of models and tools while minimizing pressures to compromise these goals to attain institutional sustainability.

Beyond the threat of incorporation and co-optation was that of the rapid devaluation and disappearance of our concepts, technologies, and institutions. Community accountability and transformative justice may serve the interests of grassroots, marginalized communities, so long as states do not gain the power to control and determine their content. The subtler violence of competition in the marketplace of innovation is equally threatening to our social movement's sustainability.

The act of publishing can hone analysis and disseminate knowledge across social movements and among important allies. It can also contribute to obsolescence. The market's thirst for quickly consumable information can move from public knowledge to stories of accomplishments, or even to postmortems on the failures of utopian visions. Efforts to identify limitations can unwittingly fuel skepticism and demoralization in a social movement project that is facing considerable odds. Given the ambitiousness of our collective projects and the infinitesimal resources fueling them, the pervasiveness of our efforts and doggedness in their pursuit cannot be underestimated. Lest these stories become lost archaeological remnants rather than the foundation for new and lasting structures, our radical work is to embody these lessons in daily practice and to push for greater collective impact.

# 28

# HOW WE LEARNED (ARE LEARNING) TRANSFORMATIVE JUSTICE

*adrienne maree brown*

"If I didn't define myself for myself, I would be crunched
into other people's fantasies for me and eaten alive."
—Audre Lorde[1]

FINALLY, WE BECAME TIRED OF THE SLAUGHTER, TIRED OF THE
taste of each other's shame.

It made us sick, you know. First you hunger for the taste of
a stranger, then your enemy, then anyone called a leader, then
any small difference will do. Your hands become sharp and your
words become sharp and the only move available, even with beloveds, is bloodletting.

---

1  Audre Lorde, "Learning from the Sixties," in *Sister Outsider* (New York: Ten
Speed, 1984).

What we called justice back then was the death throes of a worldview, of divine monarchy, manifest destiny, supremacy. It is dying still, but now we have contained the death within ourselves: Inside, in the gardens where we "grow our souls," in that soil, we are composting the final strains of this disease.[2]

When we define ourselves, the result is complexity. We are none of us one thing, neither good nor bad. We are complex surviving organisms. We do appalling things to each other, rooted in trauma.

We survive, we learn, we have agency about our next steps.

We rise to great kindness, great bravery, rooted in lineage and dream.

> "If you don't trust the people, they become
> untrustworthy."
> —Lao Tzu, *Tao Te Ching*[3]

We went through the untrustworthy age. It was hundreds and hundreds of years. Not trusting creates good soil for fear, terror. We were terrified of everyone, everything different than us. Our distrust was contagious, palpable. It seemed like everyone died. It seemed like we wept every day.

Then we remembered ourselves, remembered that trust is not earned—it is how we begin. It is the first thing we do. Learning to trust is returning to beginner's mind, returning to our nature. We are meant to need each other

> "We honor our ancestors by thriving."
> —Dallas Goldtooth[4]

2   Grace Lee Boggs, "Time to Grow Our Souls, ch 22, 2011, https://www.yesmagazine.org/blogs/grace-lee-boggs/wisconsin-time-to-grow-our-souls.

3   Lao Tzu, Stephen Mitchell's translation, *Tao Te Ching*, trans. Stephen Mitchell (New York: HarperCollins, 1998).

4   Dallas Goldtooth, "U.S. Army Soldiers Massacred Hundreds of Lakota Relatives

We realized we didn't know what we were doing, even the experts.

We turned to our personal relationships, to our families, our lovers, our closest friends, and we said to each other, "I want justice between us."

We put down our masks and projections.

We began speaking to each other only truth.

We found a center within ourselves and began to listen there.

We cultivated curiosity.

Enough of us were in practice to be able to say the word "community" and mean it, not aesthetically, not based in shared oppression, but in our visionary practices of justice rooted in love, in connection.

We began to question our own actions, our participation in systems designed around our subjugation.

We relinquished judgment rooted in superiority. We shook off individual righteousness as a symptom of supremacy thinking. We were not better than each other. We worked together to generate ways forward.

We outgrew the survival technology of politeness-in-the-face-of-injustice, which had gotten us as far as it could get us, the presidency of nations. It could not get us to liberation, so we adapted.

Not all of us could be in one place, so we made room—room for many ways of being.

We learned to place our attention where we wanted it. When someone acted against community, instead of flooding them with our attention, we pulled collective attention away from them, while a healer would move in and give attention to that someone's root system, supporting wholeness.

We learned what forgiveness lets us release, and how to use time to heal that which feels too painful to forgive.

We turned to look back at our traumas and understand how they shaped us. We created more room for the traumas of other people, for the weight of ancestral trauma.

at Wounded Knee Creek," Facebook, December 29, 2016, https://m.facebook.com/story.php?story_fbid=10106137024011493&id=1216853.

We practiced deep patience with each other.

We created boundaries around our joy, around our love, around our children. Only offers of love could be felt, seen, heard, inhaled, and tasted.

We accepted more and more pathways to change as not only legitimate but necessary.

> "You're nobody until you're somebody to a bunch of other somebodies."
> —Jimmy Boggs[5]

We surrendered to how deeply we need each other.
All of us matter, to ourselves, to each other.

---

5   Grace Lee Boggs, *Living for Change: An Autobiography* (Minneapolis: University of Minnesota Press, 1998).

# ACKNOWLEDGMENTS

THANK YOU TO THE WRITERS, FOR TRUSTING US WITH YOUR STO-
ries and strategies, for writing hard and giving us the sacred gift
of your knowledge.

Spirit for guiding this work and holding us, reminding us why
we are doing this.

Amirah Mizrahi for her vital, skillful support transcribing
multiple interviews. Chrystal Stone for her formatting support.

Charles, Zach, Andrew and the entire AK Press team, for saying yes and helping birth this book into the world.

A deep and heartfelt thank you to the generations of Black,
Indigenous, Latinx, Asian/Pacific Islander, Arab/North African
survivors, organizers, and activists, many of whom are queer and
trans, who created and are creating a rich legacy of addressing violence outside of prisons and policing. Thank you whether you're
in big cities and small towns, publicly celebrated or unknown,
whether you call it transformative justice or not.

To the co-editors and authors of *The Revolution Starts At Home*
for their groundbreaking work creating the first anthology of
Community Accountability and Transformative Justice essays.

## EJERIS'S THANK YOUS:

Thank you Leah for asking me to do this, for pushing me when
I said no repeatedly, and for seeing me in this type of project
in the first place I've learned so much within this project, and

from you. Thank you for demystifying the process, holding things down when I was in the midst of holding multiple crises, for shifting your original vision and co-creating a vision for this book with me. Thank you for the coffee, the tinctures, for loving me, and this work (in that order). Thank you for the late-night calls, the book meetings that turned into co-commiseration about our lives. Your fire, brilliance, and perseverance are the foundation of this book. This book, one among your many contributions, has been a joy and a gift. And thank you for holding me down when I wasn't ready, or had so so many deeply difficult times during the creation of this book. I am grateful for a process that made so much room for access, grief, our bodies, shared trauma, joy.

Thanks Mom for your stories of community safety, Dad for teaching me to never trust the police, and for the rest of my blood family for the honest questions, hard truths, love and support quiet and loud.

Thank you to the Vision Change Win Team past and present, especially to YaliniDream, Taylor Money Worthy, Krystal Portalatin, Lindsey Charles, and Celiné Justice, for holding me down and creating space in our shared work for this book to be possible.

Thank you to Ang Hadwin, for pushing me to write my very first article which opens this book, and pushing me to apply to work at the Audre Lorde Project, which started my own transformative justice journey.

Thank you to my dear friends, movement comrades, and chosen family—you keep me honest, remind me to drink water, make me laugh, and love me so so hard, especially: V. Tobar, Mai-Lee Wong, Evelyn Lynn, Adaku Utah, Maura Bairley, Ingrid Benedict, Andrea Durojaiye, Tiffany James, Shelby Chestnut, Edith Sargon, Kay Barrett, Che J Rene Long, Deesha Narichania, Holiday Simmons, Amita Swadhin, Aishah Shahidah Simmons, Toshi Reagon, Erica Woodland, Bran Fenner, Shira Hassan, Cara Page, Rachel Herzing, Mimi Kim, Sondra Youdelman, Henry Serrano, Beverly Corbin, Michael Bell, RJ Maccani, Ora Wise, Wanda Imasuen, Ken Montenegro, Dove Kent, and many many more.

Thank you to the current and former members of the Safe OUTside the System Collective at the Audre Lorde Project where I first learned to build work that could hold our safety and survivorship. I'm so grateful for our work of co-creating my first experience of having a political home. Thank you to all the members that co-shaped my entire TJ practice and process. Special thank yous to Tasha Amezcua, Rashawn Chisolm, Jai Dulani, Yvonne Fly Onakame Etaghene, Ryann Holmes, Sherman Jones, Joseph Reaves, Tahira Pratt, Colleen Thompson, Veronica Tirado, and so so many more.

Thank you to the Safe OUTside the System Collective at the Audre Lorde Project, for being my first political home. Thank you to all the members that co-shaped my entire TJ practice and process.

Thank you to the organizers within New York City's anti-police violence movement, the transformative justice movement, LGBTQ antiviolence movements, racial justice movements, and economic justice movement. Y'all raised and shaped every move I make.

Thank you to every survivor and surviving family member that I had the honor of supporting and collaborating with. Your brilliance, bravery, heart, and heartache inspire me. I strive to do this work in a way that is continually accountable to your sacrifices. I am beyond grateful for the lessons we learned together and the trust you bestowed in me.

## LEAH'S THANK YOUS:

Thank you, Ejeris, for being the co-editor of my wildest dreams, for bringing your wide and deep organizer, writer and facilitator genius to this work. For making me laugh my ass on a regular basis, for our four-hour storytelling phone calls and buying each other flowers as part of the editing process, and the rigor, joy and clear integrity of your work and soul. For telling me to pay for Internet on a cross country flight and to get a damn massage already. I love how the process of sweating this book into being made us closer. You teach me so much and I celebrate your joy and brilliance. Thank you for loving me, yourself and this book.

Thank you to my beloved, Jesse Manuel Graves, for your steady love, persistence, brilliance, making me laugh, bringing me coffee sometimes when I'm on another conference call and sticking around. I never take for granted having a partner who cheers me on. The way we build love without abuse as a daily choice and practice has transformed my life and healed my heart. Thank you for being my femme of color love of my life.

Thank you to my community of friends and comrades for holding me down, making me laugh and being disabled together with joy and care: Billie Rain, Lisa Amin, Syrus Marcus Ware, Stacey Milbern Park, Amirah Mizrahi, Chanelle Gallant, Tina Zavitsanos, Setareh Mohammed, Leroi Newbold, Elena Rose, Cyree Jarelle Johnson, Dori Midnight, Jonah Aline Daniel, Kai Cheng Thom, Aaron Ambrose, Neve Kamilah Bianco-Mazique, Tony Riccardi, Satchél Silvette, Aruna Zehra, Max Reynolds, Kim Murray, Elliot Fukui, Vero Vengara, Caitlin Ehlers, Carolyn Lazard, Jina Kim and Lucia Leandro Gimeno. Thank you to my roommates, Reilly Joy and Eze Klanet, for being OK with my sitting in my bathrobe at 2PM writing emails at the kitchen table.

Thank you to my comrades over the past two decades of community accountability and transformative justice work, from my friends in Toronto in the 1990s who created a safety team before there was a name for it to protect me from a violent ex partner, to Ching-In Chen, Jai Dulani and Sham-e-Ali Nayeem and all the contributors to *The Revolution Starts At Home*, all the versions. To my co-workers on the crisis line at the Women's Counseling Referral and Education Centre (WCREC) in Toronto from 1999–2007, who were ahead of the curve in co-creating a feminist of color, queer, trans and working-class lead sexual and partner violence crisis line that was critical of psychiatry and the medical industrial complex and got people therapy for five bucks, along with being my first good, accessible unionized job. To my comrades in CUAV's Safetyfest, Toronto's Learning To Action Transformative Justice Study Group, generationFIVE, the North

American TJ Convening of 2010, API Chaya, Femme Heartshare Circle, and everyone who worked on the Allied Media Conference Building and Growing Safer Communities Tracks and Safetyteam from 2010–2015. To Femme Secret Society, Femmes of Colour: A Transnational Solidarity Group and Sick and Disabled Queers for being online homes.

Thank you to my comrades in the disability and healing justice movement and my therapists, Vanissar Tarakali and Tamara Lewis, for the essential support you have provided to me that allows me to do trauma and anti violence work as a long term neurodivergent survivor.

Finally, thank you the most to the hundreds of people who have trusted me with their stories of abuse, attempts at justice, healing and survival, and held my own. I cherish the ways we have shown up for each other, and honor the ways we've failed and made mistakes. Our stories are sacred.

# CONTRIBUTOR
# BIOGRAPHIES

Ejeris Dixon is an organizer, consultant, and political strategist with twenty years of experience working in racial justice, LGBTQ, antiviolence, transformative justice, and economic justice movements. She is the Founding Director of Vision Change Win Consulting (www. visionchangewin.com) where she partners with organizations to build their capacity and deepen the impact of their organizing strategies. From 2010–2013 Ejeris served as Deputy Director at the New York City Anti-Violence Project where she directed national, statewide, and local organizing, rapid response, education and policy initiatives on hate violence, domestic violence, police violence, and sexual violence. From 2005–2010, Ejeris worked as the Founding Program Coordinator of the Safe OUTside the System Collective at the Audre Lorde Project where she worked on creating transformative justice strategies to address hate and police violence. Her essay, " Building Community Safety: Practical Steps Toward Liberatory Transformation," is featured in the anthology *Who Do You Serve, Who Do You Protect? Police Violence and Resistance in the United States.* Her writing and analysis have been featured in Truthout, the *New York Times, Everyday Feminism*, the *Huffington Post, SPIN Magazine*, and CNN.

Leah Lakshmi Piepzna-Samarasinha is a disability and transformative justice movement worker, writer, poet, and teacher. The Lambda Award winning author of *Care Work: Dreaming Disability Justice, Tonguebreaker, Bridge of Flowers, Dirty River, Bodymap*, and other books, and co-editor of *The Revolution Starts At Home: Confronting Intimate Violence in*

*Activist Communities*, her work has been shortlisted for the Publishing Triangle and Pushcart Prizes. A Burgher/Tamil Sri Lankan/Irish/Roma nonbinary disabled femme raised in Worcester, MA, she co-founded Toronto's Asian Arts Freedom School and the QTBIPOC performance troupe and tour Mangos With Chili. Since 2009 she has been a lead artist with the disability justice performance collective Sins Invalid. Her work has been widely anthologized, with recent pieces in *Laura Hershey: An American Master, Pleasure Activism, Octavia's Brood*, PBS Newshour, *Vice, Yes, Guernica*, Poets.org, *The Deaf Poets Society, Bitch, Guts, Self, TruthOut*, and *The Body Is Not an Apology*. She has a MFA from Mills College and is a VONA fellow. She is also a rust belt poet, a femme over forty, a Sri Lankan with a white mom, an autistic kid who grew up, a survivor who is hard to kill.

Amanda Aguilar Shank is a queer, mixed, Salvadoran mom, organizer, writer, trainer, and abolitionist living in Portland, Oregon. I have a commitment to be free, embracing political education, campaigning, art, healing, community care as modalities for practicing transformation and resilience that starts with the self and extends outwards. I am currently Deputy Director at Freedom to Thrive, a national Black & brown network organizing for abolition.

The Audre Lorde Project is a Lesbian, Gay, Bisexual, Two Spirit, Trans, and Gender Non-Conforming People of Color center for community organizing, focusing on the New York City area. Through mobilization, education, and capacity-building, we work for community wellness and progressive social and economic justice. Committed to struggling across differences, we seek to responsibly reflect, represent, and serve our various communities.

Blyth Barnow is a white queer femme who was raised working class in Ohio. She is a preacher, harm reductionist, writer, and community organizer. She is the founder of Femminary and works nationally to develop harm reduction resources for faith communities. Blyth graduated from Pacific School Of Religion where she received a Master of Divinity and the Paul Wesley Yinger preaching award. She served as a survivor advocate for ten years, was an Everyday Feminism Writing Fellow, and was a Collective Safety Fellow at Yerba Buena Center for the Arts. You can learn more at femminary.com.

The Bay Area Transformative Justice Collective (BATJC) is a community collective of individuals working to build and support transformative justice responses to child sexual abuse. We are based in Oakland, California. We envision a world where everyday people can intervene in incidences of child sexual abuse in ways that not only meet immediate needs such as stopping current violence, securing safety, and taking accountability for harm; but that also prevent future violence and harm by actively cultivating things such as healing, accountability, and resiliency for all—survivors, bystanders, and those who have abused others.

Janaé Bonsu is a Chicago-based organizer and researcher from Columbia, SC. She currently serves as National Co-Director of BYP100, a national member-based organization of eighteen to thirty-five-year-old Black activists and organizers dedicated to creating justice and freedom through a Black queer feminist lens. Janaé is also a PhD candidate in social work at the University of Illinois-Chicago where her research focuses on Black women's multidimensional experiences of interpersonal and state violence as it relates to their contact with police. Janaé is dedicated to an abolitionist praxis through her organizing and scholarship.

Lara Brooks consults, trains, and teaches on accessible and visionary program design, program and system evaluation, harm reduction, and community accountability practices. A long-time Chicago-based youth worker and organizer, Brooks has been a part of projects and organizations that support LGBTQ youth, survivors of violence, and youth experiencing homelessness since 2001. Currently, Brooks is the Chief Program Officer at San Francisco AIDS Foundation. Before joining SFAF, Brooks was a driving force behind the Chicago Youth Storage Initiative, a citywide storage project for youth experiencing homelessness, and worked at Howard Brown Health's Broadway Youth Center between 2005 and 2013.

adrienne maree brown is the author of *Emergent Strategy* and *Pleasure Activism*, coeditor of *Octavia's Brood*, mediator/facilitator for social justice work focused on Black liberation, cohost of the "How to Survive the End of the World" podcast, and an enthusiastic auntie living in Detroit.

Creative Interventions is a resource for *community-based interventions to interpersonal violence* or what is also referred to as *community accountability and transformative justice.* Based upon its work from 2004 to 2010, Creative Interventions created *Creative Interventions Toolkit: A Practical Guide to Stop Interpersonal Violence* documenting a model, tools, and lessons learned from its interventions to domestic and sexual violence. It also has a website featuring audio and transcripts of everyday stories of people confronting violence from StoryTelling & Organizing Project (STOP). See www.creative-interventions.org and www.stopviolenceeveryday.org for free resources.

The Fireweed Collective/The Icarus Project is a support network and education project by and for people who experience the world in ways that are often diagnosed as mental illness. We advance social justice by fostering mutual aid practices that reconnect healing and collective liberation. We transform ourselves through transforming the world around us.

Monica Forrester is a Two Spirit Trans queer woman of colour. Working and advocating for the decriminalization of sexwork. Currently Program Manager of Maggie's Toronto Sexwork Action Project. Founder of Trans Pride Toronto to bring inclusion equality and awareness of Trans:Nonbinary issues.

Chanelle Gallant is a transformative organizer, writer, and trainer with a focus on sex and justice. She is a member of the national leadership team for Showing Up For Racial Justice (SURJ) and co-founded the Migrant Sex Workers Project and the first SURJ chapter in Canada. She has published and presented widely on sex and/or social and economic justice. She is working on her first book—a theory of sexual labour.

Founded nearly fifteen years ago, the Georgia Latino Alliance for Human Rights (GLAHR) is a non-profit, community-based organization that educates, organizes, and empowers Latino immigrants across Georgia to defend and advance their civil and human rights. Established in 2001 by Adelina Nicholls and Theodoro Maus, former Mexican Consul General in Atlanta, GLAHR developed out of the Coordinating Council of Latino Community Members, an organization that supported the right of undocumented immigrants to obtain drivers licenses. Today, GLAHR has become the largest Latino grassroots organization in Georgia as a result of its efforts to organize Latinos to defend and campaign for their rights and human dignity.

Alexis Pauline Gumbs is working to become your favorite cousin. She is the author of *Spill: Scenes of Black Feminist Fugitivity*, *M Archive: After the End of the World*, and co-editor of *Revolutionary Mothering: Love on the Front Lines*. She is a founding member of UBUNTU a women of color survivor-led coalition to end gendered violence and create sustainable transformative love that rose up in the aftermath of the Duke Lacrosse Case. She is also a member of SpiritHouse—a Black women led arts-based abolitionist tribe, which also facilitates the Durham Harm Free Zone.

Staci K. Haines is the founder of generative somatics, and committed the interdependence of personal, community, and systemic transformation. Staci integrates her extensive experience in somatics, social change, and healing trauma into this powerful work: www.generativesomatics. org. Staci also founded generationFIVE, whose mission is to end the sexual abuse of children within five generations—through survivor leadership, community organizing, and transformative justice: www.genera tionFIVE.org. Staci is the author of *Healing Sex: A Mind Body Approach to Healing Sexual Trauma* and the DVD *Healing Sex*. She is also the author of *The Politics of Trauma: Somatics, Healing and Social Justice* (Fall 2019).

Shira Hassan is the former executive director of the Young Women's Empowerment Project, a movement building project led by and for young people of color that have current or former experience in the sex trade and street economics. A lifelong harm reductionist and prison abolitionist, Shira has been working on community accountability for nearly twenty-five years and has helped young people of color start their own organizing projects across the country. She is the founder and principle consultant for Just Practice, a capacity building project for those working at the intersection of transformative justice, harm reduction, and collective liberation. Shira's work has been discussed on National Public Radio, the *New York Times*, *The Nation*, *In These Times*, Bill Moyers, Scarleteen, Everyday Feminism, Bitch Media, TruthOut, and Colorlines.

Audrey Huntley is a filmmaker and the co-founder of the Toronto-based network No More Silence, which works to honor MMIWGT2S and support community efforts to end violence, land reclamation, and defense while asserting sovereignty. In her day job she is the victim rights paralegal at Aboriginal Legal Services. She is an army brat of mixed

European and Indigenous ancestry. She grew up in Calgary, Alberta and moved to Europe as a young adult where she got involved in the autonomist movement, anti-fascist and anti-racist political organizing. She visited Palestine as part of a delegation of women from Germany during the first Intifada and co-wrote a collection of stories upon the group's return. She has been back on Turtle Island since 1998, living and organizing with Indigenous women in Vancouver's Downtown Eastside and Toronto, where she resides with her street dog rescue, Kimei.

Mariame Kaba is an organizer, educator, and curator who is active in movements for racial, gender, and transformative justice. She is the founder and director of Project NIA, a grassroots organization with a vision to end youth incarceration. Mariame is also a co-organizer of the Just Practice Collaborative, a training and mentoring group focused on sustaining a community of practitioners that provide community-based accountability and support structures for all parties involved with incidents and patterns of sexual, domestic, relationship, and intimate community violence.

Mimi E. Kim is the founder of Creative Interventions and a co-founder of Incite! She has been a long-time activist and advocate challenging gender-based violence at its intersection with state violence. As a second generation Korean American, she locates her political work in global solidarity with feminist anti-imperialist struggles, seeking not only the end of oppression but the creation of liberation here and now. Mimi is also an Assistant Professor of social work at California State University, Long Beach.

Elene Lam holds a Master of Law (Human Rights), Bachelor of Law, Master of Social Work and Bachelor of Social Work. She is the founder and executive director of Butterfly (Asian and migrant sex workers support network) and co-founder of Migrant Sex Workers Project. She has been involved in the sex work, gender, migrant, and labour movement for almost twenty years. She has provided trainings for community members, services providers, and policy markers on sex work, migration, anti-oppression practice, and human rights in different countries. She also participated the meeting of the Committee on the Elimination of Discrimination Against Women (CEDAW) of the United Nations in Geneva to advocate for the rights and safety of migrant sex workers.

Raquel Laviña has over thirty years of experience in activism and organizing. As an organizer she focused on helping to build youth organizing as a discipline within a broader community-organizing field. She served as the National Program Director of the Ella Baker Center for Human Rights, supervising twenty staff in three cities; the Executive Director of the Youth Empowerment Center, which housed five youth groups in Oakland, CA including SOUL, the School of Unity and Liberation; and as the Deputy Director of Social Justice Leadership, which supported groups in integrating analysis, organizing, and personal transformation. She is now Deputy Director of the National Domestic Workers' Alliance, with a focus on leadership development and organizational sustainability, where she's honored to contribute her skills and experience to a movement that centers dignity and justice.

Elisabeth Long is a community organizer, educator, and facilitator rooted in anticarceral feminism and focused on transformative justice, prison abolition, and racial justice. She has spent the last decade working at various points within the antiviolence/anti-criminalization venn diagram, and her heart and political home lie in the overlap.

Adrian Lowe has organized for the past three decades in movements for queer civil rights, economic justice, prison abolition and health justice.

Chris Lymbertos was born and raised in Iran, from Syrian and Armenian parents. She lives deeply in the contradictions of an exiled identity and made a commitment to transform the lives and conditions of her family, community, and peoples. She is a leader member of the Arab Resource and Organizing Center (AROC) and has spent the last twenty-five-plus years working with organizations and efforts committed to the liberation of people impacted by racism, homophobia, xenophobia, capitalism, and imperialism. She has trained in embodied transformation through generative somatics (gs) since 2008, is a Trainer/Teacher for gs and as much as possible, integrates what she learns into her life and movement work. When not working, she looks for ways to get friends and family to join and share in being outside in beauty and adventure with good food.

RJ Maccani's work brings together three complementary passions: transformative justice, somatic coaching, and the creative arts. He is a parent; a lead teacher and board member of Generative Somatics; and

Assistant Director of Intervention for Common Justice in Brooklyn, a groundbreaking restorative justice organization. RJ served on the leadership team of generationFIVE and co-founded the Challenging Male Supremacy Project. He also co-led the Foundry Theatre, worked as an Associate Producer and Story Advisor on the documentary film *Slingshot Hip Hop*, and was a participant performer in Ping Chong and Company's oral history theatre work and documentary film *Secret Survivors*.

Mijente is a new national hub for Latinx and Chicanx organizing. Using a hybrid offline and online platform, we're creating a political home that brings together leadership, advocacy, culture, and media to spark the culture and policy change we need.

Oakland Power Projects (OPP) works to shift resources through building skills, knowledge, and access. Its demands scale up from personal practice, to community practice and priorities and beyond, by challenging common-sense prioritization of the cops through imagining and creating solutions based in building people's capacities and desires for well-being. OPP is a project of Critical Resistance Oakland, an organization working to abolish the prison industrial complex. This chapter was produced by the CR Oakland Anti-Policing working group and the OPP health workers cohort, a group of volunteer health workers from a range of fields, backgrounds, and types of expertise.

Jenna Peters-Golden is a queer, white, anti-zionist Jew living in Philadelphia. They have been doing transformative justice and anti-violence work since 2007, and offering social justice facilitation and organizational planning with AORTA since 2010. When Jenna isn't in meetings and working on projects, she loves living collectively, drawing comics, cooking up meals and plans, and adventuring with her dog, her little wonder child, her partner, and friends.

Philly Stands Up is a queer, multiracial collective committed to ending violence and abolishing prisons. From 2005–2016, PSU facilitated accountability processes for people who perpetrated violence. In addition, PSU taught community-based workshops and helped convene transformative justice organizers across borders. Today, Philly Stands Up remains a network of activists dedicated to transformative justice.

The Puente Human Rights Movement is a grassroots migrant justice organization based in Phoenix, Arizona. We develop, educate, and empower migrant communities to protect and defend our families and ourselves.

Nathan Shara is a queer South Asian trauma therapist and educator who is committed to transformative justice as a spiritual path. Politicized through queer, feminist, and racial justice organizing, he has spent the last decade in collective experiments with liberatory responses to intimate and community violence. Nathan maintains a small private practice in Oakland, CA, applying TJ principles through his 1:1 work with survivors of violence and with people who have caused harm. Nathan is a lead teacher and practitioner with generative somatics, building capacity within our organizations and communities to heal, transform, and win.

Amita Y. Swadhin is an organizer, educator, storyteller, and strategist working to end interpersonal and institutional violence against young people. Their work stems from their experiences as a non-binary, femme, queer woman of color, daughter of immigrants from India, and years of childhood abuse by their parents, including eight years of rape by their father. They are the founding director of Mirror Memoirs, a national storytelling and organizing project uplifting the narratives, healing and leadership of queer, transgender, non-binary, and intersex people of color who survived child sexual abuse, as a strategy to end rape culture and other forms of oppression.

Kai Cheng Thom is a writer, performer, healer, lasagna lover, and wicked witch. She is the author of three award-winning books as well as many articles and essays. She would love to live by the sea again, someday.

Trans Lifeline was founded in 2014 to connect trans people to the community, resources, and support they need to survive and thrive—building a resilient trans community through trans-led direct services. Trans Lifeline's Hotline is there to care for trans people through moments of crisis and suicidality. Their Microgrants program provides low-barrier grants to trans people in need of legal name changes and updated government IDs—as well as specialized support for trans people who are incarcerated or undocumented. By providing care, Trans Lifeline identifies the trans community's most pressing needs and brings that expertise to the broader LGBT equality movement.

Ilankai Tamil blood, Texas-bred, and Brooklyn-brewed, YaliniDream conjures spirit through a unique blend of poetry, theater, song, and dance—reshaping reality and seeking peace through justice in lands of earth, psyche, soul, and dream. YaliniDream has twenty years experience using artistic tools for healing, organizing, and dignity with communities contending with violence and oppression. Yalini is a consultant with Vision Change Win, a wellness specialist with EM Arts, tours with hip-hop storytelling group Brooklyn Dreamwolf, and teaches "Social Justice Pedagogy and the Arts" at University of San Francisco's graduate program in Human Rights and International Multicultural Education.

# INDEX

**AK PRESS** is small, in terms of staff and resources, but we also manage to be one of the world's most productive anarchist publishing houses. We publish close to twenty books every year, and distribute thousands of other titles published by like-minded independent presses and projects from around the globe. We're entirely worker-run and democratically managed. We operate without a corporate structure—no boss, no managers, no bullshit.

The **FRIENDS OF AK PRESS** program is a way you can directly contribute to the continued existence of AK Press, and ensure that we're able to keep publishing books like this one! Friends pay $25 a month directly into our publishing account ($30 for Canada, $35 for international), and receive a copy of every book AK PRESS publishes for the duration of their membership! Friends also receive a discount on anything they order from our website or buy at a table: 50% on AK titles, and 30% on everything else. We have a Friends of AK ebook program as well: $15 a month gets you an electronic copy of every book we publish for the duration of your membership. *You can even sponsor a very discounted membership for someone in prison.*

Email **friendsofak@akpress.org** for more info, or visit the website: **https://www.akpress.org/friends.html**.

There are always great book projects in the works—so sign up now to become a Friend of AK Press, and let the presses roll!